IMPERIAL GLASS

Coordinated
and
Arranged By

Margaret & Douglas Archer

With the cooperation
of the

Imperial Glass Corporation
Bellaire, Ohio

COLLECTOR BOOKS
A Division of Schroeder Publishing Co., Inc.

Additional copies of this book may be ordered from:

COLLECTOR BOOKS
P.O. Box 3009
Paducah, Kentucky 42001
or
Margaret & Douglas Archer
P.O. Box 423
Ballwin, Missouri 63011

@ 14.95 Postpaid

Copyright: Douglas Archer & Bill Schroeder, 1978
ISBN: 0-89145-074-2

This book or any part thereof may not be reproduced
without the written consent of the Publisher.

GLASS IMPERIAL COLLECTORS

SOCIETY

The Imperial Glass Collectors Society was established in 1977 for the benefit of collecting and identifying Imperial Glass. Those who wish to further their knowledge in this outstanding glassware are cordially invited to apply for membership in the society. This may be accomplished by submitting your name, complete mailing address, city, state, and zip code, plus your Imperial Glass specialty to IGCS HEADQUARTERS, P.O. Box 4012, Silver Spring, Maryland 20904. Dues are $3.00 per year. Each additional family member $1.00.

FOREWORD

From the banks of the Nile, where the recorded history of glass begins, to the banks of the Ohio, Imperial's birthplace, is a distance measured in both miles and years. Yet, one of our very first industries in this country was the making of glass in Jamestown, Virginia in 1608.

Even with the struggle that the Jamestown Glass Makers had, the glass industry took hold in other parts of the "Colonies". Swedes opened a plant in New Amsterdam in 1654; Wistar in New Jersey about 1750; Stiegel in Pennsylvania about 1760; Amelung in Maryland in 1785; O'Hara in Pittsburg in 1797; Duval in (West) Virginia in 1813; Carothers in Wheeling in 1820; and Jarvis began the famed Boston and Sandwich Glass Company in Massachusetts in 1825. Glassmaking spread into New York State and further into the Ohio Valley, where today are found the best of the still existing handmade glass factories, among them Imperial Glass in Bellaire, Ohio.

With the beginning of Imperial in 1901, to a period between 1935 to 1938, we have selected a representative from five of the Company's sales catalogs of the glass made during these years.

None of the catalogs selected, were dated; therefore we have established the dates from history information and from dates that certain trademarks were registered.

A lot of the glass shown has been given names by various authors. We have not carried these names in this presentation. If the sales catalogs used did not list the glass by name, we have not altered the pages to comply with anything other than the original listing, the majority being catalog numbers only.

With this, we are pleased to present to you Imperial Glass - 1904 to 1938.

Margaret & Douglas Archer

This Book is Dedicated to

LUCILE J. KENNEDY

Manager, Marketing Services
IMPERIAL GLASS CORPORATION

With great pleasure we acknowledge the efforts of Lucile J. Kennedy with heart-felt thanks for:

The consideration, help and thoughtfulness that has made our's and many other publications possible;

Devoting her valuable time and energy from a very demanding schedule to assist others in research involving, not only Imperial Glass, but also Cambridge and Heisey Glass;

And, last but not least, for the many years of unwavering dedication to Imperial and the manufacturing of fine glass, that undoubtedly bears her mark of quality.

TRADEMARKS

The following information concerning trademarks is not as inclusive as we would like it to be. Some of the statements made are our own opinions, derived from reviewing the registration of trademarks which were available to us.

The  trademark, we believe to be one of the first trademarks registered by Imperial. We have not been able to establish a date that it was registered. It was used very early on the gas and electrical shades (one of the first products produced). The patent for "Nuart" could have been filed at the same time that "Nearcut" was applied for. In the latter part of 1911, Imperial had adopted the term "Nearcut". The trademark was used on pressed and blown table glassware, commonly known in the trade as tableware. On March 17, 1913, Imperial filed an application at the U.S. Patent office to register the term "Nearcut". It appears that the Cambridge Glass Company registered the trademark first, as Imperial was not granted a patent. Following the same style, on September 15, 1914, Imperial was granted the trademark ⟨NUCUT⟩ (Patent No. 99,747).

In between, on December 31, 1913, an application was filed for this Trademark **IM PE RI AL** and registration was granted on June 2, 1914 (Patent No. 97,422). On the same date, (December 31, 1913) another application was filed for this trademark ←┼→ and again, granted on June 2, 1914 (Patent No. 97,423). Although we have not seen the two used together, it is our opinion that the intent was to use them as such: ⬦IMPE RIAL⬦. The registrations indicated that the trademark is usually applied to the goods by being impressed or formed in the same and is applied to the receptacles containing the goods by being printed directly thereon, or by means of labels, on which the trademark is shown.

During the same year, an application was filed for ⊢┼┤ . Registration was granted on September 15, 1914 (Patent No. 99,748). It is not known if the "Double - I" was used prior to these dates, although the "Double - I" seems to be an expansion of the "Double Arrow" above.

To combine the "Double - I" with the word "Imperial", on May 19, 1920, an application was filed for **IMPE RIAL** and a patent granted on August 16, 1921.

HISTORY

A new century...
...a new company

In 1901, Imperial Glass was organized by a group of Wheeling, West Virginia and Bellaire, Ohio investors, with the aim of making the company the "most modern glass factory in America."

Glassmaking was not new to Bellaire. In fact, at its founding, Imperial became the newest of 14 "glass houses" in Bellaire. Despite this, on January 13, 1904, amid much celebration and after the completion of several years of construction, installing furnaces, and creating a number of initial molds, the first Imperial glass was made.

Imperial's first sale was to the F.W. Woolworth Co. Woolworth's initial order, for almost 500 stores, included approximately 20 items such as a covered butter dish, pickle dish, and a berry bowl. Future years saw Imperial produce items for such retailers as McCrory and Kresge. Imperial's earliest products were for the "mass markets": jelly glasses with tin lids; pressed tumblers with horseshoe and star designs on the bottoms; and assorted tableware items.

1910 to 1920 heralded the beginning of change in Imperial's markets, as machine glassware companies began flooding the market, previously held by the hand-glass factories, with machine glassware.

From 1910 to 1929, Imperial's product lines expanded. First came "Nuart" iridescent ware.

Another line of Imperial's iridescent glassware that proved popular was a group of colored and satin frosted electric lamp shades in an imitation "Tiffany" style.

Following "Nuart," Imperial introduced "Nucut" Crystal: handpressed reproductions of early English cut glass pieces. "Nucut" sold well, particularly as premiums. In fact, the Grand Union Tea Company purchased approximately $15,000 worth per month for several years. In the 1950's, "Nucut" was reintroduced as "Collectors Crystal", today one of Imperial's most popular giftware lines.

In its early years, Imperial produced a variety of glassware, including pressed glass shades for gas and electric fixtures, other illuminating ware; and gasoline pump cylinders.

In 1916, the Company introduced "Imperial Jewels"... exquisite free hand, iridescent "stretch glass" items. At this time, Imperial's scope of glassmaking activity was at a high point: numerous shops were busy making not only pressed ware but many varieties of blown and freehand ware.

In 1922, the "mass markets" further decline caused Imperial to seek new products and outlets. The Company imported a shop of Venetian glassmakers who created Imperial "Art Glass," an unsuccessful but highly distinctive collection of offhand decorative pieces in colored and cased glass.

In 1929, the forces of the Depression and Imperial's further loss of major markets to machine-glass companies combined, and in 1931, Imperial entered bankruptcy. Fortunately, the plant continued operation, primarily through the efforts of court-appointed receivers.

Additional impetus was given to Imperial's rebirth when the company secured a five-carload order for a premium from the Quaker Oats Company. This premium was the forerunner of today's "Cape Cod" pattern.

In 1937, Imperial's Candlewick pattern was introduced. Today the many beautiful Candlewick shapes are still among Imperial's best selling items.

1940 saw the beginning of Imperial's acquisition program with the purchase of the Central Glass Works of Wheeling (estab. 1860). In 1958 Imperial purchased the molds of the famous Heisey Company (estab. 1895), and in 1960 the Cambridge Glass Company of Cambridge, Ohio (estab. 1873).*

In 1973, Imperial became a subsidiary of Lenox, where equal quality of glass is produced today, as in the past.

---

* The history and parts of the foreward were taken from a pamphlet published by Imperial titled "A Consumer and Retail Guide to Handcrafted Glassware."

INDEX

CATALOG 100F

Circa: 1904-1910

Lamp Shades - Gas & Electric .... 1 thru 19
Smoke Shades 20

CATALOG 104E

Circa: 1904-1920

Forepage 21
Banana Dish or Bowl 26, 28, 41, 42
Berry Dish or Bowl 22, 27, 28, 29
Berry Dish or Bowl 30, 31, 32, 38
Berry Dish or Bowl 39, 41, 42, 44
Bon Bon Dish 44
Bonquet Vase 36, 38
Bowls (unnamed) 45
Brandy Bottles 31, 46
Card Plate 27, 45
Casserole 39
Celery 25, 26, 28, 30
Celery 40, 48
Compote 24, 25, 26, 32
Cracker Jar 48
Cream Pitcher (single) 50
Cucumber Dish 30
Custard Cup 44, 51
Goblet 46
Grape Bowl 26, 29, 44
Green Onion Dish 43
Ice Cream Dishes, Plates & Bowls 27, 29, 39
Ice Cream Dishes, Plates & Bowls 41, 44
Jelly Bowl 45, 51
Lemonade Set 32, 33, 40
Lily Bowl 47
Milk Jar 48
Molasses Can 33, 34, 47
Nappy 39
Nut Bowl 26, 27, 29, 30
Nut Bowl 39, 41
Oil Bottle 31, 32, 38, 47
Olive Dish 44
Orange Bowl 42
Pear Bowl 40, 41, 44
Pitchers 23, 31, 34, 35
Pitchers 46, 50
Plates 27, 28, 29, 30
Plates 38, 43
Punch Bowl Set 51
Radish Dish 31
Rose Bowl 36, 37, 51
Salt or Pepper 32, 34, 38, 47
Salver 27
Sherbet 51
Spoon Trays 42, 50
Sugar Bowls 50
Sugar & Cover (single) 31
Sugar Shaker 33, 34
Sweet Pea Holder 36, 37

Table Sets: 22, 24, 25, 38
    Consisting of 48, 49
        Butter & Cover
        Sugar & Cover
        Cream Pitcher
        Spoon Tumbler
Tumblers 23, 31, 46, 50
Vases (General Use) 36, 37, 47, 51
Violet Holder 36
Whiskey Glass 46
Water Bottle 32, 34
Wine Glasses & Wine Sets 46, 47

CATALOG 101D

Circa: 1920-1932

Forepage 52, 53
Berry Bowl or Dish 63, 75
Blanks (for cutting) 70
Bon Bon Dish 66, 69, 70
Bowls (Unnamed) 66, 69, 70, 73
Bread & Butter Plate 75
Butter & Cover (Single) 75, 77
Candy Bowl 58
Celery 60, 64
Cream Pitcher 66, 69, 70, 76
Cream Pitcher 77
Custard Cup 65, 68
Finger Bowl 65, 68
Ice Cream Dishes & Bowls 65, 68
Ice Tea Tumblers 55, 60, 64, 71
Jelly Bowl 65, 68
Jugs (Pitchers) 54, 57, 67, 71
Jugs (Pitchers) 72
Mayonnaise & Plate 72
Molassis Can 64
Nut Bowl 54, 56, 58, 59
Nut Bowl 61, 62
Oil Bottle 74
Olive Dish 66, 69, 70
Pickle Dish 66, 69, 70
Plates 56, 58, 59, 61
Plates 62, 65, 68
Salad Bowls & Plates 56, 58, 59, 61
Salad Bowls & Plates 62, 72
Salt (Open) 73
Salt or Pepper 55, 60, 64, 74
Sherbet 65, 68
Spoon Holder 77
Sugar Bowl (single) 66, 69, 70, 76
Sugar Bowl (single) 77
Sundae Cup 65, 68
Syrup Can 55, 60
Tumblers 55, 60, 64, 71
Tumblers 72
Vases 55, 60, 64, 76
Water Bottle 73

CATALOG 101D

Hand Cutting Design Patterns

Design Number:

102	55, 56
110	57, 58
112	59
113	60, 61
114	62, 63
115	54
300	64, 65, 66
301	67, 68, 69

BARGAIN BOOK

Circa: 1910-1929

Forepages	78, 79, 80, 81, 82
Basket	101, 111
Berry Bowl or Dish	103, 104, 116, 123,
Berry Bowl or Dish	125, 127, 128
Bon Bon Dish	102
Bowls (unnamed)	90, 103, 107, 108
Bowl Base	107
Bud Vase	91
Butter & Cover (single)	116, 124, 130
Cafe Parfail	120
Candlesticks (holder)	99, 107, 108, 115
Candy Jar & Cover	132
Celery	101, 122, 124, 125,
Champagne	121
Cheese & Cracker Set	94, 95, 113
Child's Mug	120
Claret	121
Compote	122, 126
Console Set	90, 108
Cordial	121
Cream Pitcher (single)	101, 102, 116, 122
Cream Pitcher (single)	123, 124, 125, 129
Cream Pitcher (single)	130
Cup & Saucer	117, 120
Custard Cup	120
Fruit Bowl	93, 105, 106, 113
Goblet	121
Graduated Jug (Pitcher)	132
Ice Cream Dishes, Bowls & Plates	120
Ice Tea Tumbler	100
Jelly Bowl	123, 126
Jugs (pitchers)	100, 116, 119, 126
Jugs (pitchers)	132
Lemonade Tumbler	120
Lily Bowl	101, 125, 126
Milk Pitcher	124
Nappy	101, 102, 125 126
Night Set	99
Oil Bottle	101
Olive Dish	123, 125
Pickle Dish	102, 125
Plates	108, 112
Rose Bowl	88, 91, 112
Salad Bowls, Plates & Sets	96, 97, 98, 101
Salad Bowls, Plates & Sets	104, 105, 106, 107

Salad Bowls, Plates & Sets 110, 112, 113, 126
Salad Bowls, Plates & Sets 127
Salt (open) 120
Sandwich Tray 93, 94, 95, 113
Sherbet Dishes & Plates 102, 112, 123, 129
Spoon Holder 116, 120, 124, 130
Square Dish & Plate 126, 130
Sugar Bowl (single) 101, 102, 122,
Sugar Bowl (single) 123, 125, 129
Sugar Bowl & Cover (single) 116
Sugar Bowl & Cover (single) 124
Sugar Bowl & Cover (single) 130
Sundae Cups & Set 111
Tooth Pick Holder 120
Tumbler 116
Vases 83, 84, 85, 86
Vases 87, 88, 89, 91
Vases 92, 114, 115, 132
Water Sets 118, 119, 131
Wine Glasses & Sets 117, 121

BARGAIN BOOK

Iridescent Colors
Amber 115
Azur 104, 119
Blue Glow 122
Helios 104, 119
Mulberry 115
Nuruby 103,106, 107
Nuruby 108, 109, 111
Nuruby 112, 114, 115, 117
Peacock 103, 105, 106, 107
Peacock 108, 109, 111, 112
Peacock 114, 115, 117
Plain Mulberry 107
Plain Nugreen 109
Purple Glaze 112
Red Glow 122
Rubigold 104, 105, 116
Rubigold 117, 118, 119, 120
Rubigold 121
Sapphire 103, 105, 106, 107
Sapphire 108, 112, 114, 117

Special Colors (Stritch Glass)
Amber Ice 112
Amethyst Ice 112
Blue Ice 110, 111, 112, 113
Green Ice 111
Iris Ice 110, 111, 112, 113
Rose Ice 110, 111, 112, 113

BOOK "E"

Circa: 1914-1937
Patterns & Specialty Glass

Forepages **133, 134**
Nucut:
    (Molded Glass to Simulate Cut Patterns) 135, 136
    (Molded Glass to Simulate Cut Patterns) 137, 138, 139, 140

(Molded Glass to Simulate Cut Patterns) 141, 142, 143, 144
(Molded Glass to Simulate Cut Patterns) 145

Imperial Patterns:
    Candlewick 169, 170
    Cape Cod 160, 161, 162
    Console Sets 159
    Early American Hobnail 146, 147
    Fancy Punch Sets 158
    Impire 167, 168
    Intaglio 174, 175, 176, 177
    Intaglio 178
    Laced Edge 156, 157
    Miscellaneous 152, 155
    Monticello* 162, 163, 164
    Mount Vernon 153, 154
    Niagara 149, 150
    Octagon & Square Luncheon Sets 171
    Old English 148
    Pillar Flute 172, 173
    Reeded 165, 166
    Specials - Plates & Trays 151
    Tradition 148

Cut Patterns By Crown
    Allard 184
    Anniversary 182, 183
    Canadian Wreath 179
    Chatham Rock 194
    Corona 185
    Danube 186, 187
    Flora 179
    Georgian Shape (shape only) 193
    Hand Cut 200
    Laurel 181
    Miscellaneous 180
    Monticello Ringing Rock** 188, 189, 190, 191
    Monticello Ringing Rock** 192, 193
    Navarro 195
    Oak Leaf 179
    Primrose 185
    Regina 179
    Ruby Glass 199
    Viking Rock 196, 197, 198

Specialty Glass
    Extra Highly Fire Polished Glass 206
    Georgian Shape 203
    Hand Cut Patterns 205
    Milk or Opal Glass 210, 211, 212
    Miscellaneous 204, 207, 208, 209
    Novelties 201
    Tumblers (Hand Decorated) 202

* Do not confuse with Monticello Ringing Rock
  (See Page 188, 189, 190, 191, 192)

** Do not confuse with IMPERIAL Pattern Monticello
  (See Page 162, 163, 164)

VARIOUS EXECUTIONS
ON OUR NUART SHADES

TRADE-MARK

PEARL WHITE:
ALL NUMBERS END
WITH 1

This is a satin finish or mat iridescent color, often in crizzled effects. The basic color is white, with all the colors of the rainbow in the iridescence. This color looks very much like the "mother of pearl" color in certain tropic sea shells, hence the name.

PEARL GREEN:
ALL NUMBERS END
WITH 2

This is the darkest of the three Pearl colors. Green predominates, though other colors, especially Blue, Purple, Red and Yellow, all help to create the beautiful color variations. The finish is usually satin and often shows the crizzled effects, characteristic of certain high priced vases and other art goods.

PEARL RUBY:
ALL NUMBERS END
WITH 3

As the name indicates, the main color in this execution is red, a deep, warm, ruby like color, with golden tints shining through. However, all other colors combine in this pearl color, which is the most popular, though the most expensive of the three. The finish is usually mat or satin with crizzled effects.

ON THE OPPOSITE PAGE 2F WE TRY TO GIVE YOU SOME IDEA OF ABOVE PEARL COLORS, THOUGH IT IS IMPOSSIBLE TO FIX THEIR BEAUTY ON PAPER. THERE ARE ALL KINDS OF VARIATIONS IN THESE COLORS AS THE TERRIFIC HEAT NECESSARY TO DEVELOP THEM, MAKES AN ABSOLUTE CONTROL IMPOSSIBLE. HARDLY TWO SHADES IN THESE EFFECTS ARE ENTIRELY ALIKE, BUT EVERY ONE OF THEM IS BEAUTIFUL AND IN HARMONY WITH THE OTHERS.

PURA:
ALL NUMBERS END
WITH 0

Our Pura glass is a white, semi-opaque glass, of the highest value for commercial lighting and for all other occasions, where a soft, mellow light is wanted. This glass is superior to most other similar creations, being nearly free from air bubbles and other imperfections.

CUT:

All our cut shades are not only cut by hand, but also polished by hand. With other words, they are produced by the same process which, as a rule, is used only for the best grades of hand cut table ware and art goods.

NOT DUPLICATED
BY ANYBODY!

Your special attention is drawn to our PEARL NUART SHADES in 3 colors, cut and polished by hand,—which are illustrated on pages 2 F and 12 F to 33 F of this catalog.

We do not know of anyone else offering this class of shades, and the difficulties which we had to overcome, before being able to put these novelties on the market at reasonable prices, were so great, that we do not believe, many manufacturers will care to imitate us on this particular line.

THESE HAND CUT AND HAND POLISHED NUART PEARL IRIDESCENT SHADES

are so novel, that there is really nothing to compare them with—

You will notice however from the prices, that we have succeeded in keeping them in a class where they can be used regularly and not only for the exclusive work, for which their beauty fits them.

Please bear in mind, that

ALL OUR CUT SHADES

both the cuttings on CRYSTAL ROUGHED OUTSIDE and the cuttings on OUR THREE PEARL COLORS, are cut by hand and polished by hand, representing the highest kind of workmanship, which is usually confined to art goods and cut table glassware.

TRY A FEW OF THESE HAND CUT NUART PEARL SHADES IN YOUR NEXT ORDER

PRESSED SHADES and BLOWN BALL

No. S. 601/2 Electric, square
2¼-inch holder
Panels roughed outside, Crystal edges
Packed 8 dozen in barrel
Per dozen, $1.75

No. S. 561/2 Electric, square
2¼-inch holder
Panels roughed outside, Crystal edges
Packed 7 dozen in barrel
Per dozen, $1.75

No. S. 559/2 Electric
Melon shape, 2¼-inch holder
Panels roughed outside, Crystal edges
Packed 7 dozen in barrel
Per dozen, $1.75

No. 0279 Stalactite
Pressed, 3¼-inch holder
Crystal, roughed inside
Packed 5 dozen in barrel
Per dozen, $2.25

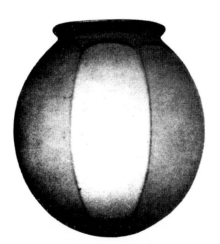

No. S. 551 Ball, blown
6-in. diameter, 3¼-in. holder
Crystal, roughed outside
Packed 2⅓ dozen in barrel
Per dozen, $2.00

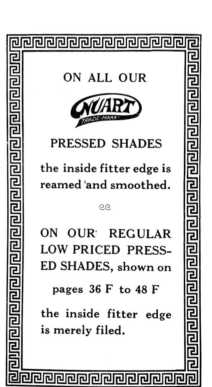

ON ALL OUR

NUART

PRESSED SHADES

the inside fitter edge is reamed 'and smoothed.

ce

ON OUR REGULAR LOW PRICED PRESS-ED SHADES, shown on

pages 36 F to 48 F

the inside fitter edge is merely filed.

½ size cuts—For terms see inside front cover

PRESSED SHADES

No. S. 601/6 Electric, square
Crystal, frosted outside
Sandblast engraved
Packed 8 dozen in barrel
Per dozen, $1.50

No. S. 591/6 Electric
Crystal, frosted outside
Sandblast engraved
Packed 7 dozen in barrel
Per dozen, $1.50

No. S. 583/6 Electric
Crystal, frosted outside
Sandblast engraved
Packed 6½ dozen in barrel
Per dozen, $1.50

All the shades on this page are for 2¼-inch holder.

No. S. 601/38 Electric, square
Crystal, frosted outside
Sandblast engraved
Packed 8 dozen in barrel
Per dozen, $1.50

No. S. 591/38 Electric
Crystal, frosted outside
Sandblast engraved
Packed 7 dozen in barrel
Per dozen, $1.50

No. S. 583/38 Electric
Crystal, frosted outside
Sandblast engraved
Packed 6½ dozen in barrel
Per dozen, $1.50

On all our pressed Nuart shades the inside fitter edge is reamed and smoothed.

½ size cuts--For extra package charge see inside front cover

PRESSED  SHADES

No. 0591/37 Electric
Crystal, roughed inside
Sandblast engraved
Packed 7 dozen in barrel
Per dozen, $1.75

No. 0583/37 Tall Electric
Crystal, roughed inside
Sandblast engraved
Packed 6½ dozen in barrel
Per dozen, $2.00

No. 0559/33 Electric
Melon Shape
Crystal, roughed inside
Sandblast engraved
Packed 7 dozen in barrel
Per dozen, $1.75

All the shades on this page are for 2¼-inch holder.

No. S. 561/39 Electric
Crystal, roughed outside
Sandblast engraved
Packed 6 dozen in barrel
Per dozen, $1.50

No. S. 561/34 Electric
Crystal, roughed outside
Sandblast engraved
Packed 7 dozen in barrel
Per dozen, $1.50

No. S. 561/40 Electric
Crystal, roughed outside
Sandblast engraved
Packed 7 dozen in barrel
Per dozen, $1.50

On all our pressed Nuart shades the inside fitter edge is reamed and smoothed

½ size cuts—Help us, by ordering as much as possible in straight barrel lots

PRESSED SHADES

The shades on this and the following page are all frosted by sandblasting on the inside and the patterns are sandblasted on the outside. This creates a very mellow and subdued light

No. 0553/31 Cluster Electric
3¼-inch holder, Crystal, roughed inside, sandblast engraved
Packed 1 dozen in barrel
Per dozen, $5.00

No. 0544/31 Electric
2¼-inch holder
Crystal, roughed inside
Sandblast engraved
Packed 7 dozen in barrel
Per dozen, $1.75

No. 0553/232 Cluster Electric
3¼-inch holder, Crystal, roughed inside, sandblast engraved
Packed 1 dozen in barrel
Per dozen, $6.00

No. 0544/232 Electric
2¼-inch holder
Crystal, roughed inside
Sandblast engraved
Packed 7 dozen in barrel
Per dozen, $2.25

½ size cuts—For terms see inside front cover

PRESSED NUART SHADES

Low priced, yet really artistic

No. 0591/36 Electric
2¼-inch holder
Crystal, roughed inside
Sandblast engraved
Packed 7 dozen in barrel
Per dozen, $1.75

No. 0583/36 Tall Electric
2¼-inch holder
Crystal, roughed inside
Sandblast engraved
Packed 6½ dozen in barrel
Per dozen, $2.00

No. 0561/35 Electric
Fancy square
2¼-inch holder
Crystal, roughed inside
Sandblast engraved
Packed 7 dozen in barrel
Per dozen, $2.00

No. 0601/35 Electric
Plain square
2¼-inch holder
Crystal, roughed inside
Sandblast engraved
Packed 8 dozen in barrel
Per dozen, $1.75

No. 0591/35 Electric
2¼-inch holder
Crystal, roughed inside
Sandblast engraved
Packed 7 dozen in barrel
Per dozen, $1.75

No. 0583/35 Tall Electric
2¼-inch holder
Crystal, roughed inside
Sandblast engraved
Packed 6½ dozen in barrel
Per dozen, $2.00

½ size cuts—For extra package charge see inside front cover

PRESSED  SHADES, Hand Cutting No. 101

R. O. means: ROUGHED OUTSIDE

Electric—Colonial flute	Electric—Colonial flute	Electric—Colonial flute
6 stars, hand cut and hand polished	12 stars, hand cut and hand polished	18 stars, hand cut and hand polished
Packed 7 dozen in barrel	Packed 7 dozen in barrel	Packed 7 dozen in barrel
Made in the following executions	Made in the following executions	Made in the following executions
No. S. 544/1016 Crystal, R.O. **$2.25**	No. S. 544/10112 Crystal, R.O. **$3.00**	No. S. 544/10118 Crystal, R.O. **$3.50**
No. 5441/1016 Pearl White. **3.75**	No. 5441/10112 Pearl White. **4.50**	No. 5441/10118 Pearl White. **5.25**
No. 5442/1016 Pearl Green. **4.25**	No. 5442/10112 Pearl Green. **5.00**	No. 5442/10118 Pearl Green. **5.75**
No. 5443/1016 Pearl Ruby.. **4.75**	No. 5443/10112 Pearl Ruby.. **5.50**	No. 5443/10118 Pearl Ruby.. **6.25**

All for 2¼-inch holder

Electric—Melon shape	Electric—Melon shape	Electric—Melon shape
6 stars, hand cut and hand polished	9 stars, hand cut and hand polished	12 stars, hand cut and hand polished
Packed 7 dozen in barrel	Packed 7 dozen in barrel	Packed 7 dozen in barrel
Made in the following executions	Made in the following executions	Made in the following executions
No. S. 559/1016 Crystal, R.O. **$2.75**	No. S. 559/1019 Crystal, R.O. **$3.00**	No. S. 559/10112 Crystal, R.O. **$3.25**
No. 5591/1016 Pearl White. **4.50**	No. 5591/1019 Pearl White. **4.75**	No. 5591/10112 Pearl White. **5.00**
No. 5592/1016 Pearl Green. **5.25**	No. 5592/1019 Pearl Green. **5.50**	No. 5592/10112 Pearl Green. **5.75**
No. 5593/1016 Pearl Ruby.. **5.75**	No. 5593/1019 Pearl Ruby.. **6.00**	No. 5593/10112 Pearl Ruby.. **6.25**

½ size cuts—Prices per dozen—For various executions see pages 2 and 3

Pressed Electric—Square
4 stars, hand cut and hand polished
2¼-inch holder
Packed 8 dozen in barrel
Made as follows
No. S. 601/102 Crystal, R.O. . .$3.25
No. 6011/102 Pearl White. . 5.25
No. 6012/102 Pearl Green. . 5.75
No. 6013/102 Pearl Ruby . . . 6.25

Pressed Electric—Square
4 stars, hand cut and hand polished
2¼-inch holder
Packed 7 dozen in barrel
Made as follows
No. S. 561/102 Crystal, R.O. . .$3.50
No. 5611/102 Pearl White. . 5.50
No. 5612/102 Pearl Green. . 6.00
No. 5613/102 Pearl Ruby . . . 6.50

Pressed Electric—Melon shape
6 stars, hand cut and hand polished
2¼-inch holder
Packed 7 dozen in barrel
Made as follows
No. S. 559/102 Crystal, R.O. . .$3.75
No. 5591/102 Pearl White. . 5.75
No. 5592/102 Pearl Green. . 6.25
No. 5593/102 Pearl Ruby . . . 6.75

Above prices are per dozen

No. S. 279/102 Stalactite—Pressed
Roughed outside
6 stars, hand cut and hand polished
Packed 5 dozen in barrel
Per dozen, $5.50

No. S. 551/1029 Ball—Blown
Roughed outside
9 stars, hand cut and hand polished
Packed 2⅓ dozen in barrel
Per dozen, $6.00

Above ball is also made with 5 stars in the same design
as No. S. 551/1025 at
$4.75 per dozen

R. O. means: ROUGHED OUTSIDE

½ size cuts—For additional package charge see inside front cover

PRESSED SHADES, Hand Cutting No. 103

R. O. means: ROUGHED OUTSIDE
All for 2¼-inch holder

Electric—Colonial flute
Hand cut and hand polished
6 figures
Packed 7 dozen in barrel
Made as follows

No. S. 544/103	Crystal, R.O.	**$5.25**
No. 5441/103	Pearl White..	**7.25**
No. 5442/103	Pearl Green..	**7.75**
No. 5443/103	Pearl Ruby...	**8.25**

Electric—Perfectly plain
Hand cut and hand polished
6 figures
Packed 7 dozen in barrel
Made as follows

No. S. 591/103	Crystal, R.O.	**$5.00**
No. 5911/103	Pearl White..	**7.00**
No. 5912/103	Pearl Green..	**7.50**
No. 5913/103	Pearl Ruby...	**8.00**

Electric—Plain, square
Hand cut and hand polished
4 figures
Packed 8 dozen in barrel
Made as follows

No. S. 601/103	Crystal, R.O.	**$4.25**
No. 6011/103	Pearl White..	**6.25**
No. 6012/103	Pearl Green..	**6.75**
No. 6013/103	Pearl Ruby...	**7.25**

Electric—Tall
Hand cut and hand polished
6 figures
Packed 6½ dozen in barrel
Made as follows

No. S. 583/103	Crystal, R.O.	**$5.00**
No. 5831/103	Pearl White..	**7.00**
No. 5832/103	Pearl Green..	**7.50**
No. 5833/103	Pearl Ruby...	**8.00**

Tungsten—Light optic flute
Hand cut and hand polished
8 figures
Packed 2¾ dozen in barrel
Made as follows

No. S. 552/103	Crystal, R.O.	**$ 6.50**
No. 5521/103	Pearl White.	**9.00**
No. 5522/103	Pearl Green.	**10.00**
No. 5523/103	Pearl Ruby..	**11.00**

Tall Electric—Light optic flute
Hand cut and hand polished
6 figures
Packed 6 dozen in barrel
Made as follows

No. S. 548/103	Crystal, R.O.	**$5.00**
No. 5481/103	Pearl White..	**7.00**
No. 5482/103	Pearl Green..	**7.50**
No. 5483/103	Pearl Ruby...	**8.00**

½ size cuts —Prices per dozen—For colors see pages 2 and 3

PRESSED SHADES, Hand Cutting No. 104

Pressed Electric—Square
Grapes, hand cut and hand polished
2¼-inch holder
Packed 8 dozen in barrel
Made as follows
No. S. 601/104   Crystal, R.O. ..**$4.25**
No.   6011/104   Pearl White..   **6.25**
No.   6012/104   Pearl Green..   **6.75**
No.   6013/104   Pearl Ruby...   **7.25**

Pressed Electric—Square
Grapes, hand cut and hand polished
2¼-inch holder
Packed 7 dozen in barrel
Made as follows
No. S. 561/104   Crystal, R.O. ..**$4.50**
No.   5611/104   Pearl White..   **6.50**
No.   5612/104   Pearl Green..   **7.00**
No.   5613/104   Pearl Ruby...   **7.50**

Pressed Electric—Melon shape
Grapes, hand cut and hand polished
2¼-inch holder
Packed 7 dozen in barrel
Made as follows
No. S. 559/104   Crystal, R.O. ..**$4.50**
No.   5591/104   Pearl White..   **6.50**
No.   5592/104   Pearl Green..   **7.00**
No.   5593/104   Pearl Ruby...   **7.50**

R. O. means: ROUGHED OUTSIDE   Above prices are per dozen

No. S. 551/104—Ball—Blown
Roughed outside
Grapes, hand cut and hand polished
Packed 2⅓ dozen in barrel
Per dozen, $6.50

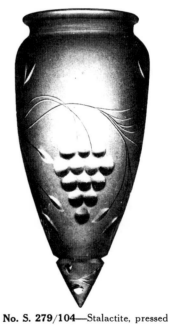

No. S. 279/104—Stalactite, pressed
Roughed outside
Grapes, hand cut and hand polished
Packed 5 dozen in barrel
Per dozen, $6.50

½ size cuts—For additional package charge see inside front cover

PRESSED SHADES, Hand Cutting No. 105

R. O. means: ROUGHED OUTSIDE

Electric—Colonial flute 12 fans and diamonds, hand cut and hand polished Packed 7 dozen in barrel Made as follows	Electric—Light optic flute 10 fans and diamonds, hand cut and hand polished Packed 7 dozen in barrel Made as follows	Electric—Perfectly plain 8 fans and diamonds, hand cut and hand polished Packed 7 dozen in barrel Made as follows
No. S. 544/105 Crystal, R.O. . .$5.50	No. S. 535/105 Crystal, R.O. . .$5.50	No. S. 591/105 Crystal, R.O. . .$5.50
No. 5441/105 Pearl White . . 7.50	No. 5351/105 Pearl White . . 7.50	No. 5911/105 Pearl White . . 7.50
No. 5442/105 Pearl Green . . 8.00	No. 5352/105 Pearl Green . . 8.00	No. 5912/105 Pearl Green . . 8.00
No. 5443/105 Pearl Ruby . . . 8.50	No. 5353/105 Pearl Ruby . . . 8.50	No. 5913/105 Pearl Ruby . . . 8.50

All for 2¼-inch holders

Tall Electric—Plain 6 fans and diamonds hand cut and hand polished Packed 6½ dozen in barrel Made as follows	Tall Electric—Light optic flute 6 fans and diamonds, hand cut and hand polished Packed 6 dozen in barrel Made as follows	Tungsten—Light optic flute 12 fans and diamonds, hand cut and hand polished Packed 2¾ dozen in barrel Made as follows
No. S. 583/105 Crystal, R.O. . .$5.50	No. S. 548/105 Crystal, R.O. . .$5.75	No. S. 552/105 Crystal, R.O. .$ 9.00
No. 5831/105 Pearl White . . 7.50	No. 5481/105 Pearl White . . 7.75	No. 5521/105 Pearl White . 12.00
No. 5832/105 Pearl Green . . 8.00	No. 5482/105 Pearl Green . . 8.25	No. 5522/105 Pearl Green . 13.50
No. 5833/105 Pearl Ruby . . . 8.50	No. 5483/105 Pearl Ruby . . . 8.75	No. 5523/105 Pearl Ruby . . 15.00

½ size cuts— Prices per dozen—For colors see pages 2 and 3

PRESSED SHADES, Hand Cutting No. 106

OUR NEW ASTER STAR CUTTING!

Electric—Colonial flute
4 stars, hand cut and hand polished
Packed 7 dozen in barrel
Made as follows

No. S. 544/1064	Crystal, R.O.	**$4.50**
No. 5441/1064	Pearl White.	**6.50**
No. 5442/1064	Pearl Green.	**7.00**
No. 5443/1064	Pearl Ruby..	**7.50**

Electric—Colonial flute
6 stars, hand cut and hand polished
Packed 7 dozen in barrel
Made as follows

No. S. 544/1066	Crystal, R.O.	**$5.50**
No. 5441/1066	Pearl White.	**7.50**
No. 5442/1066	Pearl Green.	**8.00**
No. 5443/1066	Pearl Ruby..	**8.50**

Electric—Light optic flute
4 stars, hand cut and hand polished
Packed 7 dozen in barrel
Made as follows

No. 535/106	Crystal, R.O..	**$5.50**
No. 5351/106	Pearl White..	**7.50**
No. 5352/106	Pearl Green..	**8.00**
No. 5353/106	Pearl Ruby...	**8.50**

R. O. means: ROUGHED OUTSIDE.
All for 2¼-inch holder

Electric—Perfectly plain
4 stars, hand cut and hand polished
Packed 7 dozen in barrel
Made as follows

No. S. 591/106	Crystal, R.O..	**$5.50**
No. 5911/106	Pearl White..	**7.50**
No. 5912/106	Pearl Green..	**8.00**
No. 5913/106	Pearl Ruby...	**8.50**

Electric—Plain square
4 stars, hand cut and hand polished
Packed 8 dozen in barrel
Made as follows

No. S. 601/106	Crystal, R.O..	**$4.50**
No. 6011/106	Pearl White..	**6.50**
No. 6012/106	Pearl Green..	**7.00**
No. 6013/106	Pearl Ruby...	**7.50**

Electric—Fancy square
4 stars, hand cut and hand polished
Packed 7 dozen in barrel
Made as follows

No. S. 561/106	Crystal, R.O..	**$4.75**
No. 5611/106	Pearl White..	**6.75**
No. 5612/106	Pearl Green..	**7.25**
No. 5613/106	Pearl Ruby...	**7.75**

½ size cuts—Prices per dozen—Extra charge for packages

PRESSED GAS and ELECTRIC SHADES, Crystal

All the globes on this page are mould frosted all over— The various figures are crystal

No. 358½C gas shade
4-inch holder
Packed 5 dozen in barrel
Per dozen, $0.65

No. 358½C electric shade
2¼-inch holder
Packed 12 dozen in barrel
Per dozen, $0.40

No. 359½ B gas shade
4-inch holder
Packed 5 dozen in barrel
Per dozen, $0.65

No. 359½B electric shade
2¼-inch holder
Packed 12 dozen in barrel
Per dozen, $0.40

No. 359½C gas shade
4-inch holder
Packed 5 dozen in barrel
Per dozen, $0.65

No. 359½C electric shade
2¼-inch holder
Packed 12 dozen in barrel
Per dozen, $0.40

½ size cuts—Order as much as possible in straight barrel lots

PRESSED GAS and ELECTRIC SHADES, Crystal

All the globes on this page are mould frosted all over.
The various figures are crystal.

No. 342½C electric shade
2¼-inch holder
Packed 12 dozen in barrel
Per dozen, $0.50

No. 342½C gas shade
4-inch holder
Packed 4½ dozen in barrel
Per dozen, $0.75

No. 486C electric shade
2¼-inch holder
Packed 12 dozen in barrel
Per dozen, $0.45

No. 486C gas shade
4-inch holder
Packed 5 dozen in barrel
Per dozen, $0.70

No. 474C electric shade
2¼-inch holder
Packed 12 dozen in barrel
Per dozen, $0.45

No. 474C gas shade
4-inch holder
Packed 5 dozen in barrel
Per dozen, $0.70

½ size cuts--For extra package charge see inside front cover

PRESSED GAS and ELECTRIC SHADES, Crystal

No. 430C gas shade, crimped
4-inch holder
Packed 5 dozen in barrel
Per dozen, $0.70

No. 430C electric shade, crimped
2¼-inch holder
Packed 12 dozen in barrel
Per dozen, $0.50

No. 430B gas shade, bell shape
4-inch holder
Packed 5 dozen in barrel
Per dozen, $0.70

No. 430B electric shade, bell shape
2¼-inch holder
Packed 12 dozen in barrel
Per dozen, $0.50

No. 48C gas shade, extra large
4-inch holder
Packed 4½ dozen in barrel
Per dozen, $1.00

No. 48C electric shade, large
2¼-inch holder
Packed 12 dozen in barrel
Per dozen, $0.75

½ size cuts—Order as much as possible in straight barrel lots

PRESSED GAS and ELECTRIC SHADES, Crystal

No. 49½ electric shade
Mould frosted all over
2¼-inch holder
Packed 12 dozen in barrel
Per dozen, $0.50

No. 49½ gas shade
Mould frosted all over
4-inch holder
Packed 5 dozen in barrel
Per dozen, $0.75

No. 45½C electric shade
Mould frosted all over
2¼-inch holder
Packed 12 dozen in barrel
Per dozen, $0.50

No. 45½C gas shade
Mould frosted all over
4-inch holder
Packed 5 dozen in barrel
Per dozen, $0.75

No. 46C electric shade, crystal
2¼-inch holder
Packed 12 dozen in barrel
Per dozen, $0.50

No. 46C gas shade, crystal
4-inch holder
Packed 4½ dozen in barrel
Per dozen, $1.00

½ size cuts—For extra package charge see inside front cover

PRESSED GAS AND ELECTRIC SHADES

CRYSTAL ROUGHED INSIDE

THE PRICES OF No. 279 AND No. 255 GAS AND ELECTRIC SHADES, PLAIN AS WELL AS ENGRAVED, ON THIS AND THE FOLLOWING 3 PAGES ARE FOR CRYSTAL ONLY. HOWEVER, WE ALSO SELL THESE SHADES WITH ROUGHING ON THE INSIDE, WHICH CREATES A VERY MELLOW EFFECT ON THE LIGHT.

THESE ROUGHED INSIDE SHADES
COST 30 CENTS PER DOZEN MORE
THAN THE FOLLOWING PRICES.

ORDER THE ROUGHED INSIDE SHADES BY PLACING AN O BEFORE THE FOLLOWING NUMBERS, FOR INSTANCE 0279C GAS SHADE AT $1.10 PER DOZEN, 0279C ELECTRIC SHADE AT $0.85 PER DOZEN, ETC., ETC.

No. 279C gas shade
All crystal
4-inch holder
Packed 6 dozen in barrel
Per dozen, $0.80

No. 279C electric shade
All crystal
2¼-inch holder
Packed 12 dozen in barrel
Per dozen, $0.55

No. 255C gas shade
All crystal
4-inch holder
Packed 5 dozen in barrel
Per dozen, $0.90

No. 255C electric shade
All crystal
2¼-inch holder
Packed 12 dozen in barrel
Per dozen, $0.60

½ size cuts—For extra package charge see inside front cover

PRESSED GAS AND ELECTRIC SHADES

No. 255/10 electric shade
Sandblast engraved on crystal
2¼-inch holder
Packed 12 dozen in barrel
Per dozen, $0.90

No. 255/10 gas shade
Sandblast engraved on crystal
4-inch holder
Packed 5 dozen in barrel
Per dozen, $1.25

No. 255/4 electric shade
Sandblast engraved on crystal
2¼-inch holder
Packed 12 dozen in barrel
Per dozen, $0.90

No. 255/4 gas shade
Sandblast engraved on crystal
4-inch holder
Packed 5 dozen in barrel
Per dozen, $1.25

No. 255C/2 electric shade
Sandblast engraved on crystal
2¼-inch holder
Packed 12 dozen in barrel
Per dozen, $0.90

No. 255C/2 gas shade
Sandblast engraved on crystal
4-inch holder
Packed 5 dozen in barrel
Per dozen, $1.25

½ size cuts—For roughed inside add 30 cents per dozen

PRESSED SMOKE SHADES WITH METAL RINGS

No. 54 Pressed smoke shade, with metal ring
All crystal
Made in 7-inch only
Packed 12 dozen in barrel
Per dozen, $0.80

No. 054 Pressed smoke shade, with metal ring
The plain flutes are roughed; the figured flutes are crystal
Made in 7-inch only
Packed 12 dozen in barrel
Per dozen, $1.35

No. 47 Pressed smoke shade, with metal ring
All crystal
Made in the following sizes
6-inch—Packed 15 dozen in barrel, per dozen. .$0.70
7-inch—Packed 12 dozen in barrel, per dozen. . 0.80
8-inch—Packed 8 dozen in barrel, per dozen. . 0.90

No. 047 Pressed smoke shade, with metal ring
The edge is roughed; the figured part is crystal
Made in the following sizes
6-inch—Packed 15 dozen in barrel, per dozen. .$1.30
7-inch—Packed 12 dozen in barrel, per dozen. . 1.40
8-inch—Packed 8 dozen in barrel, per dozen. . 1.50

No. 252 Pressed smoke shade, with metal ring
All crystal
Made in the following sizes
6-inch—Packed 15 dozen in barrel, per dozen. .$0.70
7-inch—Packed 12 dozen in barrel, per dozen. . 0.80
8-inch—Packed 8 dozen in barrel, per dozen. . 0.90

No. 0252 Pressed smoke shade, with metal ring
Roughed all over on the upper side
Made in the following sizes
6-inch—Packed 15 dozen in barrel, per dozen. .$1.15
7-inch—Packed 12 dozen in barrel, per dozen. . 1.25
8-inch—Packed 8 dozen in barrel, per dozen. . 1.35

½ size cuts—For terms see inside front cover

CATALOG 104F

This catalog contained a variety of tableware which appeared to be some of the first glass manufactured at Imperial. As the first few pages indicate, the "Mirror Bottoms" were featured. We believe this to be a prelude for the glass being called "Nearcut" (See Trademarks for the use of the word "Nearcut").

The latter part of this catalog featured molded glass which was the fore-runner of "Nucut" and again, was referred to as "Nearcut".

Special Notice:

These goods have Imperial mirror bottoms, which are ground to the stars and heavily polished. The bottoms are actually cut, and the pressed star looks as bright as a cut one. The knobs of sugar and butter cover are really cut, like a cut glass stopper for a cut glass oil bottle.

No. 283A 9 inch berry.
actual diameter 9¼ inches.
packed 2½ dozen in barrel.

No. 283C 9 inch berry.
actual diameter 9¼ inches.
packed 2½ dozen in barrel.

No. 2831 set, consisting of 4 articles shown, is packed 1 dozen sets in barrel,
also sold separately, as follows:

No. 2831 butter and cover, really cut knob, (not imitation cut) packed 4 dozen in barrel.
"   sugar and cover, really cut knob, (not imitation cut)   "   5   "   "   "
"   cream   "   9   "   "   "
"   spoon   "   8   "   "   "

Before ordering, read terms and other information on front pages of our price list.

Every article shown on this page, has our famous Imperial mirror bottom, which is not to be compared with the regular ground bottom, but which is ground to the figure, and well polished, so that it might be justly called a cut bottom with a pressed star.

No. 283 pressed pitcher.
capacity 3 pints.
packed 2 dozen in barrel.

No. 2831 pressed tumbler.
½ sham bottom.
3¾ inches high.
packed 15 dozen in barrel.

No. 2832 pressed pitcher.
capacity ½ gallon.
packed 1¾ dozen in barrel.

No. 283 pressed tumbler.
full sham bottom.
3¾ inches high
packed 15 dozen in barrel.

No. 2831 pressed pitcher.
capacity ½ gallon.
packed 2 dozen in barrel.

No. 281A pressed tumbler.
heavy bottom.
3¾ inches high.
packed 15 dozen in barrel.

No. 281A pressed pitcher.
capacity ½ gallon.
packed 2 dozen in barrel.

The goods shown on this page, make very fine lemonade sets. (see price list).

Before ordering, read terms and other information on front pages of our price list.

23

Good glass shows up to the best advantage in a plain pattern; that is why we make so many plain patterns.

No. 274C 8 inch comport, crimped.
actual diameter 8¼ inches.
packed 3¾ dozen in barrel.

No. 274B 8 inch comport, flared.
actual diameter 8¾ inches.
packed 3¾ dozen in barrel.

No. 274 set, consisting of 4 articles shown, is packed 1½ dozen sets in barrel.

or sold separately, as follows:

No. 274   butter and cover, packed 4 dozen in barrel.
   "   sugar   "   "   " 6 "   "
   "   cream   " 9 "   "
   "   spoon   " 10 "   "

Before ordering, read terms and other information on front pages of our price list.

24

No. 274A 4½ inch comport.
diameter 4½ inches
packed 15 dozen in barrel.

No. 274A 8 inch comport.
actual diameter 8 inches.
packed 3 dozen in barrel.

No. 274 celery, tall.
packed 5 dozen in barrel.

A winner, and that is all.

No. 302 Set, consisting of 4 articles shown, is packed 1½ dozen sets in barrel.
also sold separately, as follows:
No. 302 butter and cover, packed 4 dozen in barrel.
"   sugar and cover,   "   6   "   "   "
"   cream   "   9   "   "   "
"   spoon   "   9   "   "   "

Before ordering, read terms and other information on front pages of our price list.

25

No. 2461N   6 inch nut bowl.
actual diameter 5¾ inches.
packed 4½ dozen in barrel.

No. 2461E   8 inch banana dish.
8½ inches long.
packed 3 dozen in barrel.

No. 2461A   7 inch comport.
actual diameter 7¼ inches.
packed 4½ dozen in barrel.

No. 2461C   7 inch grape dish.
actual diameter 7 inches.
packed 3 dozen in barrel.

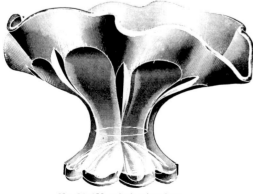

No. 2461M   8 inch celery boat.
8¼ inches long.
packed 3 dozen in barrel.

No. 2461P   7 inch nut bowl, 3 corners.
actual diameter 7 inches.
packed 4 dozen in barrel.

Before ordering, read terms and other information on front pages of our price list.

26

No. 2461D 9 inch salver.
actual diameter 9 inches.
packed 3 dozen in barrel.

No. 2461R 8 inch card receiver.
actual diameter 8½ inches.
packed 3 dozen in barrel.

No. 2461F 7 inch ice cream dish.
actual diameter 7½ inches.
packed 3 dozen in barrel.

No. 276C 7 inch berry.
ground bottom ; actual diameter 8 inches.
packed 5 dozen in barrel.

No. 276N 7 inch nut bowl.
ground bottom; actual diameter 7 inches.
packed 3½ dozen in barrel.

No. 276D 10 inch plate.
ground bottom; actual diameter 10¼ inches.
packed 6 dozen in barrel.

No. 276A 7 inch berry.
ground bottom; actual diameter 8 inches.
packed 5 dozen in barrel.

Before ordering, read terms and other information on front pages of our price list.

27

No. 88B 7 inch berry, flared.
actual diameter 8½ inches.
packed 5 dozen in barrel.

No. 88C 7 inch berry, crimped.
actual diameter 8¼ inches.
packed 5 dozen in barrel.

No. 88C 4½ inch berry, crimped.
actual diameter 5 inches.
packed 30 dozen in barrel.

No. 88D 10 inch plate.
packed 6 dozen in barrel.

No. 46E celery boat.
11½ inches long.
packed 3 dozen in barrel.

No. 88D 6 inch plate.
packed 25 dozen in barrel.

No. 46M banana dish.
10 inches long.
packed 3 dozen in barrel.

For terms and other information see front pages of our price list.

No. 89B 7 inch berry, flared.
actual diameter 8½ inches.
packed 5 dozen in barrel.

No. 89B 4 inch berry, flared.
actual diameter 4½ inches.
packed 30 dozen in barrel.

No. 89D 10 inch plate.
packed 6 dozen in barrel.

No. 89C 7 inch berry, crimped.
actual diameter 8½ inches.
packed 5 dozen in barrel.

No. 46D 10 inch ice cream plate, deep.
actual diameter 10½ inches.
packed 5 dozen in barrel.

No. 89C 4 inch berry, crimped.
actual diameter 4½ inches.
packed 30 dozen in barrel.

No. 46C 8 inch grape dish.
actual diameter 8 inches.
packed 4 dozen in barrel.

No. 46N 7 inch nut bowl.
actual diameter 7 inches.
packed 3½ dozen in barrel.

For terms and other information see front pages of our price list.

No. 47A 7 inch berry, round.
actual diameter 8 inches.
packed 5 dozen in barrel.

No. 47D 10 inch plate.
actual diameter 10 inches.
packed 6 dozen in barrel.

No. 47N 7 inch nut bowl.
actual diameter 7 inches.
packed 3½ dozen in barrel.

No. 47E 10 inch celery boat.
11 inches long.
packed 3 dozen in barrel.

No. 263 berry set.

consists of one 8 inch and
six 4½ inch berries.
packed 2 dozen sets in barrel.

No. 263 4½ inch berry.
packed 20 dozen in barrel.

No. 263 7 inch berry.
actual diameter 7¼ inches.
packed 3½ dozen in barrel

No. 263 8 inch berry.
actual diameter 8¼ inches.
packed 2½ dozen in barrel.

No. 280 cucumber dish.
packed 10 dozen in barrel.

Before ordering read terms and other information on front pages of our price list.

30

No. 47C 7 inch berry, crimped.
actual diameter 8½ inches.
packed 5 dozen in barrel.

No. 47B 7 inch berry, flared.
actual diameter 8¼ inches.
packed 5 dozen in barrel.

No. 293 radish.
7½ inches diameter.
packed 9 dozen in barrel.

No. 272 sugar and cover.
packed 6 dozen in barrel.

No. 286 pressed oil bottle.
capacity 5 ounces.
packed 16 dozen in barrel.

These 3 bottles are sold with pressed stoppers
or with ground and cut stoppers.

No. 300 lemonade
set.

consists of one 300 pitcher
and six 300 tumblers.
packed 1 dozen sets in barrel.

No. 300 pitcher.
9 inches high
including lip.
packed
2½ dozen in barrel.

No. 300 tumbler.
height 3¾ inches.
packed 16 dozen in barrel.

No. 277 oil bottle.
capacity 2¾ oz.
packed 16 dozen in barrel.

No. 40 brandy bottle.
capacity 9 ounces.
packed 8 dozen in barrel.

Before ordering, read terms and other information on front pages of our price list.

31

No. 6 4½ inch comport.
packed 18 dozen in barrel.

No. 6 8 inch comport.
packed 3½ dozen in barrel.

Celluloid tops.

The 286A salts and peppers
and several other of our pressed
and blown shakers are also sold
with celluloid tops.

We use only the genuine,
patented celluloid tops which
are better in every way than
any other kind in the market.

Try them.

No. 099A pressed water bottle, optic.
packed 2½ dozen in barrel.

No. 099A pressed oil bottle.
capacity 6½ ounces.
packed 12 dozen in barrel.
sold with pressed or with cut stopper.

No. 286A blown salt
or pepper.
dome top.
packed 36 dozen
in barrel.

No. 286A blown salt
or pepper.
silver top.
packed 36 dozen
in barrel.

This lemonade set is also sold, with No. 232 metal
tray, packed 1 dozen sets in barrel, or without tray
packed 1 dozen sets in barrel.

No. 082A lemonade set, shown with 231 metal tray.
the optic tumblers in this set are pressed, with ground bottoms, the pitcher is blown.
packed 1 dozen sets in barrel.

For terms and other information see front pages of our price list.

No. 69A blown molasses can.
optic, with common tin top.
capacity 13 ounces.
packed 8 dozen in barrel.

No. 69A blown molasses can.
optic, with patent tin top.
capacity 13 ounces.
packed 8 dozen in barrel.

No. 69A blown molasses can.
optic, with nickel top.
capacity 13 ounces.
packed 8 dozen in barrel.

No. 69A blown molasses can.
optic, with silver top.
capacity 13 ounces.
packed 8 dozen in barrel.

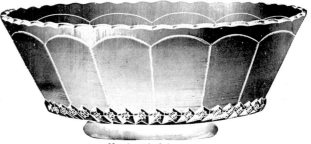

No. 6   4½ inch berry.
packed 30 dozen in barrel.

No. 6   8 inch berry.
packed 5 dozen in barrel.

No. 68A blown sugar shaker.
optic, with flat top.
packed 14 dozen in barrel.

This lemonade set is also sold with
No. 232 metal tray.
packed 1 dozen sets in barrel.
or without tray.
packed 1 dozen sets in barrel.

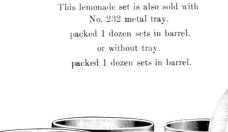

No. 68A blown sugar shaker.
optic, with silver top.
packed 14 dozen in barrel.

No. 083A lemonade set, shown with No. 231 metal tray.
The optic tumblers in this set are pressed, with ground bottoms; the pitcher is blown.
packed 1 dozen sets in barrel.

For terms and other information see front pages of our price list.

No. 286   blown molasses can.
with common tin top.
capacity 7 ounces.
packed 12 dozen in barrel.

No. 286   blown molasses can.
with patent tin top.
capacity 7 ounces.
packed 12 dozen in barrel.

No. 286   blown molasses can.
with nickel top.
capacity 7 ounces.
packed 12 dozen in barrel.

No. 286   blown molasses can.
with silver top.
capacity 7 ounces.
packed 12 dozen in barrel.

No. 291 blown restaurant salt or pepper.
flat top.
packed 24 dozen
in barrel.

No. 286 blown sugar duster.
flat top.
packed 14 dozen in barrel.

No. 286 blown sugar duster.
silver top.
packed 14 dozen in barrel.

No. 286   blown salt
or pepper.
silver top.
packed 36 dozen
in barrel.

No. 286   blown salt
or pepper.
dome top.
packed 36 dozen
in barrel.

No. 286   blown salt
or pepper.
flat top.
packed 36 dozen
in barrel.

Sold also with the genuine, patented celluloid top.

A good hotel or restaurant sugar duster.

No. 337 pressed sugar shaker.
shown with silver top.
packed 14 dozen in barrel.
also sold with flat top.

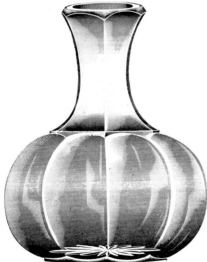

No. 287 blown water bottle.
ground and polished top.
packed 3 dozen in barrel.

No. 84B blown ½ gallon pitcher.
polka dots on the inside.
packed 2 dozen in barrel.

Before ordering, read terms and other information on front pages of our price list.

Novelties which will become staple goods.

No. 83A blown $\frac{1}{2}$ gallon pitcher.
optic flutes on the inside.
packed $1\frac{3}{4}$ dozen in barrel.

No. 299 blown $\frac{1}{2}$ gallon pitcher.
ribbed flutes on the outside.
packed 2 dozen in barrel.

No. 82A blown $\frac{1}{2}$ gallon pitcher.
optic flutes on the inside.
packed $1\frac{3}{4}$ dozen in barrel.

No. 289 blown $\frac{1}{2}$ gallon pitcher.
ribbed flutes on the outside.
packed 2 dozen in barrel.

Before ordering, read terms and other information on front pages our price list.

No. 246A bouquet.
packed 15 dozen in barrel.

No. 246B bouquet.
packed 8 dozen in barrel.

No. 246D violet holder.
packed 10 dozen in barrel.

No. 294 vase.
5 to 8 inches high.
packed 12 dozen in barrel.

This vase is hand finished, varying in height from 5 to 8 inches.

Because of the low price, no selection of sizes will be made.

No. 294H violet holder.
packed 20 dozen in barrel.

No. 246C bouquet.
packed 8 dozen in barrel.

No. 2461A vase.
packed 6 dozen in barrel.

No. 2461C vase, crimped.
packed 6 dozen in barrel.

No. 2461N rose bowl, footed.
packed 4 dozen in barrel.

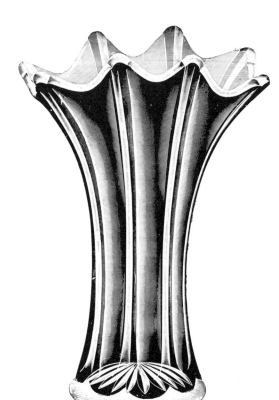

No. 284E 10 inch sweet pea holder.
packed about 3 dozen in barrel.
above vase being hand made, varies from 8 to 10 inches in height.

Before ordering, read terms and other information on front pages of our price list.

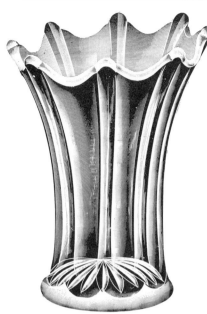

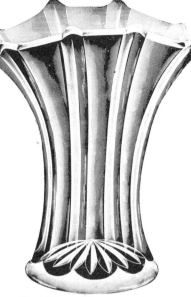

No. 284H rose bowl, fancy.
packed about 4 dozen in barrel.

No. 284A   8 inch sweet pea holder, round.
packed about 3 dozen in barrel.
above vase being hand made, varies from
6 to 8 inches in height.

No. 284E   8 inch sweet pea holder.
packed about 3 dozen in barrel.
above vase being hand made, varies from
6 to 8 inches in height.

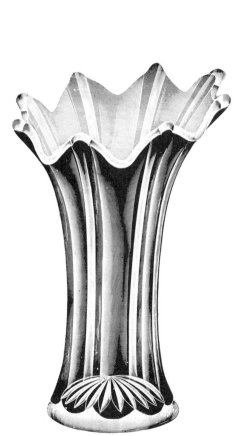

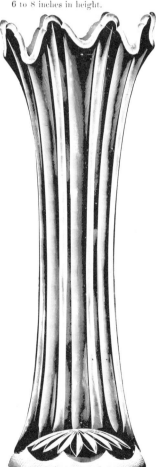

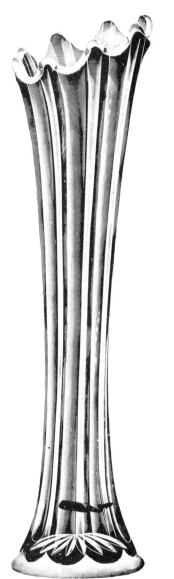

No. 284A   10 inch sweet pea holder, round.
packed about 2½ dozen in barrel.
above vase being hand made, varies from
8 to 10 inches in height.

No. 284   12 inch vase.
packed about 3 dozen in barrel.
above vase being hand made, varies from
10 to 12 inches in height.

No. 284   16 inch vase.
packed about 2½ dozen in barrel.
above vase being hand made, varies from
12 to 16 inches in height.

Before ordering, read terms and other information on front pages of our price list.

37

No. 256 oil bottle.
capacity 1½ oz.
packed 25 dozen in barrel.

No. 256 salt or pepper.
shown with dome top.
packed 36 dozen in barrel.
also sold with flat top
or with silver top.
also with the genuine,
patented celluloid top.

No. 256 set, consisting of above 4 articles, is packed 2 dozen sets in barrel.
also sold separately, as follows:
No. 256 butter and cover, packed 4 dozen in barrel.
" sugar and cover " 6 " " "
" cream " 10 " " "
" spoon " 10 " " "

No. 256 8 inch bouquet.
packed 6½ dozen in barrel.

No. 2566D 8 inch plate.
actual diameter 8¼ inches.
packed 9 dozen in barrel.

No. 256U 3½ inch berry

packed 40 dozen in barrel.

No. 256D 4½ inch plate.
actual diameter 4¾ inches.
packed 35 dozen in barrel.

For terms and other information see front pages of our price list.

No. 2567A 7 inch berry, round.
actual diameter 8 inches.
packed 5 dozen in barrel.

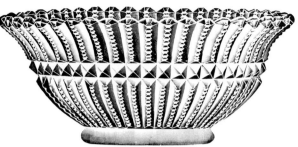

No. 2567B 7 inch berry, flared.
actual diameter 8¼ inches.
packed 5 dozen in barrel.

No. 2567C 7 inch berry, crimped.
actual diameter 8¼ inches.
packed 5 dozen in barrel.

No. 2567F 8 inch ice cream nappy.
actual diameter 8½ inches.
packed 4 dozen in barrel.

No. 2567N 7 inch nut bowl.
actual diameter 7 inches.
packed 3½ dozen in barrel.

No. 2567 8 inch casserole.
actual diameter (including flange) 8½ inches.
packed 4 dozen in barrel.

No. 2567S 7 inch berry, square.
actual diameter 6½ inches.
packed 3½ dozen in barrel.

No. 2567W 7 inch berry, straight.
actual diameter 8½ inches.
packed 5 dozen in barrel.

For terms and other information see front pages of our price list.

No. 2567E 10 inch celery boat.
10½ inches long.
packed 3 dozen in barrel.

No. 2567P 7 inch pear bowl.
actual diameter 7½ inches.
3½ dozen in barrel.

No. 256 lemonade set with No. 243 glass tray.
packed ¾ dozen sets in barrel.

also sold with 231 or with 232 metal tray.
packed 1 dozen sets in barrel.

or without any tray.
packed 1 dozen sets in barrel.

For terms and other information see front pages of our price list.

The following 8 articles can be retailed at 10 cents very profitably!

No. 2826A　6 inch berry, round.
actual diameter 7 inches.
packed 10 dozen in barrel.

No. 2826B　6 inch berry, flared.
actual diameter 7 inches.
packed 10 dozen in barrel.

No. 2826C　6 inch berry, crimped.
actual diameter 7 inches.
packed 10 dozen in barrel.

No. 2826F　6 inch ice cream dish.
actual diameter 7¼ inches.
packed 10 dozen in barrel.

No. 2826N　6 inch nut bowl.
actual diameter 5½ inches.
packed 7 dozen in barrel.

No. 2826O　8 inch banana dish.
8¼ inches long.
packed 5 dozen in barrel.

No. 2826P　6 inch pear bowl.
actual diameter 6¼ inches.
packed 5 dozen in barrel.

No. 2826S　6 inch berry square.
actual diameter 5½ inches.
packed 7 dozen in barrel.

For terms and other information see front pages of our price list.

No. 2823C 3½ inch berry, crimped.
packed 45 dozen in barrel.

No. 2824C 4 inch berry, crimped.
packed 36 dozen in barrel.

No. 2829O 12 inch banana dish.
12½ inches long.
packed 2 dozen in barrel.

No. 2825C 4½ inch berry, crimped.
packed 25 dozen in barrel.

No. 2827O 9 inch banana dish.
9¾ inches long.
packed 3½ dozen in barrel.

No. 2827C 7 inch berry, crimped.
actual diameter 8½ inches.
packed 5 dozen in barrel.

No. 2825O 6 inch spoon tray.
6 inches long.
packed 12 dozen in barrel.

No. 2829C 9 inch orange bowl, crimped.
actual diameter 10½ inches.
packed 2½ dozen in barrel.

No. 2820 6 inch spoon tray, handled.
6½ inches long.
packed 10 dozen in barrel.

Before ordering, read terms and other information on front pages of our price list.

No. 2829R 13 inch plate, crimped.
packed 3 dozen in barrel.

No. 2824E 5 inch green onion dish.
5½ inches long.
packed 12 dozen in barrel.

No. 2825E 6 inch green onion dish.
6¼ inches long.
packed 10 dozen in barrel.

No. 2829D 13 inch plate or tray.
packed 3 dozen in barrel.
This is the tray which is used for 282 lemonade sets and
wine sets, also for other lemonade sets.

No. 2824D 5 inch plate.
actual diameter 5¼ inches.
packed 30 dozen in barrel.

No. 2825D 6 inch plate.
actual diameter 6¾ inches.
packed 25 dozen in barrel.

Before ordering, read terms and other information on front pages of our price list.

43

No. 2820A handled berry.
diameter (not including handle) 4½ inches.
packed 16 dozen in barrel.

No. 2829H 10 inch grape dish.
diameter 10 inches.
packed 2 dozen in barrel.

No. 2820B bon bon, handled.
diameter (not including handle) 5½ inches.
packed 12 dozen in barrel.

No. 2825P bon bon.
diameter 5 inches.
packed 13 dozen in barrel.

No. 2820C olive, crimped.
diameter (not including handle) 5 inches.
packed 14 dozen in barrel.

No. 282 custard.
ground bottom.
packed 30 dozen in barrel.

No. 2827P 7 inch pear bowl.
actual diameter 8 inches.
packed 3½ dozen in barrel.

No. 2820S olive, square.
diameter (not including handle) 4½ inches.
packed 12 dozen in barrel.

No. 2820P bon bon, handled.
diameter (not including handle) 5 inches.
packed 12 dozen in barrel.

No. 282F 11 inch ice cream dish, footed.
actual diameter 11¼ inches.
packed ¾ dozen in barrel.

Before ordering, read terms and other information on front pages of our price list.

No. 2822A 4½ inch footed jelly, round.
packed 8 dozen in barrel.

No. 282A 10 inch footed bowl, round.
height 9 inches.
packed ¾ dozen in barrel, or 3 dozen in cask.

No. 2822B 4½ inch footed jelly, flared.
packed 8 dozen in barrel.

No. 2822C 4½ inch footed jelly, crimped.
packed 8 dozen in barrel.

No. 282B 10 inch footed bowl, flared.
height 8½ inches.
packed ¾ dozen in barrel, or 3 dozen in cask.

No. 2822D 6 inch card plate.
packed 6 dozen in barrel.

For terms and other information see front pages of this catalog.

No. 282 pitcher.
8½ inches high.
packed 2 dozen in barrel.

No. 282B pitcher.
8½ inches high.
packed 2 dozen in barrel.

No. 282 tumbler.
ground bottom.
height 3⅞ inches.
packed 16 dozen in barrel.

No. 282 whiskey.
ground bottom.
capacity 2½ oz.
packed 50 dozen in barrel.

No. 282 brandy bottle.
packed 2 dozen in barrel.

No. 282 whiskey bottle.
packed 2 dozen in barrel.

These two bottles are sold with pressed or with cut stopper, either kind
being ground in the bottles.

No. 282 wine.
capacity 2½ oz.
packed 35 dozen in barrel.

No. 282 goblet.
capacity 10 oz.
packed 9 dozen in barrel.

For terms and other information see front pages of our price list.

46

No. 282   pressed salt
or pepper.
shown with dome top
packed 36 dozen in barrel

also sold with flat top
or with silver top;
also with the genuine,
patented celluloid top.

No. 282B vase, flared.
packed 2 dozen in barrel.

No. 282 oil bottle.
capacity 5 ounces.
packed 12 dozen in barrel.

Our 282 oil bottle is sold with
pressed or with cut stopper.

No. 282 pressed molasses can.
capacity 6½ ounces.
shown with nickel top.
packed 6 dozen in barrel.
also sold with silver top.

No. 2827J lily bowl.
actual diameter 6½ inches.
packed 4 dozen in barrel

No. 282 wine set, shown with
2829 glass tray.

packed 1 dozen sets in barrel

also sold with
231 or 232 metal tray.
packed 1 dozen in barrel.

or without tray.
packed 1½ dozen in barrel.

The bottle in this set is furnished with pressed or with cut stopper, both kinds being ground in.

For terms and other information see front pages of our price list.

47

No. 282 milk jar and cover.
packed 8 dozen in barrel.

No. 282 celery, tall.
packed 6 dozen in barrel.

No. 282 cracker jar and cover.
packed 2½ dozen in barrel.

We are told, that our 282 pattern is the best one
known at its prices.

No. 282 set, consisting of above **4 articles**, is packed 2 dozen sets in barrel.
also sold separately, as follows:
No. 282 butter and cover, packed 4 dozen in barrel.
  " sugar and cover, " 6 " " "
  " cream,   " 10 " " "
  " spoon,   " 10 " " "

For terms and other information see front pages of our price list.

48

Our 292 pattern,

shown on the following pages, is recommended to your special attention.

This brilliant, yet simple design is not only beautiful, but altogether different from anything now in the market.

The peculiar foot is impossible to show this foot various pieces, we illustrate  very effective, and as it is plainly on the cuts of the its bottom herewith separately.

The illustrations can only give you an idea of the outlines of this pattern, but not of the dazzling reflections, caused by this peculiar design in our pure glass.

Let us send you a sample lot, to show you, how this 292 ware really looks.

No. 292 set, consisting of above 4 articles, is packed 1¼ dozen sets in barrel.

also sold separately as follows:

No. 292   butter and cover, packed 3 dozen in barrel.
     "   sugar and cover,   "   6   "   "
     "   cream,   "   8   "   "
     "   spoon,   "   8   "   "

For terms and other information see front pages of our price list.

49

No. 292 lemonade set

consists of one 292 large pitcher and six 292 tumblers, sold with or without
glass or metal trays.

No. 292 small pitcher.
6 inches high, including lip.
packed 3 dozen in barrel.

No. 292 large pitcher.
8½ inches high, including lip.
packed 1½ dozen in barrel.

No. 2927A individual sugar.
round.
packed 8 dozen in barrel.

No. 2927A individual cream.
round.
packed 10 dozen in barrel.

No. 292 tumbler.
ground bottom.
4 inches high.
packed 16 dozen in barrel.

No. 2927A individual set consists of one round individual sugar and
one round individual cream, packed 4½ dozen sets in barrel.

No. 2927S individual sugar.
square.
packed 8 dozen in barrel.

No. 2927S individual cream.
square.
packed 10 dozen in barrel.

No. 2927E handled spoon tray.
5½ inches long.
packed 6 dozen in barrel.

No. 2927S individual set consists of one square individual sugar and one
square individual cream, packed 4½ dozen sets in barrel.

For terms and other information see front pages of our price list.

No. 2921N rose bowl.
4 inches high.
packed 14 dozen in barrel.

No. 2922N rose bowl.
4½ inches high.
packed 12 dozen in barrel.

No. 2921A sherbet.
4 inches high.
packed 10 dozen in barrel.

No. 2922A footed jelly.
4½ inches high.
packed 8 dozen in barrel.

No. 2925A vase, round.
height 5 inches.
packed 8½ dozen in barrel.

No. 2925E vase, fan shape.
height 4¾ inches.
packed 8 dozen in barrel.

No. 2925B vase, flared.
height 4¼ inches.
packed 6 dozen in barrel.

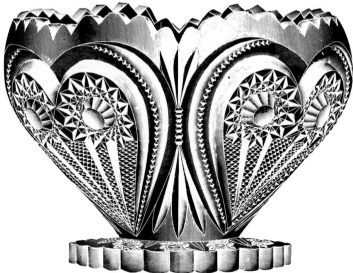

No. 292 10 inch punch bowl.
packed 1 dozen in barrel.

No. 292 punch set

consists of one 292 10 inch
punch bowl and twelve
292 custards.
packed ¾ dozen sets in barrel.

No. 292 custard.
packed 20 dozen in barrel.

For terms and other information see front pages of our price list.

Catalog No. 101D

This is one of the most important catalogs of table glassware ever issued by us or by any other factory.

On pages 4D to 21D we show our beautiful *No. 582 pattern of open stock table glass*, [IMPERIAL] brand, brought up to date with all the new pieces, which were added since the publication of our catalog No. 100 D.

On pages 22D to 28D we show for the first time the beginning of a wonderful new line of *perfectly plain table glass*, also in the [IMPERIAL] brand, which, we feel sure, will become most popular with the better class of trade very rapidly and stay popular for many years to come.

On pages 29D to 87D new lines of hand-engraved, hand cut and hand polished staple table glasswares are shown for the first time. Every single buyer who has seen these new goods, has complimented us for having produced *something really new in table glassware.*

If you will carefully study the prices, the novel shapes and the usefulness of these cut goods, you will readily admit, *that nothing like this has ever been offered before to you.* If you are impressed by the illustrations, *the goods will impress you still more.*

PLACE YOUR TRIAL ORDER TO-DAY.

The balance of our products is illustrated in the following 5 catalogs:

No. 100A General line of low and medium priced Crystal table glass.
No. 100B Iridescent glass novelties.
No. 101C NUCUT GLASS, cut glass effects in fancy goods.
No. 100E Jelly tumblers, common table tumblers, and other packers' glass.
No. 100F Glassware for illumination, both electric and gas.

Imperial glass company
Bellaire, Ohio, U. S. A.

The above is an exact reproduction of an

Advertising Sign

which we supply, free of charge, at his request, to every distributor of the goods shown in this catalog.

By placing some of these signs on your tables over these wares, you will attract the attention of your customers to the fact that you are selling the highest grade of moulded open stock table glass ever offered by anybody—while this is still further proved by the above trade mark, which is in the bottoms of most pieces, excepting a few blown and cut pitchers, molasses cans and salt shakers.

It will pay you to keep a representative assortment of pieces in this unusual ware always on hand, for many of your customers, being pleased with a few first articles bought from you, will come back to your store for additional pieces in the same design.

As you can buy the goods in this catalog at our lowest prices in any quantity to suit yourself, it will require an investment of only very little money to keep a representative assortment always in stock.

HAND CUTTING, DESIGN No. 115.

This wonderfully effective design was added by us, since the catalog went into the printers' hands. We could not illustrate therefore every shape, but the two illustrations will show you the pattern. The blanks are the same as used on the HAND CUTTING No. 102, illustrated on pages 46D to 53D of this catalog.

MADE IN THE FOLLOWING PIECES:

No. 5927N/115—6½-inch nut bowl
Moulded star in cut bottom

No. 6025/115	5 inch ice cream nappy	per dozen $3.60	For shapes
No. 6028/115	8¾ inch ice cream nappy	per dozen 7.80	see
No. 5925A/115	5½ inch berry bowl	per dozen 3.60	page 46
No. 5926A/115	6¾ inch berry bowl	per dozen 5.40	
No. 5927A/115	8 inch berry bowl	per dozen $7.80	For shapes
No. 5924A/115	4¼ inch berry	per dozen 2.00	see
No. 5928A/115	9 inch berry bowl	per dozen 9.00	page 47
No. 5924½A/115	4¾ inch berry	per dozen 2.25	
No. 5925N/115	4¾ inch nut bowl	per dozen $3.60	For shapes
No. 5926N/115	5½ inch nut bowl	per dozen 5.40	see
No. 84/115	5½ inch plate	per dozen 2.50	page 48
No. 5735B/115	7 inch salad	per dozen 6.00	
No. 5737B/115	9¼ inch salad	per dozen 9.00	
No. 5927N/115	6½ inch nut bowl	per dozen $7.80	For shapes
No. 5924N/115	3½ inch nut bowl	per dozen 2.00	see
No. 5928N/115	7½ inch nut bowl	per dozen 9.00	page 49
No. 5924½N/115	4 inch nut bowl	per dozen 2.25	
No. 6065/115	4½ inch olive	per dozen $3.60	For shapes
No. 606/115	sugar	per dozen 3.60	see
No. 606/115	cream	per dozen 3.60	page 50
No. 60251/115	5½ inch bon bon	per dozen 4.80	
No. 84/115	pickle dish	per dozen 3.60	
No. 6067B/115	7½ inch footed bowl	per dozen 15.00	
No. 91/115	custard	per dozen $2.50	For shapes
No. 84/115	finger bowl	per dozen 2.75	see
No. 2091/115	5¼ inch ice cream	per dozen 3.60	page 51
No. 108/115	sherbet	per dozen 2.50	
No. 208/115	sundae	per dozen 2.75	
No. 209/115	footed jelly	per dozen 3.00	
No. 84/115 pint	blown jug	per dozen $5.40	For shapes
No. 84/115 quart	blown jug	per dozen 6.60	see
No. 84/115 3-pint	blown jug	per dozen 7.80	page 52
No. 84/115 ½-gal.	blown jug	per dozen 9.00	
No. 84/115 3-quart	blown jug	per dozen 12.00	
No. 84/115	table tumbler	per dozen $2.50	
No. 84/115	ice tea—14 oz.	per dozen 3.00	
No. 84/115	ice tea and plate	per dozen 5.25	For shapes
No. 572/115	vase or celery	per dozen 6.00	see
No. 286/115	blown salt or pepper	per dozen 2.25	page 53
No. 286/115 7½ oz.	blown syrup can	per dozen 5.40	
No. 286/115 12 oz.	blown syrup can	per dozen 6.00	
No. 69/115 13 oz.	blown syrup can	per dozen 6.00	

No. 84/115—½-gallon jug—blown
Hand cut and hand polished bottom star

½ size cuts — For description of patterns see pages 28 and 29.

HAND CUTTING, DESIGN No. 102.

ALL OUR CUT DESIGNS ARE CUT BY HAND INTO THE PLAIN
SURFACE OF THE GLASS. MOST OF THE BLANKS ARE PRESSED;
WE USE BLOWN BLANKS ONLY WHERE THE SHAPE CANNOT
WELL BE PRODUCED BY PRESSING. IN MANY CASES THE PLAIN,
PRESSED ARTICLES ARE MORE BEAUTIFUL THAN THE CORRE-
SPONDING BLOWN PIECES WOULD BE, AND IN ALL CASES THEY
ARE STRONGER AND THEREFORE MORE USEFUL.

PRESSED TUMBLERS
AND PRESSED VASE

No. 84/102—table tumbler
Moulded star in cut bottom
3 hand cut side stars
Per dozen, $1.75

No. 84/102—12-oz. ice tea
Moulded star in cut bottom
3 hand cut side stars
Per dozen, $2.25

No. 84/102—ice tea and plate
Moulded stars in cut bottoms
Hand cut side stars
Per dozen sets, $4.00

No. 572/102—vase or celery
Moulded star in cut bottom
3 hand cut side stars
Per dozen, $3.60

THE TOPS ON THESE BLOWN SYRUP CANS AND
SALT OR PEPPER SHAKERS ARE HEAVY CAST AND
SILVER PLATED.

No. 286/102—blown
salt or pepper
Silver top
Hand cut bottom star
3 hand cut side stars
Per dozen, $1.75

No. 286/102—7½-oz. blown
syrup can
Silver top
Hand cut bottom star
3 hand cut side stars
Per dozen, $4.20

No. 286/102—12-oz. blown
syrup can
Silver top
Hand cut bottom star
3 hand cut side stars
Per dozen, $4.80

No. 69/102—13-oz. blown
syrup can
Silver top
Hand cut bottom star
3 hand cut side stars
Per dozen, $4.80

½ size cuts.—A wonderful, popular priced line for open stock.

OPEN STOCK IMPERIAL **TABLE GLASS**

HAND CUTTING, DESIGN No. 102.

YOUR EYES TELL YOU THAT THESE PRESSED BOWLS ARE
BEAUTIFUL; WE ADD THAT THEY ARE MORE USEFUL THAN
THE OLD BLOWN ARTICLES, THE BRITTLE EDGES OF WHICH
ARE TOO EASILY CHIPPED.

No. 5925N/102—4¾-inch nut bowl
Moulded star in cut bottom
6 hand cut side stars
Per dozen, $3.00

No. 5926N/102—5½-inch nut bowl
Moulded star in cut bottom
6 hand cut side stars
Per dozen, $4.80

No. 84/102—5½-inch plate
Moulded star in cut bottom
6 hand cut side stars
Per dozen, $1.75

No. 5735B/102—7-inch salad
Moulded star in cut bottom
6 hand cut side stars
Per dozen, $4.80

No. 5737B/102—9¼-inch salad
Moulded star in cut bottom
6 hand cut side stars
Per dozen, $7.80

½ **size cuts—For description of hand cuttings see pages 28 and 29.**

HAND CUTTING, DESIGN No. 110.

ON BLOWN IRON MOULD JUGS, HAND MADE HANDLES.

No. 84/110—pint jug—blown
Hand cut and polished bottom star
3 hand cut sprays and 2 butterflies
Per dozen, $9.00

No. 84/110—quart jug—blown
Hand cut and polished bottom star
3 hand cut sprays and 2 butterflies
Per dozen, $10.80

No. 84/110—3-pint jug—blown
Hand cut and polished bottom star
3 hand cut sprays and 2 butterflies
Per dozen, $12.00

No. 84/110—3-quart jug—blown
Hand cut and polished bottom star
3 hand cut sprays and 2 butterflies
Per dozen, $18.00

For full
description
of
this design
see
pages
28 and 29

No. 84/110—½-gallon jug, blown
Hand cut and polished bottom star
3 hand cut sprays and 2 butterflies
Per dozen, $15.00

OPEN STOCK IMPERIAL TABLE GLASS

HAND CUTTING, DESIGN No. 110.

FOR DAILY USE THESE PRESSED, EXTRA POLISHED BOWLS ARE
MUCH MORE USEFUL THAN THE EASILY CHIPPED BLOWN ONES.

No. 84/110—5½-inch plate
Moulded star in cut bottom
3 hand cut sprays and 3 butterflies
Per dozen, $5.40

No. 5926N/110—5½-inch nut bowl
Moulded star in cut bottom
3 hand cut sprays and 3 butterflies
Per dozen, $8.40

No. 5735N/110—6-inch candy bowl
Moulded star in cut bottom
3 hand cut sprays and 3 butterflies
Per dozen, $9.00

No. 5735B/110—7-inch salad
Moulded star in cut bottom
3 hand cut sprays and 3 butterflies
Per dozen, $9.00

No. 5737B/110—9¼-inch salad
Moulded star in cut bottom
3 hand cut sprays and 3 butterflies
Per dozen, $15.00

½ size cuts—For description of design see pages 28 and 29.

OPEN STOCK IMPE RIAL TABLE GLASS

HAND CUTTING, DESIGN No. 112.

ON PRESSED BOWLS WHICH ARE NOT AS EASILY CHIPPED AS
THE BRITTLE EDGED, BLOWN ONES.

No. 84/112—5½-inch plate
Moulded star in cut bottom
3 hand cut sprays with flowers
Per dozen, $6.00

No. 5926N/112—5½-inch nut bowl
Moulded star in cut bottom
3 hand cut sprays with flowers
Per dozen, $7.80

No. 5735B/112—7-inch salad
Moulded star in cut bottom
3 hand cut sprays with flowers
Per dozen, $7.80

No. 5737B/112—9¼-inch salad
Moulded star in cut bottom
3 hand cut sprays with flowers
Per dozen, $15.00

½ size cuts -— For full description of pattern see pages 28 and 29.

HAND CUTTING, DESIGN No. 113.

THESE NEW LINES ARE MORE THAN MERELY A FEW NEW
PATTERNS OF CUT GLASS.
THEY ARE AN ENTIRELY NEW KIND OF MERCHANDISE, MADE
SO BY A COMBINATION OF HIGH GRADE QUALITY, ENTIRE
USEFULNESS AND MODERATE PRICES.

PRESSED TUMBLERS AND VASE

No. 84/113—table tumbler
Moulded star in cut bottom
3 hand cut side stars
Per dozen, $2.50

No. 84/113—14-oz. ice tea
Moulded star in cut bottom
3 hand cut side stars
Per dozen, $3.00

No. 84/113—ice tea and plate
Moulded stars in cut bottoms
Hand cut side stars
Per dozen sets, $6.60

No. 572/113—vase or celery
Moulded star in cut bottom
6 hand cut side stars
Per dozen, $7.20

THE TOPS ON THESE BLOWN SYRUP CANS AND SALT
OR PEPPER SHAKERS ARE HEAVY CAST AND SILVER
PLATED.

No. 286/113—blown
salt or pepper
Silver top
Hand cut bottom star
3 hand cut side stars
Per dozen, $3.00

No. 286/113—7½-oz. blown
syrup can
Silver top
Hand cut bottom star
3 hand cut side stars
Per dozen, $6.60

No. 286/113—12-oz. blown
syrup can
Silver top
Hand cut bottom star
3 hand cut side stars
Per dozen, $7.20

No. 69/113—13-oz. blown
syrup can
Silver top
Hand cut bottom star
3 hand cut side stars
Per dozen, $7.20

½ size cuts—Read both inside covers carefully.

OPEN STOCK IMPERIAL TABLE GLASS

HAND CUTTING, DESIGN No. 113.

ON EXTRA POLISHED, PRESSED BOWLS,
MORE USEFUL THAN BRITTLE EDGED BLOWN ONES.

No. 84/113—5½-inch plate
Moulded star in cut bottom
5 hand cut side stars
Per dozen, $3.60

No. 5926N/113—5½-inch nut bowl
Moulded star in cut bottom
5 hand cut side stars
Per dozen, $7.20

No. 5735B/113—7-inch salad
Moulded star in cut bottom
5 hand cut side stars
Per dozen, $7.80

No. 5737B/113—9¼-inch salad
Moulded star in cut bottom
5 hand cut side stars
Per dozen, $12.00

½ size cuts—For description of patterns see pages 28 and 29.

OPEN STOCK **IMPE RIAL** TABLE GLASS

HAND CUTTING, DESIGN No. 114.

THESE PRESSED BOWLS ARE AS BEAUTIFUL AS BLOWN ONES,
AND A GREAT DEAL MORE PRACTICAL FOR ACTUAL USE, BE-
CAUSE THE EDGES ARE STRONGER AND NOT CHIPPED AS EASILY.

No. 84/114—5½-inch plate
Moulded star in cut bottom
5 hand cut sprays
Per dozen, $2.00

No. 5926N/114—5½-inch nut bowl
Moulded star in cut bottom
5 hand cut sprays
Per dozen, $3.60

No. 5735B/114—7-inch salad
Moulded star in cut bottom
5 hand cut sprays
Per dozen, $4.20

No. 5737B/114—9-inch salad
Moulded star in cut bottom
5 hand cut sprays
Per dozen, $7.20

½ size cuts—For description of patterns see pages 28 and 29.

OPEN STOCK IMPERIAL TABLE GLASS

HAND CUTTING, DESIGN No. 114.

No. 5924A/114—4¼-inch berry
Moulded star in cut bottom
3 hand cut sprays
Per dozen, $1.50

No. 5927A/114—8-inch berry bowl
Moulded star in cut bottom
5 hand cut sprays
Per dozen, $6.00

No. 5924½A/114—4¾-inch berry
Moulded star in cut bottom
3 hand cut sprays
Per dozen, $1.75

No. 5928A/114—9-inch berry bowl
Moulded star in cut bottom
5 hand cut sprays
Per dozen, $7.20

No. 5925A/114—5½-inch berry
Moulded star in cut bottom
5 hand cut sprays
Per dozen, $2.00

½ size cuts—Read inside back cover carefully.

HAND ENGRAVING, DESIGN No. 300.

THIS PATTERN AS WELL AS ALL THE OTHER DESIGNS, SHOWN
IN THIS CATALOG, ARE DESIRABLE FOR OPEN STOCK PURPOSES.
A REPRESENTATIVE ASSORTMENT OF ANY ONE OF THESE
DESIGNS IN YOUR STOCK MEANS A CHAIN OF ORDERS FOR YOU.

PRESSED TUMBLERS AND VASE

No. 090/300—tumbler
Plain ground bottom
Hand engraved small stars
Per dozen, $0.70

No. 84/300—14-oz. ice tea
Moulded star in cut bottom
Hand engraved small stars
Per dozen, $1.50

No. 84/300—ice tea and plate
Moulded stars in cut bottoms
Hand engraved small stars
Per dozen sets, $2.75

No. 572/300—vase or celery
Moulded star in cut bottom
Hand engraved small stars
Per dozen, $3.00

THE TOPS ON THESE MOLASSES CANS AND SALT
OR PEPPER SHAKERS ARE HEAVY CAST AND SILVER
PLATED.

No. 286/300—blown
salt or pepper
Silver top
Per dozen, $1.25

No. 286/300—7½-oz. blown
molasses can
Silver top
Per dozen, $3.00

No. 286/300—12-oz. blown
molasses can
Silver top
Per dozen, $3.60

No. 69/300—13-oz. blown
molasses can
Silver top
Per dozen, $3.60

½ size cuts—Beautiful goods for practical use.

OPEN STOCK IMPERIAL TABLE GLASS

HAND ENGRAVING, DESIGN No. 300.
PRESSED BLANKS OF SUFFICIENT THICKNESS TO MAKE THEIR PRACTICAL DAILY USE POSSIBLE.

No. 91/300—custard
Puntied bottom—Hand made handle
Hand engraved stars
Per dozen, $1.00

No. 84/300—finger bowl
Moulded star in cut bottom
Hand engraved small stars
Per dozen, $1.50

No. 84/300—5½-inch plate
Moulded star in cut bottom
Hand engraved small stars
Per dozen, $1.25

No. 208/300—sundae
Hand made foot
Hand engraved stars
Per dozen, $1.25

No. 209/300—footed jelly
Hand made foot
Hand engraved stars
Per dozen, $1.50

No. 108/300—sherbet
Hand made foot
Hand engraved stars
Per dozen, $1.00

No. 1081/300—4-inch ice cream
Hand made foot
Hand engraved stars
Per dozen, $1.25

No. 2081/300—4½-inch ice cream
Hand made foot
Hand engraved stars
Per dozen, $1.50

No. 2091/300—5¼-inch ice cream
Hand made foot
Hand engraved stars
Per dozen, $1.75

½ size cuts—For description of patterns see pages 28 and 29.

OPEN STOCK IMPERIAL TABLE GLASS

HAND ENGRAVING, DESIGN No. 300.

THESE PIECES ARE NOT BLOWN WITH BRITTLE, EASILY CHIPPED
EDGES, BUT PRESSED, OF SUFFICIENT THICKNESS, TO PERMIT
THEIR PRACTICAL USE.

No. 6065/300—4½-inch olive
Moulded star in cut bottom
Hand engraved small stars
Per dozen, $1.50

No. 606/300—sugar
Moulded star in cut bottom
Hand engraved small stars
Per dozen, $1.80

No. 606/300—cream
Moulded star in cut bottom
Hand engraved small stars
Per dozen, $1.80

No. 60251/300—5½-inch handled bon bon
Moulded star in cut bottom
Hand engraved small stars
Per dozen, $2.00

No. 84/300—two-handled pickle
Moulded star in cut bottom
Hand engraved small stars
Per dozen, $1.80

No. 6067B/300—7½-inch footed bowl
Extra polished all over
Hand engraved small stars
Per dozen, $6.60

½ size cuts—For description of patterns see pages 28 and 29.

HAND CUTTING, DESIGN No. 301.

ON PLAIN, IRON MOULD BLOWN PITCHERS

No. 84/301—pint jug—blown
Hand made handle
Per dozen, $2.50

No. 84/301—quart jug—blown
Hand made handle
Per dozen $3.60

No. 84/301—3-pint jug—blown
Hand made handle
Per dozen, $4.20

**ALL
GENUINE
HAND
ENGRAVINGS.**

No. 84/301—3-quart jug—blown
Hand made handle
Per dozen, $6.00

No. 84/301—½-gallon jug—blown
Hand made handle
Per dozen, $4.80

½ size cuts—For description of patterns see pages 28 and 29.

HAND ENGRAVING, DESIGN No. 301.

THESE PRESSED PIECES ARE FULLY AS PRETTY, BUT A GREAT DEAL MORE SUBSTANTIAL THAN CORRESPONDING BLOWN PIECES, WHOSE BRITTLE, EASILY CHIPPED EDGES MAKE THEM LESS SAFE FOR DAILY USE.

No. 84/301—6-inch plate
Moulded star in cut bottom
Genuine hand engraving
Per dozen, $1.50

No. 91/301—custard
Puntied bottom—hand made handle
Genuine hand engraving
Per dozen, $1.25

No. 84/301—finger bowl
Moulded star in cut bottom
Genuine hand engraving
Per dozen, $1.50

No. 108/301—sherbet
Hand made foot
Genuine hand engraving
Per dozen, $1.20

No. 208/301—sundae
Hand made foot
Genuine hand engraving
Per dozen, $1.50

No. 209/301—footed jelly
Hand made foot
Genuine hand engraving
Per dozen, $1.80

No. 1081/301—4-inch ice cream
Hand made foot
Genuine hand engraving
Per dozen, $1.35

No. 2081/301—4½-inch ice cream
Hand made foot
Genuine hand engraving
Per dozen, $1.65

No. 2091/301—5¼-inch ice cream
Hand made foot
Genuine hand engraving
Per dozen, $2.00

½ size cuts—Read the printed matter all through this catalog.

OPEN STOCK IMPERIAL TABLE GLASS

HAND ENGRAVING, DESIGN No. 301

No. 6065/301—4½-inch olive
Moulded star in cut bottom
Genuine hand engraving
Per dozen, $1.80

No. 606/301—sugar
Moulded star in cut bottom
Genuine hand engraving
Per dozen, $1.85

No. 606/301—cream
Moulded star in cut bottom
Genuine hand engraving
Per dozen, $1.85

No. 60251/301—5½-inch handled bon bon
Moulded star in cut bottom
Genuine hand engraving
Per dozen, $2.40

No. 84/301—handled pickle
Moulded star in cut bottom
Genuine hand engraving
Per dozen, $1.85

No. 6067B/301—7½-inch footed bowl
Extra polished all over
Genuine hand engraving
Per dozen, $7.20

½ size cuts—For description of patterns see pages 28 and 29.

OPEN STOCK IMPERIAL TABLE GLASS

THE HIGHEST GRADE OF PRESSED GLASS AT POPULAR PRICES.

THESE ARE THE PRESSED BLANKS, USED IN OUR HAND CUT
WARES, ILLUSTRATED ON PAGES 28D TO 88D.

No. 6065—4½-inch olive
Moulded star in cut bottom
Packed 11 dozen in barrel
Per dozen, $1.00, any quantity

No. 606—sugar
Moulded star in cut bottom
Packed 10 dozen in barrel
Per dozen, $1.35, any quantity

No. 606—cream
Moulded star in cut bottom
Packed 10 dozen in barrel
Per dozen, $1.35, any quantity

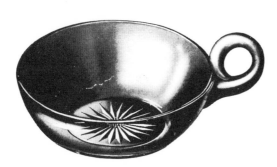

No. 60251—5½-inch handled bon bon
Moulded star in cut bottom
Packed 9 dozen in barrel
Per dozen, $1.50, any quantity

No. 84—two-handled pickle
Moulded star in cut bottom
Packed 10 dozen in barrel
Per dozen, $1.35, any quantity

No. 6067B—7½-inch footed bowl
Polished all over
Packed 1¼ dozen in barrel
Per dozen, $6.00, any quantity

½ size cuts—Our regular staple lines are shown in five other catalogs.

OPEN STOCK IMPERIAL TABLE GLASS

No. 515B—12½-oz. ice tea
Moulded star in cut bottom
Packed 10 dozen in barrel
Per dozen, $0.75, any quantity

No. 515B—table tumbler
Moulded star in cut bottom
Packed 15 dozen in barrel
Per dozen, $0.65, any quantity

No. 515A—table tumbler
Moulded star in cut bottom
Packed 17 dozen in barrel
Per dozen, $0.65, any quantity

No. 515A—12½-oz. ice tea
Moulded star in cut bottom
Packed 11 dozen in barrel
Per dozen, $0.75, any quantity

No. 0515—blown jug—½-gallon size
Deep, hand cut and hand polished star in bottom, 32 points
Packed 1 5/6 dozen in barrel
Per dozen, $6.00, any quantity

No. 515—blown jug—½-gallon size
Plain bottom
Packed 1 5/6 dozen in barrel
Per dozen, $4.50, any quantity

OPEN STOCK IMPERIAL TABLE GLASS

DESIGN AND TRADE MARK
ARE PATENTED

No. 05825—5-inch mayonnaise and plate
Packed 7 dozen sets in barrel
Per dozen sets, $2.50, any quantity

No. 05826—8-inch salad and plate
Packed 2½ dozen sets in barrel
Per dozen sets, $4.25, any quantity

**EVERYTHING
FOR THE TABLE IN
THE SAME PATTERN.**

**A STAPLE LINE
FOR
MANY YEARS.**

No. 0582—table tumbler
Moulded star in cut bottom
Packed 15 dozen in barrel
Per dozen, $0.75, any quantity

No. 5821—3-pint jug, large size
Packed 2 dozen in barrel
Per dozen, $4.75, any quantity

No. 05821—8-oz. bell tumbler
Moulded star in cut bottom
Packed 17 dozen in barrel
Per dozen, $0.75, any quantity

½ size cuts—The best quality at popular prices.

OPEN STOCK IMPERIAL TABLE GLASS

These 2 pieces are often sold together as a nut or salted almond set.

No. 582—handled table salt
Packed 50 dozen in barrel
Per dozen, $0.65, any quantity

No. 582—5-inch two-handled footed bowl
Packed 5 dozen in barrel
Per dozen, $3.00, any quantity

**EVERYTHING
FOR THE TABLE IN
THE SAME
DESIGN**

No. 5822—pressed water bottle
Plain bottom
Packed 2½ dozen in barrel
Per dozen, $4.50, any quantity

No. 05822—pressed water bottle
Hand cut and hand polished star in bottom
Packed 2½ dozen in barrel
Per dozen, $5.25, any quantity

½ size cuts—Table glass of refined taste at popular prices.

OPEN STOCK IMPE RIAL TABLE GLASS

CUT STOPPERS!

THE STOPPERS IN THE TWO OIL
BOTTLES WITH CUT STAR BOTTOMS
ARE CUT AND POLISHED BY HAND.
THE CUT STARS IN THESE TWO
BOTTLES ARE CUT AND POLISHED
BY HAND.

* * * * *

THE TOPS ON THE SALT OR PEPPER
SHAKERS ARE HEAVY CAST AND
SILVER PLATED.

No. 582—salt or pepper shaker
Heavy, silver plated top
Well polished all over
Packed 33 dozen in barrel
Per dozen, $1.00, any quantity

No. 5822—6¼-oz. oil bottle
Plain bottom
Pressed and ground-in stopper
Packed 14 dozen in barrel
Per dozen, $1.75, any quantity

No. 5821—5½-oz. oil bottle
Plain bottom
Pressed and ground-in stopper
Packed 13 dozen in barrel
Per dozen, $2.25, any quantity

No. 05821—5½-oz. oil bottle
Cut star bottom
Cut and ground-in stopper
Packed 13 dozen in barrel
Per dozen, $3.25, any quantity

No. 05822—6¼-oz. oil bottle
Cut star bottom
Cut and ground-in stopper
Packed 14 dozen in barrel
Per dozen, $2.75, any quantity

½ size cuts—Great for hotel or restaurant use.

OPEN STOCK **IMPE RIAL** TABLE GLASS

DESIGN AND TRADE MARK
ARE PATENTED

No. 05821—5¼-inch table butter and cover
Moulded star in cut bottom
Packed 9 dozen in barrel
Per dozen, $1.50, any quantity

No. 582—7½-inch two-handled berry
Packed 3¼ dozen in barrel
Per dozen, $3.00, any quantity

No. 582—7-inch bread and butter plate
Packed 12 dozen in barrel
Per dozen, $1.15, any quantity

No. 5822D—10½-inch bread and butter plate
Packed 5½ dozen in barrel
Per dozen, $1.75, any quantity

½ size cuts—If you admire this design, others will.

OPEN STOCK IMPERIAL TABLE GLASS

DESIGN AND TRADE MARK ARE PATENTED

No. 582—hotel sugar
Packed 8 dozen in barrel
Per dozen, $1.75, any quantity

No. 582—hotel cream
Packed 9 dozen in barrel
Per dozen, $1.75, any quantity

No. 582—8-inch vase
Packed 5 dozen in barrel
Per dozen, $2.50, any quantity

CUT BOTTOMS
The three 5822 vases have hand cut and hand polished bottoms with moulded stars, looking like real cut.

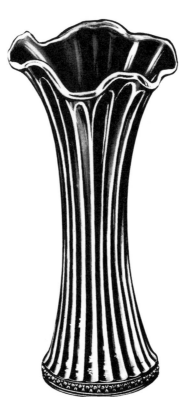

No. 5822—7-inch sweet pea vase
Varies from 6 in. to 9 in. in height
Moulded star in cut bottom
Packed about 4 dozen in barrel
Per dozen, $2.25, any quantity

No. 5822—10-inch rose vase
Varies from 9 in. to 11 in. in height
Moulded star in cut bottom
Packed about 3¾ dozen in barrel
Per dozen, $2.25, any quantity

No. 5822—12-inch long stem flower vase
Varies from 11 in. to 13 in. in height
Moulded star in cut bottom
Packed about 3½ dozen in barrel
Per dozen, $2.25, any quantity

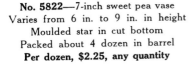

½ size cuts—**Buy this open stock ware in quantities to suit yourself.**

OPEN STOCK IMPERIAL TABLE GLASS

DESIGN AND TRADE MARK
ARE PATENTED

THESE FOUR PIECES HAVE MOULDED STARS
IN CUT AND HIGHLY POLISHED BOTTOMS

No. 0582—sugar and cover
Cover and bowl are highly polished
Packed 6 dozen in barrel
Per dozen, $2.50, any quantity

No. 0582—cream
Highly polished
Packed 8 dozen in barrel
Per dozen, $1.75, any quantity

No. 0582—butter and cover
Cover and dish are highly polished
Packed 3½ dozen in barrel
Per dozen, $3.50, any quantity

No. 0582—spoon
Highly polished
Packed 8 dozen in barrel
Per dozen, $1.75, any quantity

½ size cuts—Kept in open stock like a china dinner ware pattern.

BARGAIN BOOK

The page numbers which appear on the first four pages of the Bargain Book have no relation to the sequence page numbers of this publication. These pages are shown to give an insight to the methods used in the advertising by Imperial during these years.

The Bargain Book was a special catalog made up from a number of small catalogs and represents glass which was made between 1910 and 1929. The most interesting is the fact that the "Free-Blown" glass and some of the Imperial Jewels appear in a so-called Bargain Book.

The "Free-Blown" glass by Imperial is one of the most misrepresented line of glass collected today. It is very seldom identified as Imperial. It is usually identified as Tiffany, Duvan or other expensive antique-type glass. We expect someday it will come into its own rights as a very desirable collectible item.

DESCRIPTION OF HAND CUTTINGS

Page 16   The hand cuttings on these lead lustre, non-transparent vases are very high grade, being really stone engravings.   (Cuttings Nos. 93-94-95).

The designs are cut through the iridescent coverings and appear on the colored back grounds in pure white.

Pages 19 and 20   The hand cuttings appear in sparkling crystal on the transparent vases in bright iridescent colors.

Page 21   The hand cuttings appear in crystal on the satin iridescent colors.

This page shows the beginning of a marvelously beautiful line of decorations, entirely new.

HAND CUTTINGS ON CRYSTAL — Pages 22 to 34

Hand Cutting   2
"   "   7
"   "   10
"   "   20
"   "   28
"   "   61
"   "   66
"   "   90

These eight designs are in the satin gray color left by the cutting stone.

Hand Cutting 12
"   "   13
"   "   30
"   "   57
"   "   63
"   "   88
"   "   96
"   "   97
"   "   98
"   "   99

These ten designs are partly gray and partly brilliantly polished by hand.

ALL OUR HAND CUTTINGS, EVEN THE LOWEST PRICED ONES, ARE OF GOOD QUALITY— NOT THE CHEAP UGLY LOOKING SCRATCHES, SOMETIMES OFFERED AS CUT GLASS.

LIST OF COLORED GLASSES IN THIS BOOK

LEAD LUSTRE GLASSES   see pages 4 to 16.

Bright iridescent colors

Color No.

22	PEACOCK :	This glass has a very brilliant iridescence, but the effect is not loud. Every color of the rainbow is represented, a golden yellow predominating. Many color variations.
M	RUBIGOLD :	Our famous dark red iridescent glass with tints of other colors. The biggest selling line of iridescent glass in the world.
52	NURUBY :	Very similar to Rubigold, but because used mostly on plain designs, a slight change in the chemicals was necessary.
53	SAPHIRE :	A dark blue-gray iridescent color on crystal glass. An entirely new, expensive looking effect.
L	AZUR :	A very brilliant iridescent effect, on a dark amethyst colored glass. All colors of the rainbow such as: yellow, green, rose, combine in this treatment.
12	PURPLE GLAZE :	A very brilliant blue iridescent effect, on dark amethyst glass. The effect is similar to that of the plain blue iridescence on the expensive lead lustre glass.
K	HELIOS :	A silvery iridescence on green glass, very beautiful.

Satin iridescent colors

All in crizzled satin effects, similar to very much more expensive iridescent art pieces.   We make the following satin colors:

44	Iris Ice, white crizzled on crystal glass.
56	Rose Ice, pink crizzled on crystal glass.
50	Blue Ice, blue crizzled on crystal glass.
58	Amber Ice, crizzled on amber glass.
25	Green Ice, crizzled on green glass.
54	Amethyst Ice, crizzled on mulberry glass.

} Very dainty, modest color effects.

77 and 66   BLUE GLOW AND RED GLOW (on pages 65 and 66) are similar to Nuruby and Saphire.

PLAIN COLORS

20	Nugreen is a bluish green plain glass.
30	Mulberry is a plain amethyst glass.
40	Amber is a plain amber glass.

} Without iridescence.

NUMBERS OF LEAD LUSTRE COLORS

Shown on pages 5 to 16

Decor. No.

5	Outside plain dark green finish — Inside opal bright red.
6	Same as No. 5, but with opal leaf and web decoration, satin finish.
10	Dark blue with brilliant blue glaze, inside and outside.
11	Blue glass with fancy opal decoration, satin all over.
12	Blue glass with 4 opal festoons, satin all over.
14	Blue glass with fancy opal decoration, bright green all over.
20	Plain opal, bright red glaze all over.
21	Opal with blue fancy decoration, bright red inside only.
22	Opal with 4 blue festoons, red glaze all over.
25	Opal with green leaf and web decoration, satin outside, red inside.
29	Plain blue glass with opal leaf and web, opal edge, not iridescent.
30	Plain blue outside, opal with bright red glaze inside.
31	Opal with gray iridescence outside, bright red inside.
32	Plain blue outside, opal with satin red inside.
35	Plain canary outside, opal with bright red iridescent inside.
36	Same as No. 35, but with 4 opal festoons.
37	Opal with satin red iridescence outside, canary satin inside.
38	Plain canary outside, opal with red satin iridescent inside.
40	Opal with bright green iridescence outside, bright red inside.
44	Opal with bright green iridescence outside, gray inside.
51	Plain dark green outside, opal bright green inside.
60	Plain mulberry glass outside, opal with bright red glaze inside.
61	Plain mulberry glass outside, opal with red satin inside.

MATERIAL

In all above goods (pages 5 to 16) the very highest grade of lead glass has to be used, the same kind of lustre lead glass which distinguishes the very highest grade of hand made art glass wares from all other glass.

Our Famous Lead Lustre Glass.

is shown on the following 3 pages in colors, to give you at least an idea of a few of the fascinating effects of this art glass.

On pages 9 to 16, additional assortments of LUSTRE GLASS are shown in black and white illustrations.

All the articles on pages 6 to 16 are of the same character, all made out of our LEAD LUSTRE GLASS.

This is a very high grade of lead glass in lustre colors. In fact, nothing better is possible.

This glass is mostly non-transparent, resembling sometimes the very finest grades of Art China, only the bright colors are still brighter, and the satin colors are softer, more velvety, than they can be even in the best China Art Ware.

Glass of similar excellence has been sold heretofore at many times higher prices.

Our low prices were made possible only by our new process of manufacture, a patent for which has been applied for.

In spite of our low prices, you need not have any doubt about the high quality of our LEAD LUSTRE GLASS. We repeat: It is the best.

SPECIAL LOT 2035

This lot is shown by colored illustrations on the next 3 pages. This lot consists of two pieces each (1 pair) of the 15 vases shown, or 30 assorted vases, packed in one barrel.

FOR PRICES OF ASSORTMENTS AND INDIVIDUAL PIECES SEE PRICE LIST

Blown Lead Glass Vases, made by our own process.

619—22

412—22

418—10

417—30

618—12

Illustrations as shown are nearly one-half size of vases.

Blown Lead Glass Vases, made by our own process.

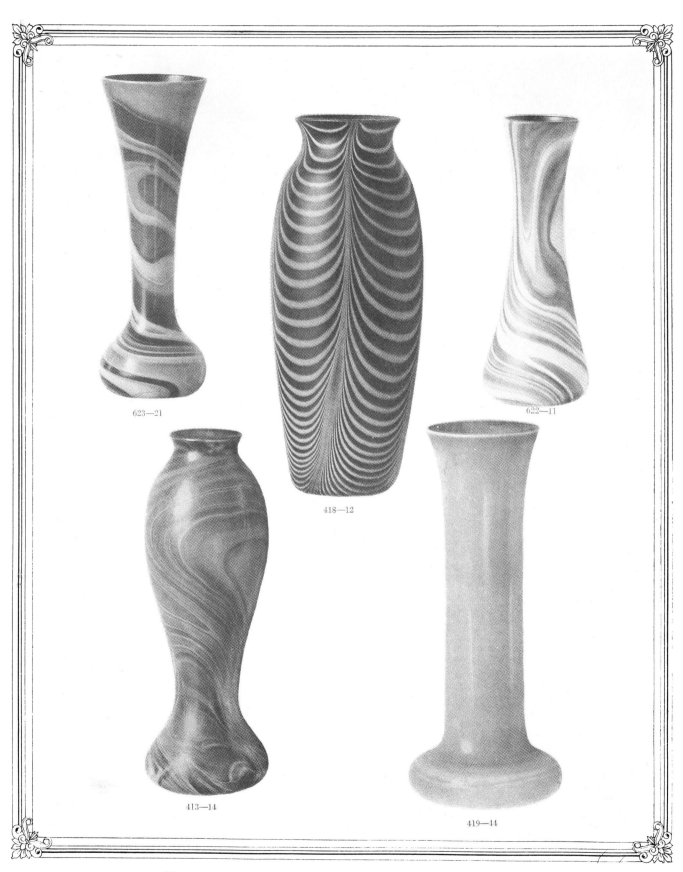

623—21

418—12

622—11

413—14

419—14

Illustrations as shown are nearly one-half size of vases.

Blown Lead Glass Vases, made by our own process.

622—21

623—10

115—11

417—20

618—10

Illustrations as shown are nearly one-half size of vases.

Not Transparent Glass (looks like finest Porcelain)

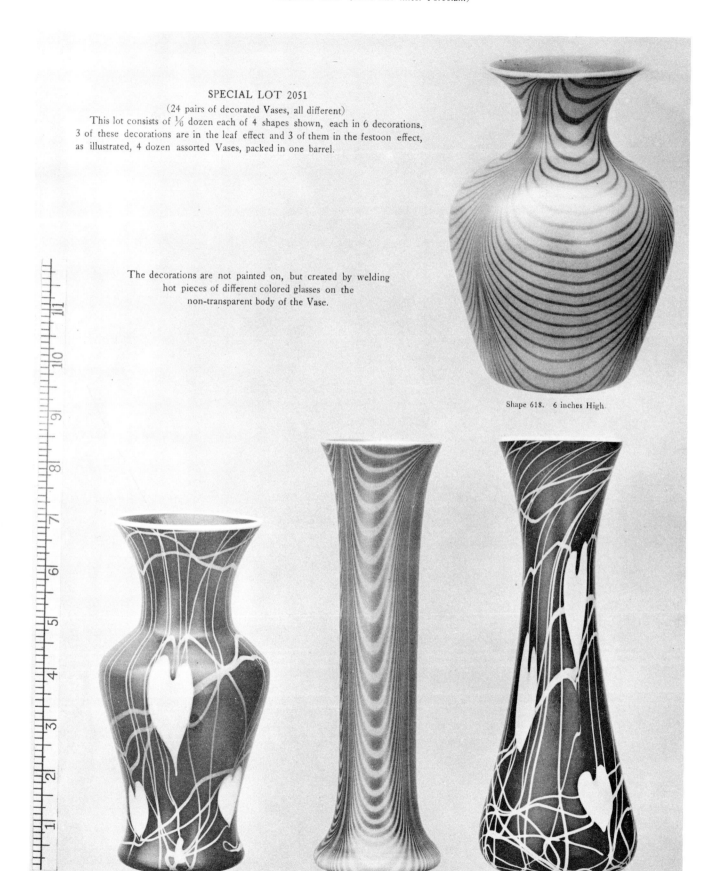

SPECIAL LOT 2051
(24 pairs of decorated Vases, all different)
This lot consists of ⅙ dozen each of 4 shapes shown, each in 6 decorations.
3 of these decorations are in the leaf effect and 3 of them in the festoon effect,
as illustrated, 4 dozen assorted Vases, packed in one barrel.

The decorations are not painted on, but created by welding
hot pieces of different colored glasses on the
non-transparent body of the Vase.

Shape 618.   6 inches High.

Shape 655.   6¾ inches High.   Shape 619.   8¾ inches High.   Shape 622.   8½ inches High.

For detailed description of colors, see Price List.

The decorations are not painted on, but created by welding hot pieces of different colored glasses on the body of the Vase.

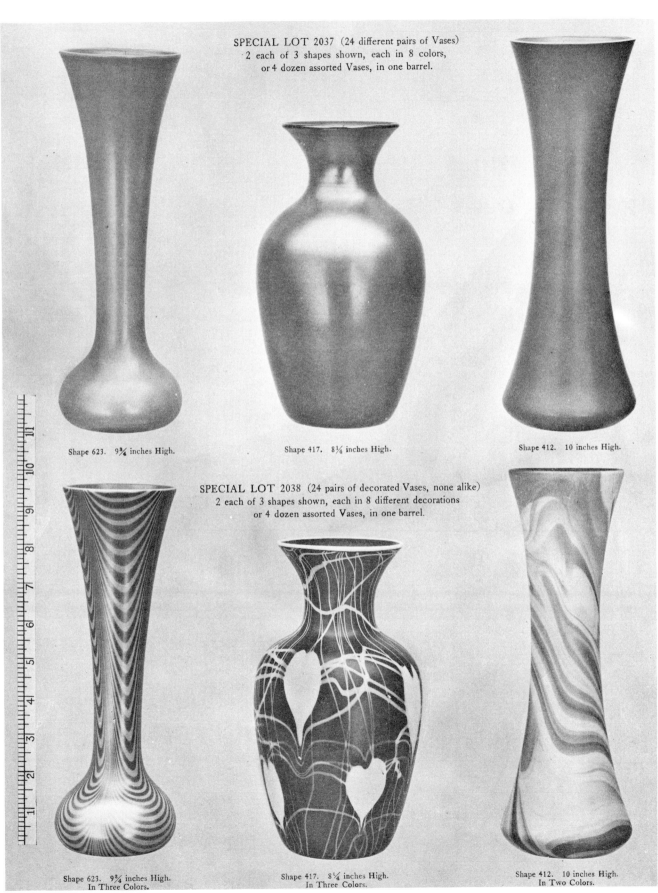

SPECIAL LOT 2037 (24 different pairs of Vases)
2 each of 3 shapes shown, each in 8 colors,
or 4 dozen assorted Vases, in one barrel.

Shape 623.   9¾ inches High.

Shape 417.   8¼ inches High.

Shape 412.   10 inches High.

SPECIAL LOT 2038 (24 pairs of decorated Vases, none alike)
2 each of 3 shapes shown, each in 8 different decorations
or 4 dozen assorted Vases, in one barrel.

Shape 623.   9¾ inches High.
In Three Colors.

Shape 417.   8¼ inches High.
In Three Colors.

Shape 412.   10 inches High.
In Two Colors.

For description of decorations and colors, see Price List.

The decorations in Lot 2040 are not painted on, but created by welding hot pieces of different colored glasses.

SPECIAL LOT 2039 contains 3 dozen Vases, assorted in one barrel,
or 2 each of 3 shapes shown, each in 6 different colors.

18 Pairs of Vases in one barrel,
not two of them alike.

3761.   8 inch Rose Bowl.   643.   9 inch Vase.   413.   10 inch Vase.

SPECIAL LOT 2040 contains 3 dozen assorted decorated Vases in one barrel,
or 2 each of **3** shapes shown, each in 6 different decorations.

18 Pairs of Vases in one barrel,
not two of them alike.

3761.   8 inch Rose Bowl.   643.   9 inch Vase.   413.   10 inch Vase.

For description of Colors see Pages 4 and 5

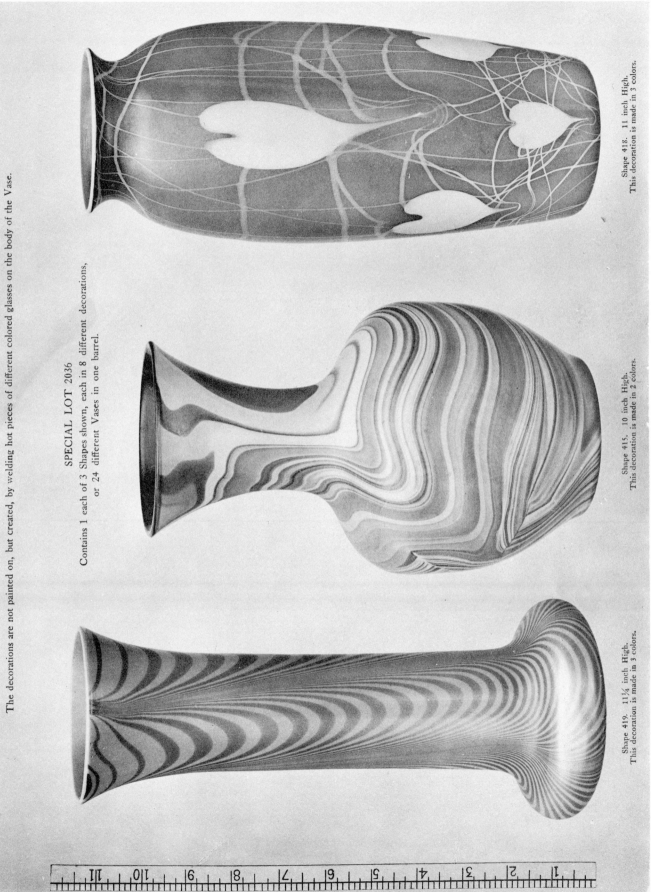

HIGHEST GRADE OF BLOWN LEAD LUSTRE GLASS.   Not Transparent Colors.

The decorations are not painted on, but created, by welding hot pieces of different colored glasses on the body of the Vase.

SPECIAL LOT 2036

Contains 1 each of 3 Shapes shown, each in 8 different decorations, or 24 different Vases in one barrel.

Shape 418.   11 inch High.
This decoration is made in 3 colors.

Shape 415.   10 inch High.
This decoration is made in 2 colors.

Shape 419.   11¼ inch High.
This decoration is made in 3 colors.

For details of decorations see Price List and Page 4 of this Book.

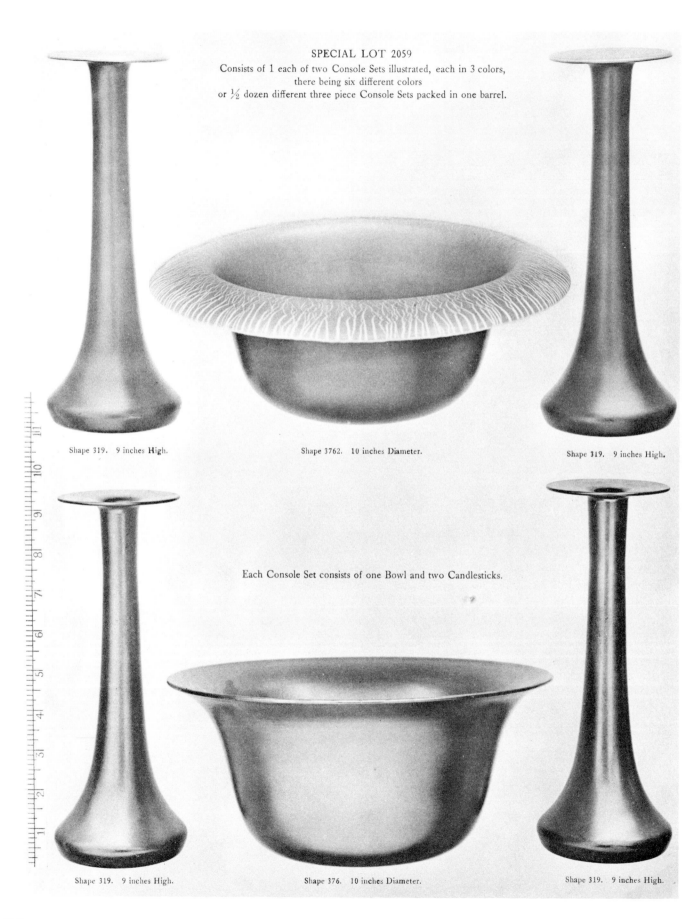

SPECIAL LOT 2059
Consists of 1 each of two Console Sets illustrated, each in 3 colors,
there being six different colors
or ½ dozen different three piece Console Sets packed in one barrel.

Each Console Set consists of one Bowl and two Candlesticks.

Shape 319.   9 inches High.

Shape 3762.   10 inches Diameter.

Shape 319.   9 inches High.

Shape 319.   9 inches High.

Shape 376.   10 inches Diameter.

Shape 319.   9 inches High.

For full description of colors, see Price List and first 4 pages of this catalog.

FINE HAND CUTTINGS ON NON TRANSPARENT LEAD LUSTRE GLASS.

The Cuttings appear in Pure White on Colored Backgrounds.

SPECIAL LOT 2072 contains 2 each of the seven shapes shown,
hand cut as shown, each in 2 colors, Gray Iridescent and Orange
Iridescent, or 2⅓ dozen assorted Vases in one barrel.

619 Cut 93.   8 inch Bud Vase.

655 Cut 93.   Vase.
6¾ inches High.

618 Cut 93.   Rose Bowl.
6 inches High.

622 Cut 93.   Vase.
8¾ inches High.

419 Cut 95.   11¼ inches High.

415 Cut 95.   10 inches High.

418 Cut 94.   11 inches High.

Each article in this Book can be ordered individually.

HAND CUTTINGS ON TRANSPARENT IRIDESCENT CRYSTAL.

The cuttings appear in Sparkling Crystal on the Iridescent Vases, assorted in NURUBY, SAPPHIRE, PEACOCK.

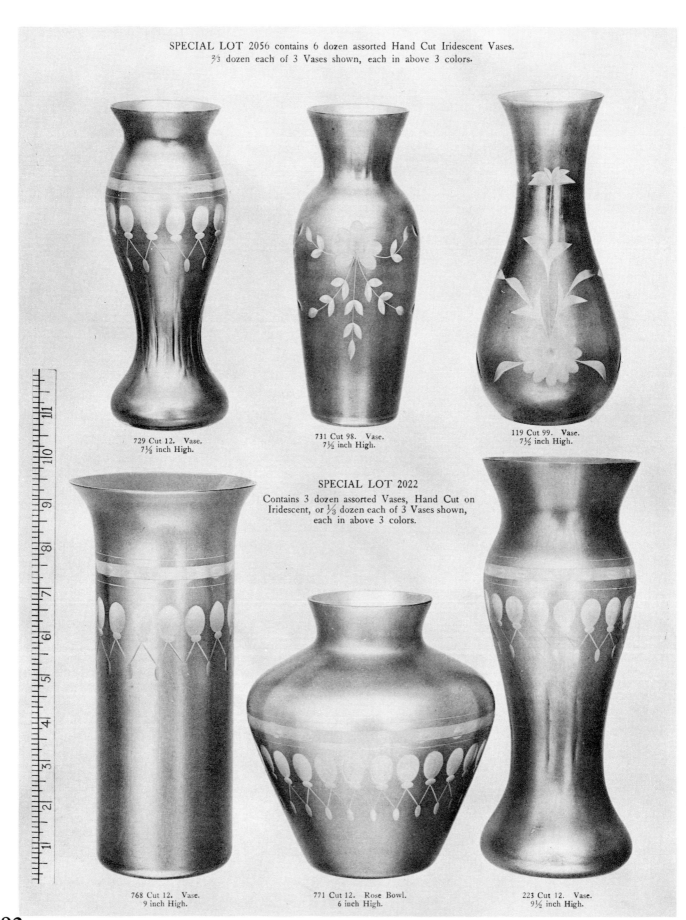

SPECIAL LOT 2056 contains 6 dozen assorted Hand Cut Iridescent Vases.
⅔ dozen each of 3 Vases shown, each in above 3 colors.

729 Cut 12. Vase.
7½ inch High.

731 Cut 98. Vase.
7½ inch High.

119 Cut 99. Vase.
7½ inch High.

SPECIAL LOT 2022

Contains 3 dozen assorted Vases, Hand Cut on
Iridescent, or ⅓ dozen each of 3 Vases shown,
each in above 3 colors.

768 Cut 12. Vase.
9 inch High.

771 Cut 12. Rose Bowl.
6 inch High.

223 Cut 12. Vase.
9½ inch High.

For detailed description of colors see Page 3

HIGH GRADE HAND CUTTINGS ON SATIN IRIDESCENT COLORS.

The Cuttings appear in Crystal on the Satin colored background.   Each made in 3 colors: Rose Satin — Blue Satin — Iris Satin.

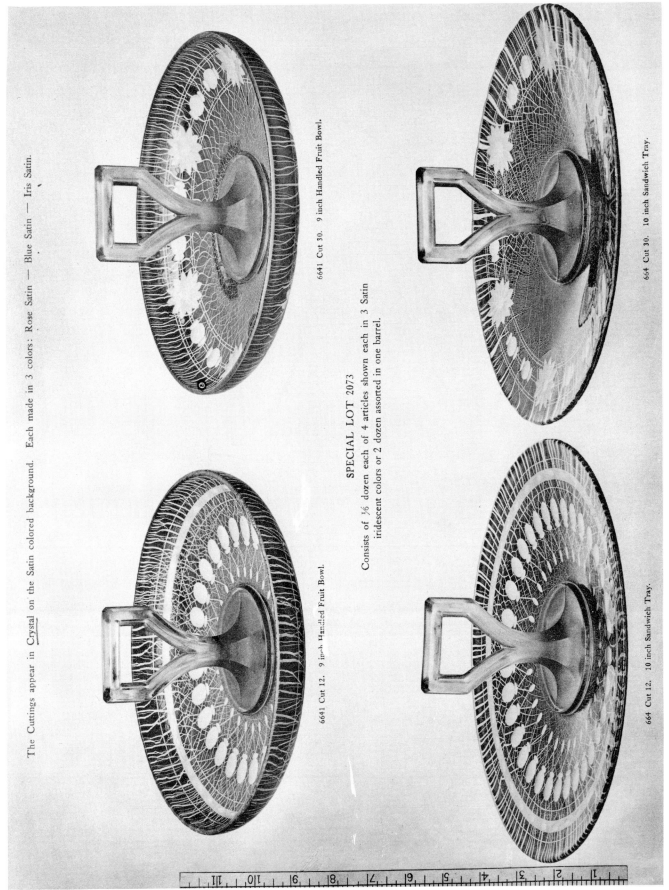

6641 Cut 30.   9 inch Handled Fruit Bowl.

664 Cut 30.   10 inch Sandwich Tray.

6641 Cut 12.   9 inch Handled Fruit Bowl.

664 Cut 12.   10 inch Sandwich Tray.

SPECIAL LOT 2073

Consists of ⅙ dozen each of 4 articles shown each in 3 Satin
iridescent colors or 2 dozen assorted in one barrel.

See Page 3 of this Book for Colors.   See Price List for Individual Prices.

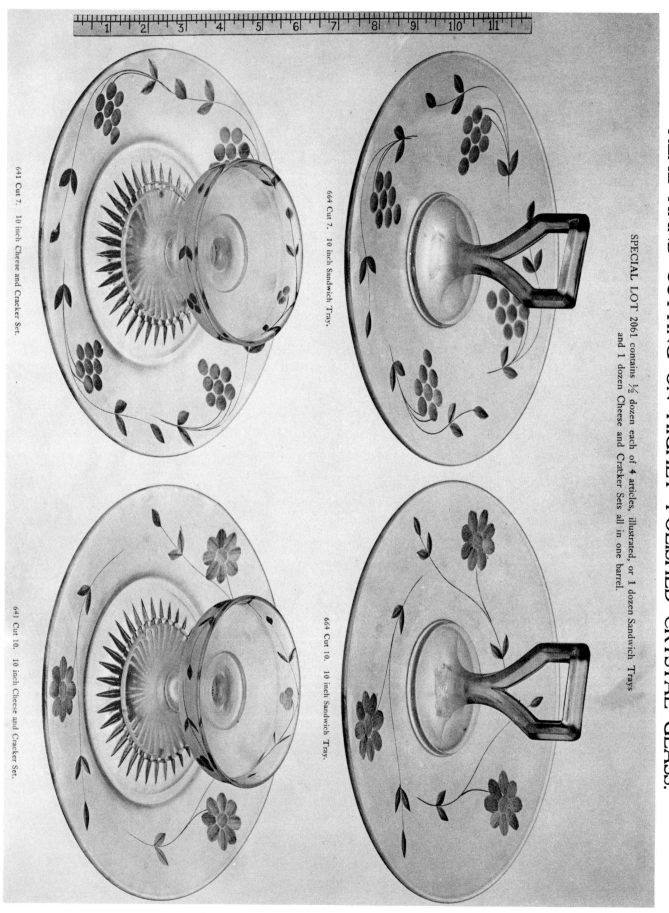

REAL HAND CUTTING ON HIGHLY POLISHED CRYSTAL GLASS.

SPECIAL LOT 2061 contains ½ dozen each of **4** articles, illustrated, or 1 dozen Cheese and Cracker Sets and 1 dozen Sandwich Trays and 1 dozen Cheese and Cracker Sets all in one barrel.

664 Cut 7.   10 inch Sandwich Tray.

641 Cut 7.   10 inch Cheese and Cracker Set.

664 Cut 10.   10 inch Sandwich Tray.

641 Cut 10.   10 inch Cheese and Cracker Set.

94

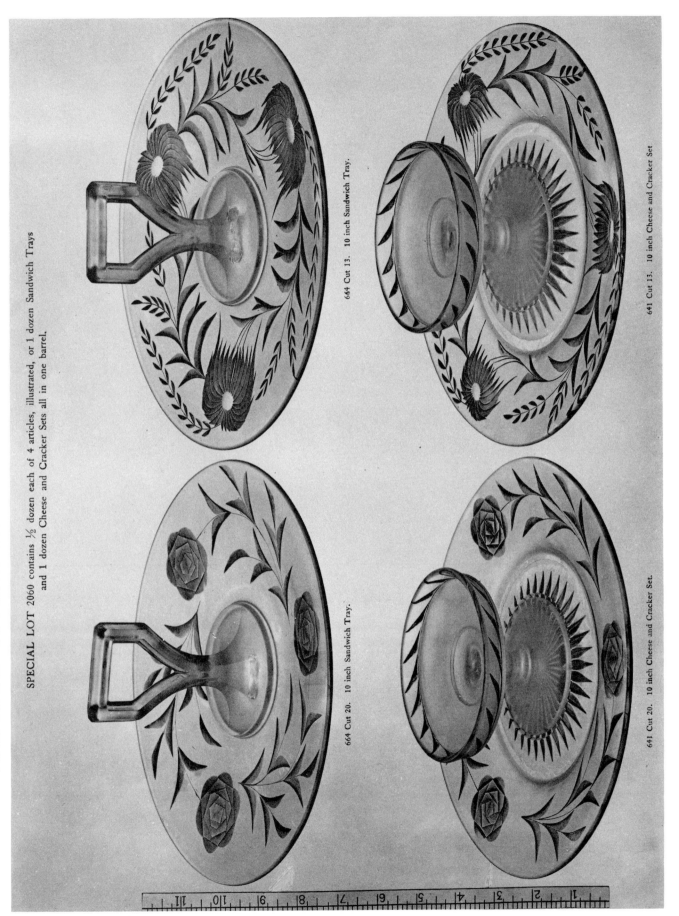

FINE HAND CUTTING ON HIGHLY POLISHED CRYSTAL GLASS.

SPECIAL LOT 2060 contains ½ dozen each of 4 articles, illustrated, or 1 dozen Sandwich Trays and 1 dozen Cheese and Cracker Sets all in one barrel.

664 Cut 13. 10 inch Sandwich Tray.

641 Cut 13. 10 inch Cheese and Cracker Set

664 Cut 20. 10 inch Sandwich Tray.

641 Cut 20. 10 inch Cheese and Cracker Set.

SPECIAL LOT 2066 contains 1 dozen assorted 8 piece Salad Sets in one barrel, or ½ dozen each of 2 designs, shown below.

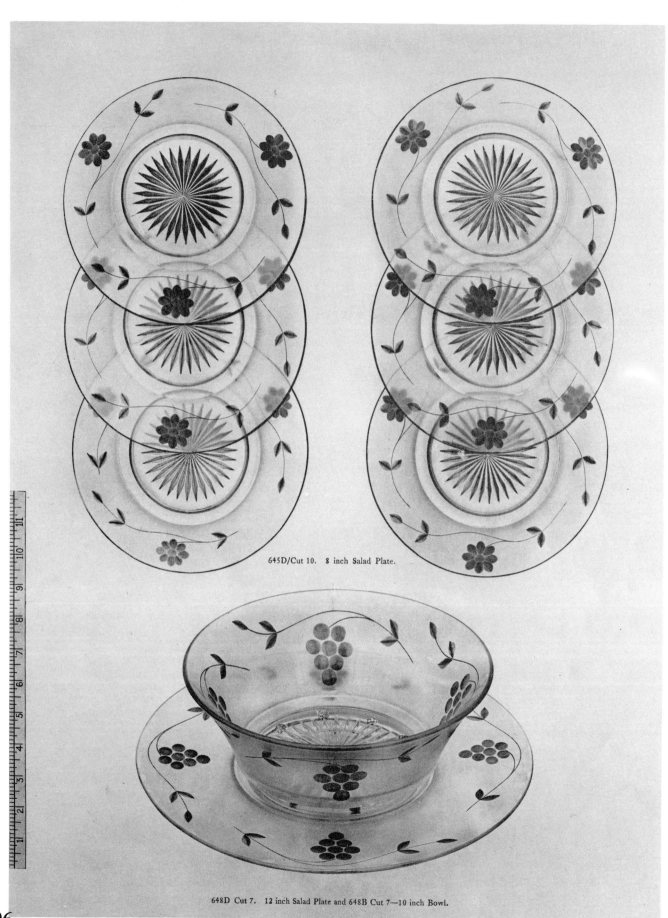

645D/Cut 10. 8 inch Salad Plate.

648D Cut 7. 12 inch Salad Plate and 648B Cut 7—10 inch Bowl.

SPECIAL LOT 2065 consists of 1 dozen assorted 8 piece Salad Sets in **one** barrel, or ½ dozen each of 2 designs, shown below.

645D Cut 20. **8 inch Salad Plate.**

648D Cut 13. 12 inch Salad Plate and 648B Cut 13—10 inch Bowl.

Each Salad Set contains one Large Bowl and Plate, with six 8 inch Plates to Match.

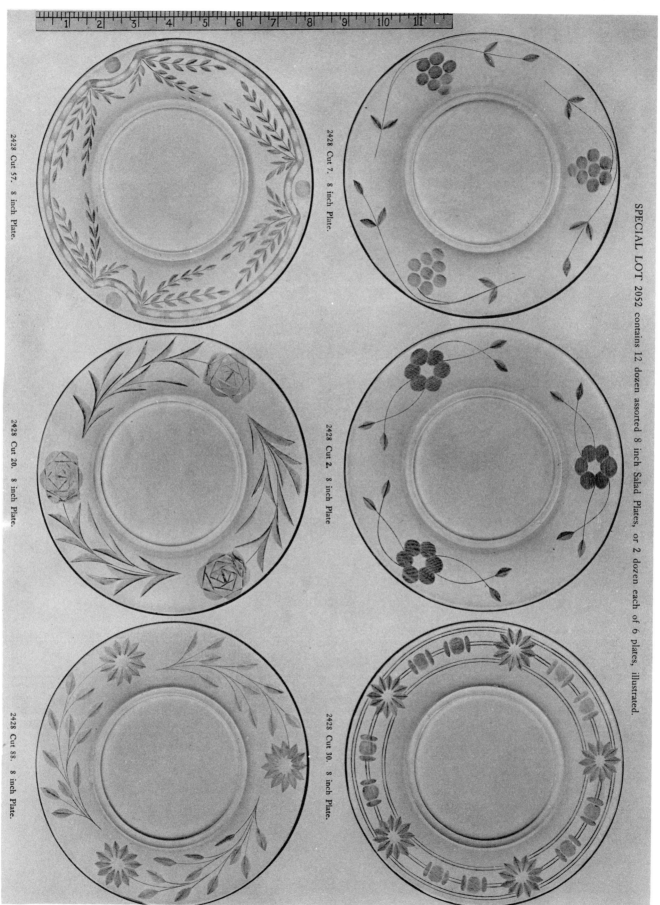

GENUINE HAND CUTTING ON GROUND BOTTOM CRYSTAL GLASS PLATES.

SPECIAL LOT 2052 contains 12 dozen assorted 8 inch Salad Plates, or 2 dozen each of 6 plates, illustrated.

2428 Cut 57. 8 inch Plate.

2428 Cut 7. 8 inch Plate.

2428 Cut 20. 8 inch Plate.

2428 Cut 2. 8 inch Plate

For description of **Hand Cuttings,** See Page 2 of this Book.

2428 Cut 88. 8 inch Plate.

2428 Cut 30. 8 inch Plate.

HIGH GRADE HAND CUTTINGS ON EXTRA POLISHED CRYSTAL.

SPECIAL LOT 2064 contains 9 pairs of Hand Cut Candlesticks, (all different) and 1 dozen assorted 2 piece Hand Cut Night Sets.

The 9 pairs of Candlesticks consist of ⅙ dozen each of 3 sizes shown, each in 3 cuttings shown.

6247 Cut 61. Square.
7 inch High.

6249 Cut 63. Square.
9 inch High.

62412 Cut 66. Square.
12 inch High.

650 Cut 57. 2 Piece Night Set.
½ dozen Sets in Lot.

650 Cut 88. 2 Piece Night Set.
½ dozen Sets in Lot.

Pitchers and Tumblers are Blown.   Each Water Set contains 1 Cut Jug and 6 Tumblers to Match.

SPECIAL LOT 2062
Contains 1 dozen assorted 7 Piece Water Sets.

There are 2 Shapes of Jugs, each in 3 designs, or six different Sets, ⅙ dozen each in one barrel.

803 Cut 88
12 oz. Ice Tea.

803 Cut 90
12 oz. Ice Tea.

803 Cut 20
12 oz. Ice Tea.

84 Cut 88. ½ Gallon Jug.

599 Cut 90. ½ Gallon Jug.

599 Cut 20. ½ Gallon Jug.

SPECIAL LOT 2032 consists of 9 pieces each of 8 items, shown below, or 6 dozen assorted in one barrel.

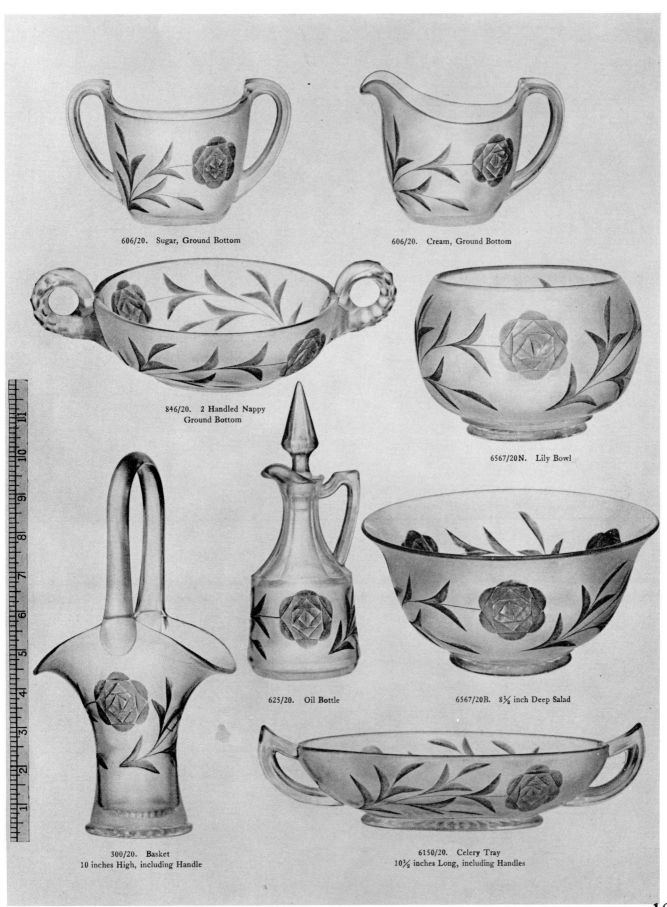

606/20. Sugar, Ground Bottom

606/20. Cream, Ground Bottom

846/20. 2 Handled Nappy
Ground Bottom

6567/20N. Lily Bowl

625/20. Oil Bottle

6567/20B. 8½ inch Deep Salad

300/20. Basket
10 inches High, including Handle

6150/20. Celery Tray
10½ inches Long, including Handles

Each item can be ordered individually, see Price List.

SPECIAL LOT 2033 consists of 2¼ dozen each of 8 items, shown below, or 18 dozen assorted in one barrel.

615/28. Sugar

615/28. Cream

6674/28. 1 Handled Nappy

6151/28. 2 Handled Bon Bon

499A/28. Sherbet
499/28. Sherbet Plate

6154½A/28. 5 inch Nappy

615/28. 2 Handled Pickle

Each item can be furnished individually, see Price List.

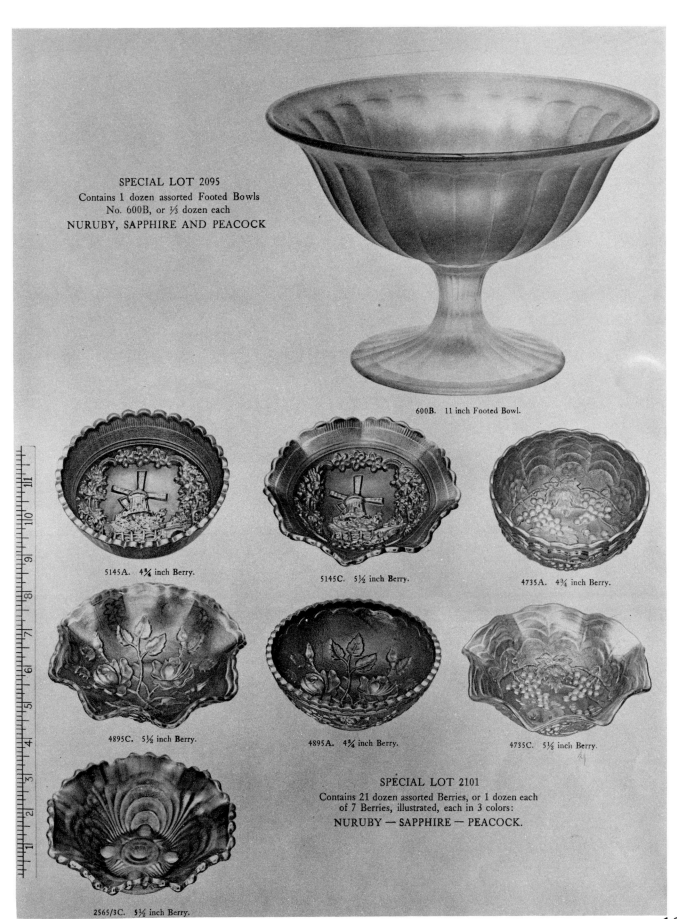

SPECIAL LOT 2095
Contains 1 dozen assorted Footed Bowls
No. 600B, or ⅓ dozen each
NURUBY, SAPPHIRE AND PEACOCK

600B. 11 inch Footed Bowl.

5145A. 4¾ inch Berry.

5145C. 5½ inch Berry.

4735A. 4¾ inch Berry.

4895C. 5½ inch Berry.

4895A. 4¾ inch Berry.

4735C. 5½ inch Berry.

SPECIAL LOT 2101
Contains 21 dozen assorted Berries, or 1 dozen each
of 7 Berries, illustrated, each in 3 colors:
NURUBY — SAPPHIRE — PEACOCK.

2565/3C. 5½ inch Berry.

For colors see Page 3 of this Book.

3 Different Colors (Rubigold — Azur — Helios) in one barrel.

SPECIAL LOT 2047 contains 1 dozen each of 5 articles illustrated, each in the color named under the respective illustration, or 5 dozen assorted in one barrel.

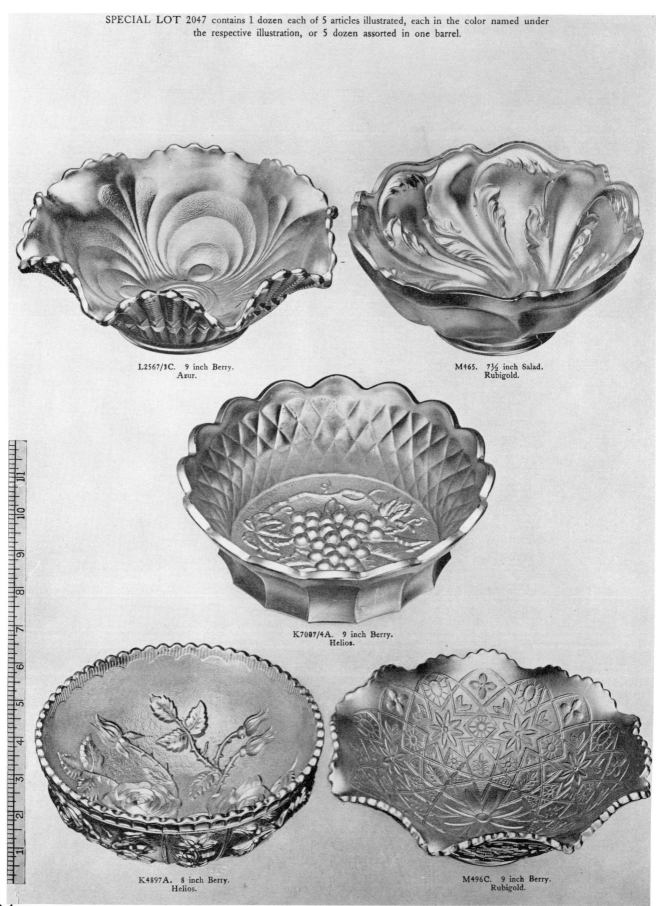

L2567/3C. 9 inch Berry.
Azur.

M465. 7½ inch Salad.
Rubigold.

K7007/4A. 9 inch Berry.
Helios.

K4897A. 8 inch Berry.
Helios.

M496C. 9 inch Berry.
Rubigold.

Each article can be ordered separately, see Price List.

THREE BRIGHT IRIDESCENT COLORS.

RUBIGOLD — SAPPHIRE — PEACOCK.

4898C. 11 inch Fruit Bowl.

4738A. 9 inch Fruit Bowl.

SPECIAL LOT 2050

Contains ½ dozen each 4898C and 4738A, each in 3 colors mentioned, or 3 dozen assorted Fruit Bowls in one barrel.

For Colors See Page 3 of this Book

4891A. 7½ inch Salad (or Fern Dish), 3 Toes.

5141C. 9 inch Salad, 3 Toes.

SPECIAL LOT 2049

Contains ½ dozen each 4891A and 5141C, each in 3 colors mentioned, or 3 dozen assorted Salads in one barrel.

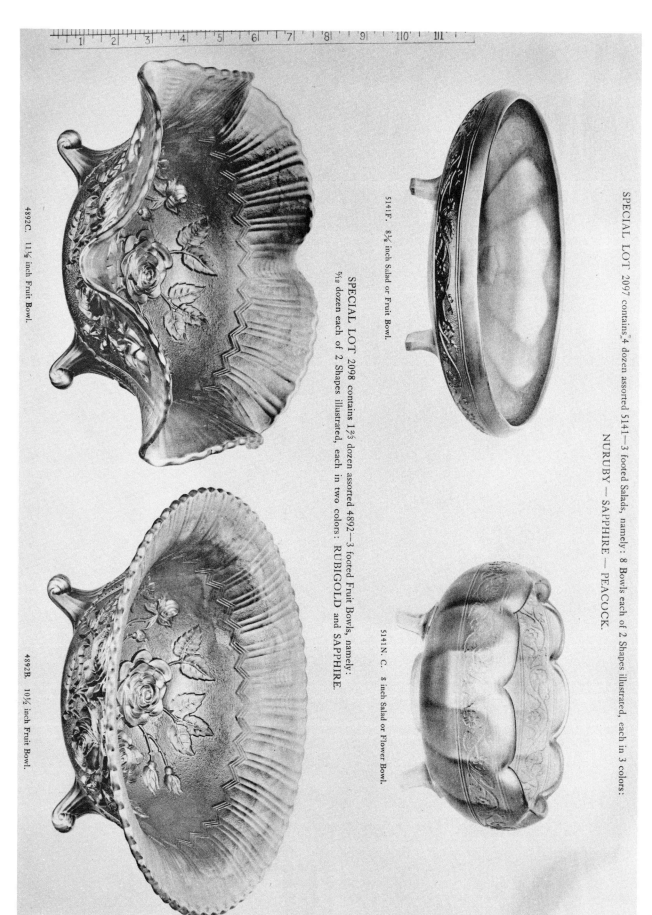

BRIGHT IRIDESCENT COLORS.

SPECIAL LOT 2097 contains 4 dozen assorted 5141—3 footed Salads, namely: 8 Bowls each of 2 Shapes illustrated, each in 3 colors:

NURUBY — SAPPHIRE — PEACOCK.

5141F.   8½ inch Salad or Fruit Bowl.

5141N. C.   8 inch Salad or Flower Bowl.

SPECIAL LOT 2098 contains 1⅔ dozen assorted 4892—3 footed Fruit Bowls, namely:
5/12 dozen each of 2 Shapes illustrated, each in two colors: RUBIGOLD and SAPPHIRE.

4892C.   11½ inch Fruit Bowl.

4892B.   10½ inch Fruit Bowl.

Barrels are always Charged Extra.

106

Three Colors in Each Lot.

SPECIAL LOT 2074
Contains 2¼ dozen 3 piece Console Sets, assorted in one barrel,
or ¾ dozen each Nuruby Iridescent, Peacock Iridescent
and Sapphire Iridescent.

6007.   7 inch Candlestick.

5141/2B.   8½ inch Salad.
3 Footed.

6007.   7 inch Candlestick.

SPECIAL LOT 2018
Contains 1½ dozen assorted 4 piece Console Sets in one barrel
or ½ dozen each in Nuruby Iridescent, Peacock Iridescent
and Plain Mulberry.

635-8⅛ inch Candlestick.

6567/2B.   8½ inch Bowl on
No. 634 Black Base.

635-8½ inch Candlestick

THREE BRIGHT IRIDESCENT COLORS.

Each Color Packed Separately.

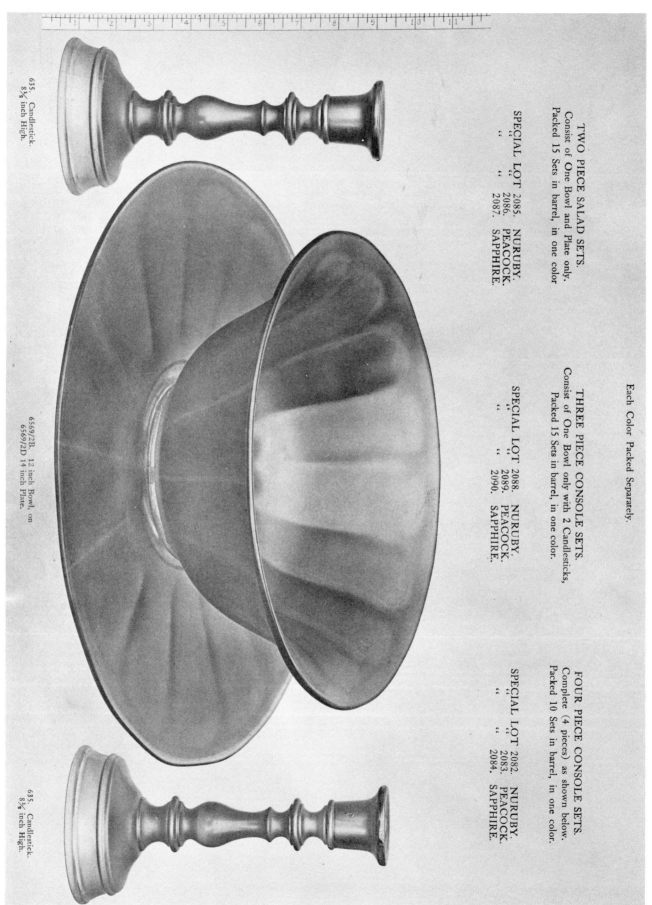

635. Candlestick.
8⅜ inch High.

TWO PIECE SALAD SETS.
Consist of One Bowl and Plate only.
Packed 15 Sets in barrel, in one color.

SPECIAL LOT	2085.	NURUBY.
" "	2086.	PEACOCK.
" "	2087.	SAPPHIRE.

THREE PIECE CONSOLE SETS.
Consist of One Bowl only with 2 Candlesticks.
Packed 15 Sets in barrel, in one color.

SPECIAL LOT	2088.	NURUBY.
" "	2089.	PEACOCK.
" "	2090.	SAPPHIRE.

FOUR PIECE CONSOLE SETS.
Complete (4 pieces) as shown below.
Packed 10 Sets in barrel, in one color.

SPECIAL LOT	2082.	NURUBY.
" "	2083.	PEACOCK.
" "	2084.	SAPPHIRE.

6569/2B. 12 inch Bowl, on
6569/2D 14 inch Plate.

635. Candlestick.
8⅜ inch **High.**

Each article in this Catalog can be bought individually.

108

This Lot consists of 1 dozen 8 piece Salad Sets, as shown, or ⅓ dozen each of the following 3 colors:
Nuruby Iridescent, Peacock Iridescent, Plain Nugreen.

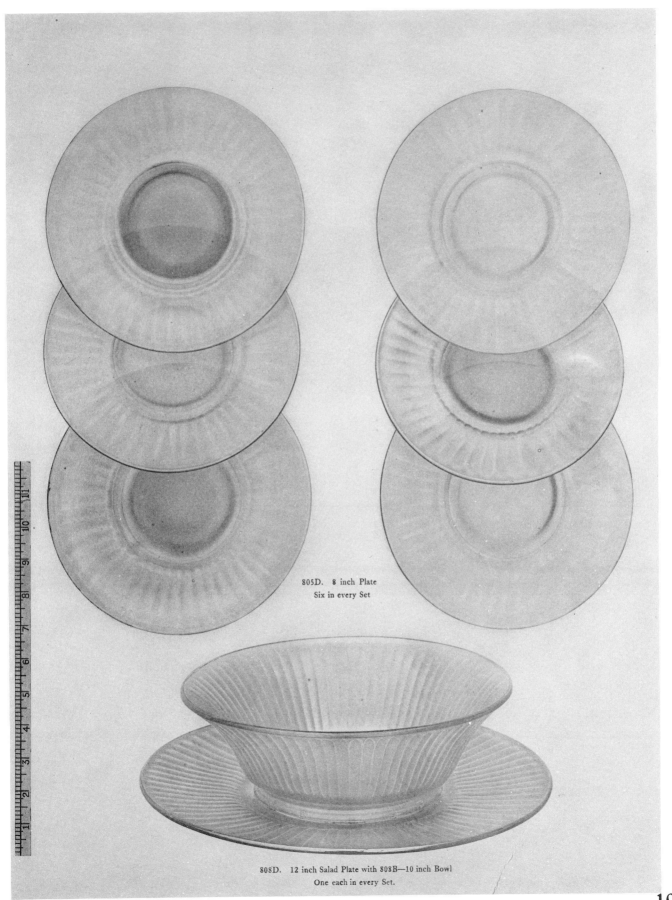

805D.   8 inch Plate
Six in every Set

808D.   12 inch Salad Plate with 808B—10 inch Bowl
One each in every Set.

Each item can be ordered by itself, see Price List.

THREE NEW SATIN IRIDESCENT COLORS.

ROSE ICE — BLUE ICE — IRIS ICE.

SPECIAL LOT 2096 contains 1 dozen 8 piece Salad Sets, evenly assorted in above 3 Satin Colors.

Each 8 piece Salad Set consists of one 647/2B. 9 inch Bowl, one 647/2D—11 inch Plate and six 645/2D—8 inch Salad Plates.

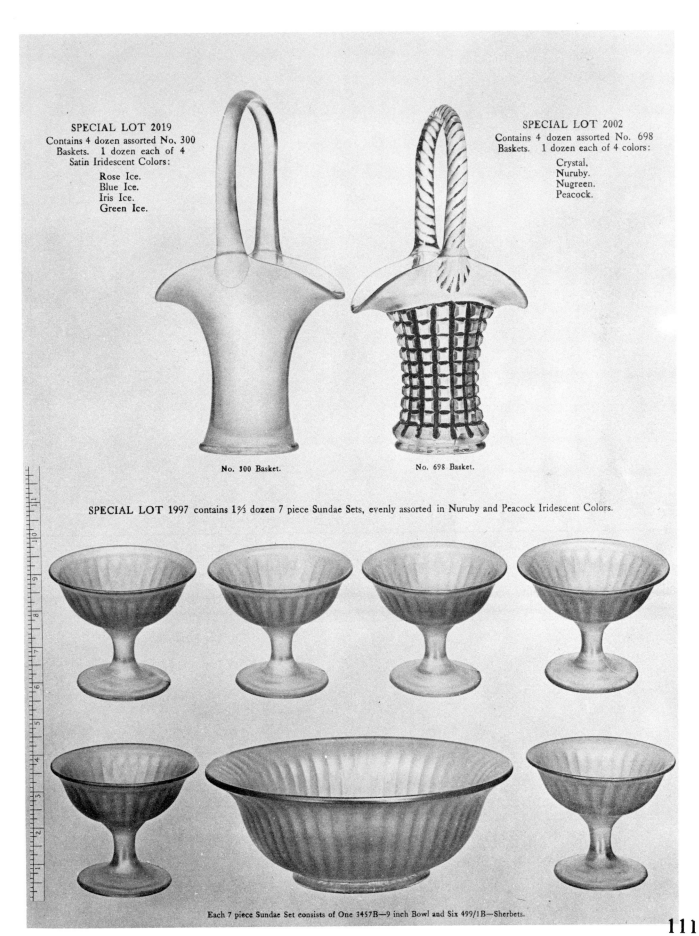

SPECIAL LOT 2019
Contains 4 dozen assorted No. 300 Baskets. 1 dozen each of 4 Satin Iridescent Colors:

Rose Ice.
Blue Ice.
Iris Ice.
Green Ice.

SPECIAL LOT 2002
Contains 4 dozen assorted No. 698 Baskets. 1 dozen each of 4 colors:

Crystal.
Nuruby.
Nugreen.
Peacock.

No. 300 Basket.

No. 698 Basket.

SPECIAL LOT 1997 contains 1⅔ dozen 7 piece Sundae Sets, evenly assorted in Nuruby and Peacock Iridescent Colors.

Each 7 piece Sundae Set consists of One 3457B—9 inch Bowl and Six 499/1B—Sherbets.

111

PEACOCK — NURUBY — SAPPHIRE — PURPLE GLAZE.

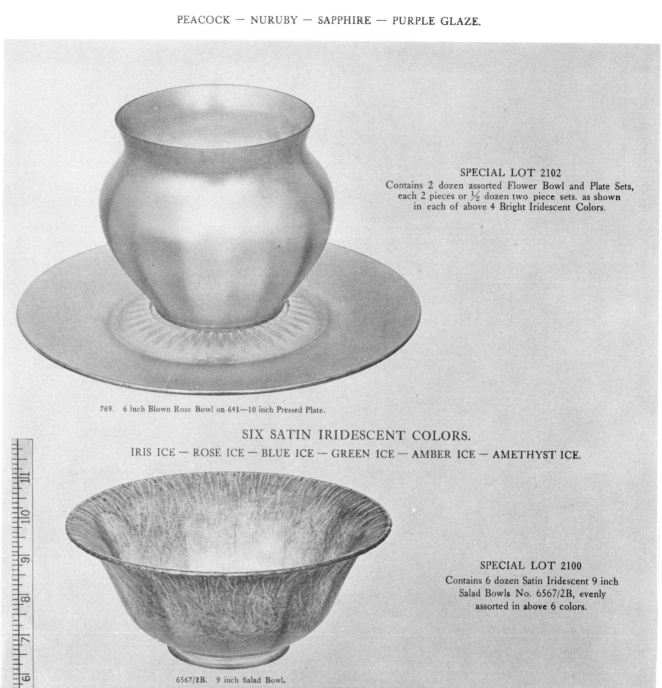

SPECIAL LOT 2102
Contains 2 dozen assorted Flower Bowl and Plate Sets, each 2 pieces or ½ dozen two piece sets, as shown in each of above 4 Bright Iridescent Colors.

769.   6 inch Blown Rose Bowl on 641—10 inch Pressed Plate.

SIX SATIN IRIDESCENT COLORS.
IRIS ICE — ROSE ICE — BLUE ICE — GREEN ICE — AMBER ICE — AMETHYST ICE.

SPECIAL LOT 2100
Contains 6 dozen Satin Iridescent 9 inch Salad Bowls No. 6567/2B, evenly assorted in above 6 colors.

6567/2B.   9 inch Salad Bowl.

SPECIAL LOT 2091
Contains 9 dozen assorted Sherbet and Plate Sets, or 1½ dozen each in above 6 Satin Iridescent Colors.

6001B.   Sherbet on 6724D—6 inch Plate.

For description of Colors, See Page 3

BEAUTIFUL SATIN IRIDESCENT COLORS.

SPECIAL LOT 2058 contains 12 dozen assorted 8 inch Salad Plates
or 2 dozen each of 6 Satin colors to match Sherbets on Page 48

641. 10 inch
Cheese and Cracker Set.

SPECIAL LOT 2057
Contains 3 dozen Cheese and Cracker Sets, equally assorted in
ROSE ICE — IRIS ICE — BLUE ICE.

SPECIAL LOT 2023
Contains 2 dozen Handled Fruit Bowls, equally assorted in
ROSE ICE — IRIS ICE — BLUE ICE.

6641. 9 inch Handled Fruit Bowl.

SPECIAL LOT 2024
Contains 2 dozen Sandwich Trays, equally assorted in
ROSE ICE — IRIS ICE — BLUE ICE.

664. 10 inch Sandwich Tray.

See Page 3 for Description.

THREE BRIGHT IRIDESCENT NEW COLORS.

NURUBY — PEACOCK — SAPPHIRE.

SPECIAL LOT 2092 contains 2 dozen assorted Vases, packed in one tierce.
⅙ dozen each of 4 shapes shown, each in above 3 colors.

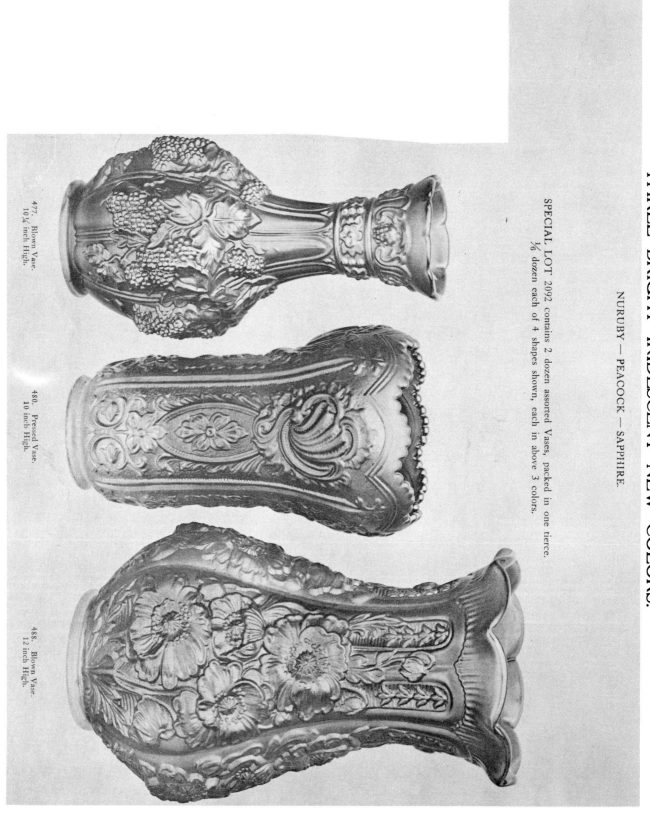

477. Blown Vase.
10¼ inch High.

480. Pressed Vase.
10 inch High.

488. Blown Vase.
12 inch High.

No risk in buying 12 pairs of Vases, packed in one tierce. Not two of them alike.

SPECIAL LOT 2114 contains 7½ dozen assorted Candlesticks in one barrel,
or 6 each of 3 Candlesticks illustrated, each in 5 colors:
CRYSTAL — AMBER — MULBERRY — PEACOCK — NURUBY.

41. 7 inch Candlestick.   635. 8½ inch Candlestick.   419. 9 inch Candlestick.

SPECIAL LOT 2115 contains 8 dozen Vases, assorted in one barrel,
or 6 each of 4 shapes illustrated, each in 4 colors:
CRYSTAL — NURUBY — PEACOCK — SAPPHIRE.

710. 6 inch Vase.   682. 6 inch Vase.   711. 8 inch Vase.

Each item in this book c:

115

18 PIECE BUFFET SET.

Bright Rubigold Color only.

SPECIAL LOT 1908 contains ⅓ dozen each of 4 piece Tea Set, 7 piece Berry Set and 7 piece Water Set, or 1 dozen Assorted Sets, RUBIGOLD only.

M489. Spoon Holder.
1 in Set.

M489. Sugar and Cover.
1 in Set.

M489. Cream.
1 in Set.

EACH SET AND EACH ARTICLE IN EACH
SET CAN BE BOUGHT SEPARATELY.

M4895A. 4¾ inch Berry.
6 in Set.

M489. Butter and Cover.
1 in Set.

M489. Tumbler.
6 in Set.

M4898A. 9 inch Berry.
1 in Set.

M489. Pitcher.
1 in Set.

Barrels are Charged Extra.

THREE NEW IRIDESCENT COL

NURUBY — PEACOCK — SAPPHIRE.

SPECIAL LOT 2077
Contains 18 dozen assorted pieces in one barrel, or 1½ dozen
of the 4 articles illustrated, each in above 3 colors.

473. Wine.

473. Cup and Saucer.

SPECIAL LOT 2078
Contains 2½ dozen assorted 7 piece Wine Sets
or 10 Sets each in above 3 colors.

For description of colors see Page 3 of this Book.

473. Blown Wine Bottle with Six 473 Pressed Wines, all in 3 colors.

Every article in each Special Lot of this Book can be ordered separately.

SPECIAL, LOT 2045. RUBIGOLD WATER SETS.

This Lot contains ¼ dozen each of the 4 Water Sets illustrated, or 1 dozen assorted 7 piece Sets in one barrel.

M484. Tumbler.

M484. ½ Gallon Pitcher.

M514. Tumbler.

M5143. ½ Gallon Pitcher.

M670. Tumbler.

M670. ½ Gallon Pitcher.

EACH WATER SET
Consists of One Pitcher and Six Tumblers.

M474. Tumbler.

M4743. ½ Gallon Pitcher.

Every Item Shown in this Book can be Ordered Separately.

118

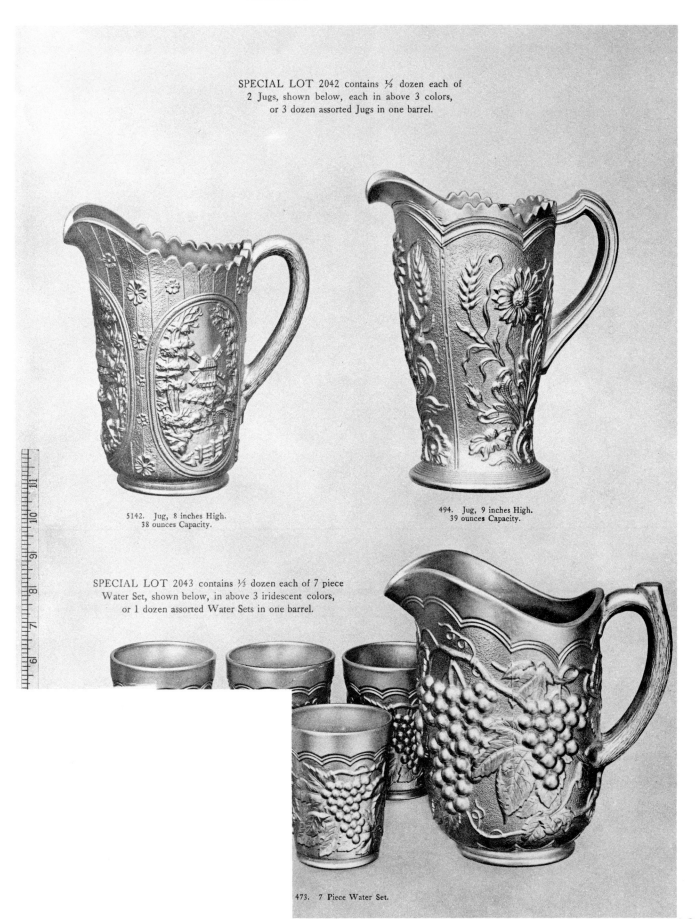

SPECIAL LOT 2042 contains ½ dozen each of
2 Jugs, shown below, each in above 3 colors,
or 3 dozen assorted Jugs in one barrel.

5142.   Jug, 8 inches High.
38 ounces Capacity.

494.   Jug, 9 inches High.
39 ounces Capacity.

SPECIAL LOT 2043 contains ⅓ dozen each of 7 piece
Water Set, shown below, in above 3 iridescent colors,
or 1 dozen assorted Water Sets in one barrel.

473.   7 Piece Water Set.

tion of colors see page 3 of this book.

BRIGHT IRIDESCENT. RUBIGOLD ONLY.

SPECIAL LOT 2107 contains 16 dozen assorted Rubigold Iridescent, or 1 dozen each of 16 articles illustrated.

M600. Table Salt.

M600. Tooth Pick.

M6000. 3½ inch Sherbet.

M6001. 4 inch Ice Cream.

M399/1. 3 inch Sherbet.

M755/1. Custard Cup.

M672. Custard Cup.

M666. Low Ice Cream on M666—6 inch Plate. (2 Pieces)

M5822B. Cup and Saucer. (2 Pieces)

M593. Child's Mug.

M5823. Cafe Parfait.

M612. Tall Ice Cream on M612—6 inch Plate (2 Pieces)

M600. 10 oz. Lemonade Glass.

120

SPECIAL LOT 2108 contains 18 dozen assorted in the 14 items illustrated, in quantities given under the illustrations.   RUBIGOLD ONLY.

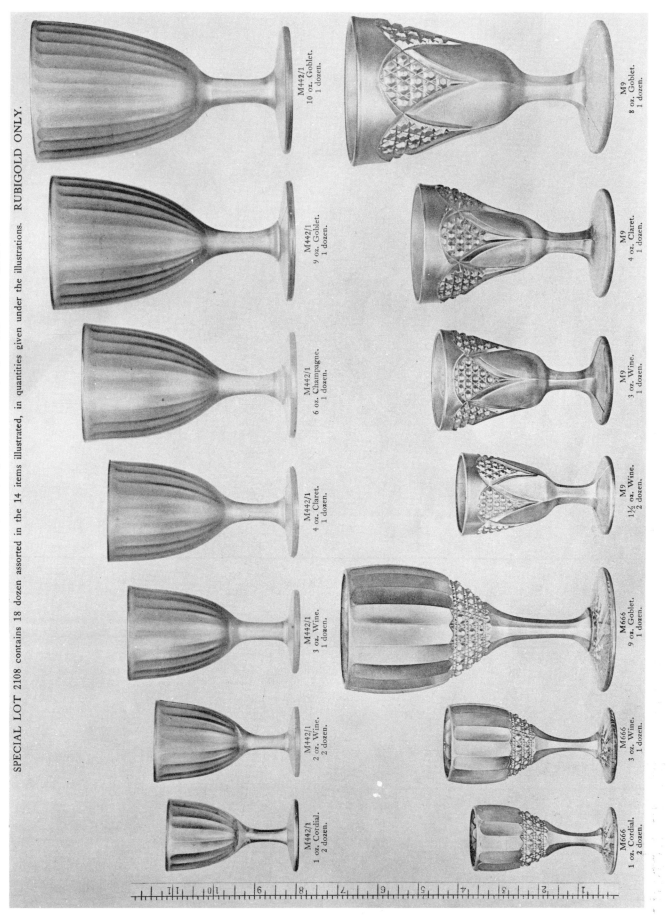

M442/1
10 oz. Goblet.
1 dozen.

M442/1
9 oz. Goblet.
1 dozen.

M442/1
6 oz. Champagne.
1 dozen.

M442/1
4 oz. Claret.
1 dozen.

M442/1
3 oz. Wine.
1 dozen.

M442/1
2 oz. Wine.
2 dozen.

M442/1
1 oz. Cordial.
2 dozen.

M9
8 oz. Goblet.
1 dozen.

M9
4 oz. Claret.
1 dozen.

M9
3 oz. Wine.
1 dozen.

M9
1½ oz. Wine.
2 dozen.

M666
9 oz. Goblet.
1 dozen.

M666
3 oz. Wine.
1 dozen.

M666
1 oz. Cordial.
2 dozen.

RED GLOW.   BLUE GLOW.

SPECIAL LOT 2104
Contains 14 dozen assorted pieces in the **New**
RED GLOW COLOR,
or 3½ dozen each of 4 articles.

SPECIAL LOT 2103
Contains 14 dozen assorted pieces in the **New**
BLUE GLOW COLOR,
or 3½ dozen each of 4 articles.

682.   Individual **Sugar.**

682.   Individual **Cream.**

BIG SPECIALS
FOR

BIG SPECIAL
SALES.

682.   5½ inch Comport.

682.   8 inch Celery Tray.

A LARGE VARIETY—SMALL QUANTITIES EACH AT THE RIGHT PRICES

THAT IS THE RESULT OF OUR SPECIAL LOTS.

OUR NEWEST DESIGN.

SPECIAL LOT 2111 contains 14 dozen assorted pieces, No. 711 Design, or 2 dozen each of 7 articles illustrated.

711. Individual Sugar.

711. Individual Cream.

711. 4½ inch Olive.

711. 5¼ inch Footed Jelly.

711. Sherbet.

7115A. 6 inch Berry.

7115B. 6¾ inch Flared Berry.

SPECIAL LOT 2117 contains 6 dozen assorted articles, 1 dozen each as shown below

671. Butter and Cover.

671. Sugar and Cover.

671. Cream.

671. Spoon Holder.

671. Tall Celery Holder.

671. Large Pint Milk Pitcher

A very brilliant design at low prices.

LOW PRICED.

SPECIAL LOT 2121 contains 12 dozen assorted pieces, or 1½ dozen each of 8 articles shown.

7105B.   6½ inch Nappy.

7105N.   5 inch Lily Bowl.

710.   Sugar.

710.   Cream.

710.   4¾ inch 2 Handled Berry.

710.   8½ inch Celery Tray.

710.   6 inch Pickle.

710.   5½ inch Olive.

Every item in every "Special Lot" can be ordered separately.

LOW PRICED.

SPECIAL LOT 2120 contains 8 dozen assorted pieces, or 1 dozen each of 8 articles illustrated.

7106A. 7 inch Nappy.

7106B. 7 inch Salad.

7106N. 6 inch Lily Bowl.

710. 4 inch Footed Jelly.

710B. Deep Comport.
5¼ inch Diameter.

710. 5½ inch Square Dish on 7½ inch Square Plate.
(2 Pieces)

710. Large Pint Jug.
6 inch High.

SPECIAL LOT 2113 contains 6 dozen assorted Bowls in one barrel, or 1 dozen each of 6 articles illustrated.

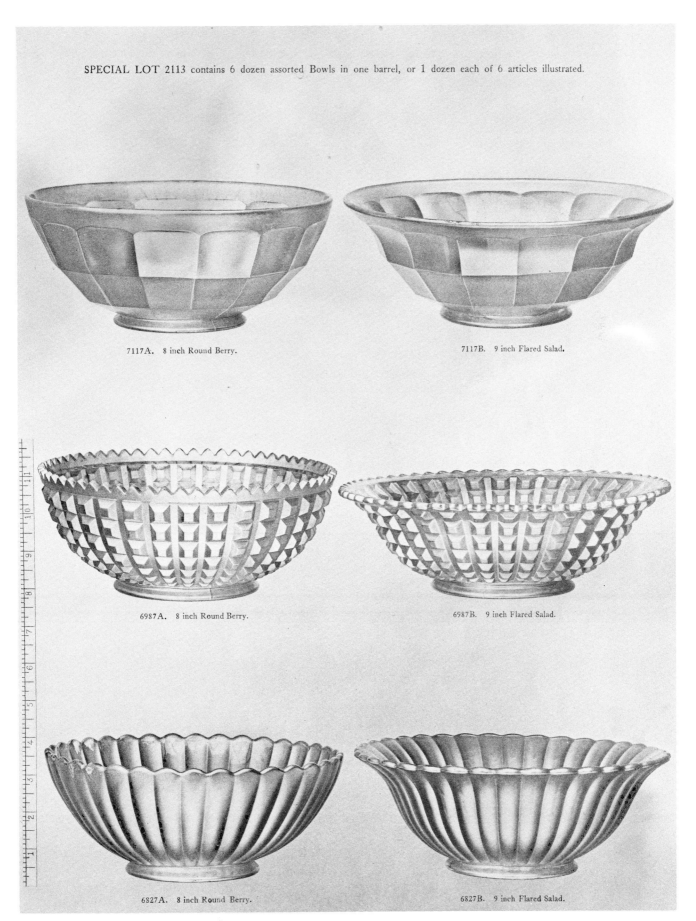

7117A. 8 inch Round Berry.

7117B. 9 inch Flared Salad.

6987A. 8 inch Round Berry.

6987B. 9 inch Flared Salad.

6827A. 8 inch Round Berry.

6827B. 9 inch Flared Salad.

Buy a ''Special Lot'' and re-order the quickest selling items.

127

SPECIAL LOT 2112 contains 2 dozen assorted 7 piece Berry Sets in one barrel,
or ⅔ dozen each of three 7 piece Berry Sets illustrated.

Each Berry Set consists of One Extra Large
Berry and Six Small Berries.

7114B. 4½ inch Berry.

7118B. 10 inch Berry.

6828B. 10 inch Berry.

6824B. 4½ inch Berry.

5824B. 4¾ inch Berry.

5828B. 10½ inch Berry.

These Berries can be sold as Sets, and also individually.

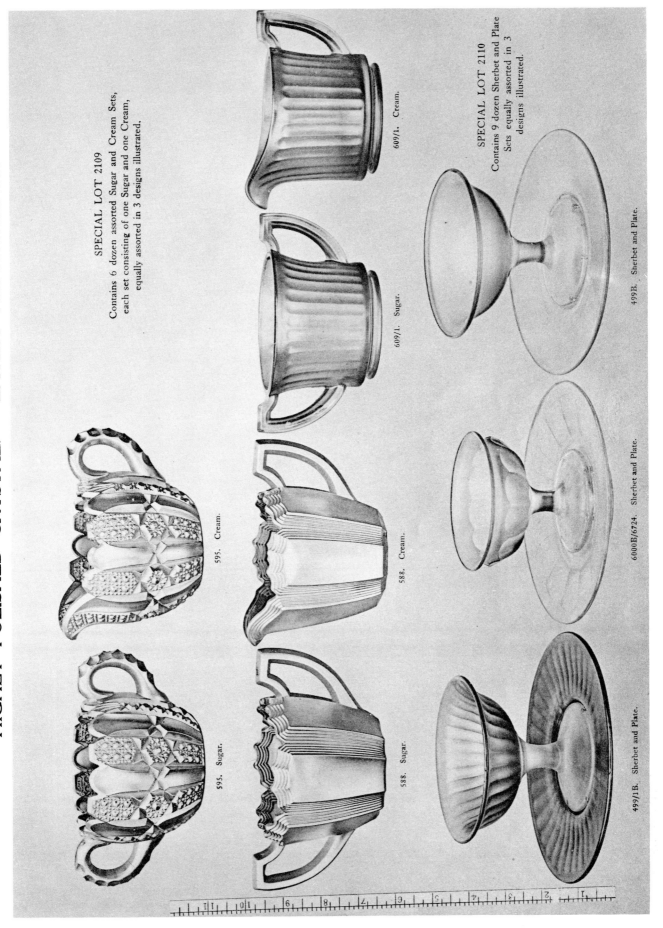

SPECIAL LOT 2109
Contains 6 dozen assorted Sugar and Cream Sets, each set consisting of one Sugar and one Cream, equally assorted in 3 designs illustrated.

609/1. Cream.

609/1. Sugar.

SPECIAL LOT 2110
Contains 9 dozen Sherbet and Plate Sets equally assorted in 3 designs illustrated.

499B. Sherbet and Plate.

595. Cream.

588. Cream.

6000B/6724. Sherbet and Plate.

595. Sugar.

588. Sugar.

499/1B. Sherbet and Plate.

698. 7½ inch Square Two Piece Salad Set.
Packed 2 dozen Sets in barrel.

698. 7½ inch Square Bowl on 10½ inch Square Plate.

698. Sugar and Cover.

698. Cream.

698. 4 Piece Tea Set
Packed 1¾ dozen Sets in barrel.

698. Spoon Holder.

698. Butter and Cover.

For Terms see inside Front Cover of Price List.

SPECIAL LOT 2116
Contains 1 dozen 7 piece Sets,
or ½ dozen each of two Sets illustrated.

This Set consists of One 7113—½ Gallon Pitcher, and Six 711—Table Tumblers.

This Set consists of One 06003—¾ Gallon Ice Jug and Cover, and Six 672—10 oz. Tumblers.

Barrels are Charged Extra.

INDIVIDUAL NEW ITEMS.

310. Jug, Quart Size.
Packed 4½ dozen in one barrel.

321. Graduated Jug, Quart Size.
Packed 3¾ dozen in one barrel.

A NEW ARTICLE

The Jar, illustrated below for the first time,
while called a Candy Jar, can be used for
many other household articles.

711. Candy Jar and Cover.
Packed 3½ dozen in one barrel.

698.   10¼ inch Vase.
Packed 3¼ dozen in one barrel.

Barrels are always charged extra.

CATALOG "E"

The entry pages of this catalog had been destroyed, therefore Imperial designated the book as Book "E". We used the same designation to simplify the identification of the catalog.

Book "E" had been made up of mostly Pattern Glass. On the first few sheets, reference is made to Catalog 100C and 101C. We have placed these sheets with those of Book "E" to keep the glass listed as "Nucut" together.

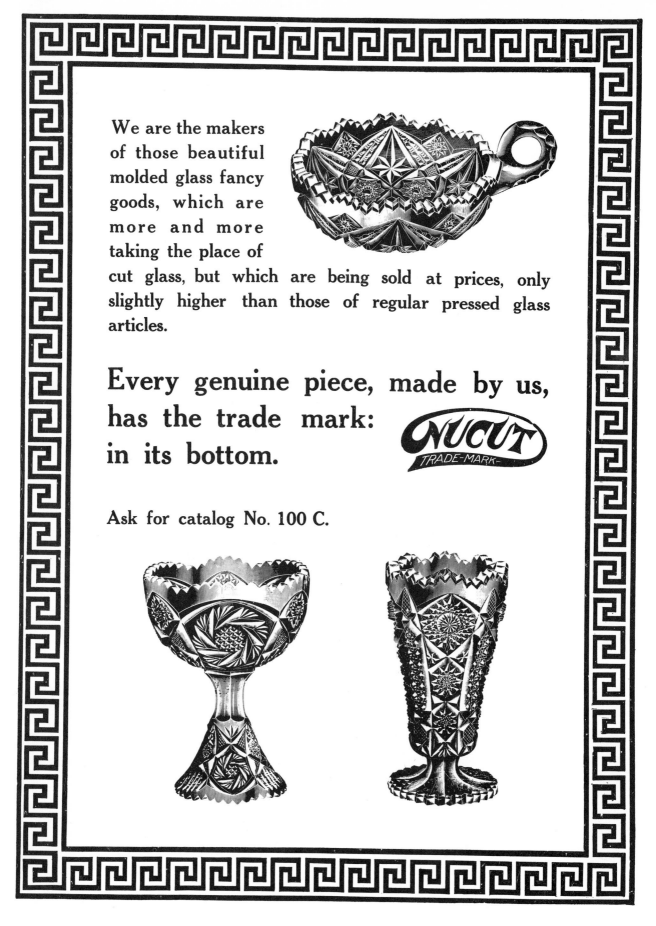

We are the makers of those beautiful molded glass fancy goods, which are more and more taking the place of cut glass, but which are being sold at prices, only slightly higher than those of regular pressed glass articles.

Every genuine piece, made by us, has the trade mark: in its bottom. *NUCUT* TRADE-MARK

Ask for catalog No. 100 C.

THE BEST IMITATION OF CUT GLASS IN EXISTENCE.

SPECIAL LOT 2122 contains 10 dozen assorted NUCUT pieces, or 1 dozen each of 10 articles illustrated.

212/8. 4½ inch Two Handled Berry, Round.

212/6. 7½ inch Spoon Tray, Oval.

212/7. 6½ inch Pickle, Oval.

212/9. 5 inch Handled Olive, Round.

212/5. 6 inch Round Nappy.

212/10. 5 inch Comoprt.

212/3. 5½ inch Round Perry.

NUCUT GLASS looks like Cut Glass, but it is made in very wonderful Moulds.

212/1. Sugar.

212/2. Cream.

212/11. 6 inch Vase.

Every piece, Shown in this Book, can be bought individually.

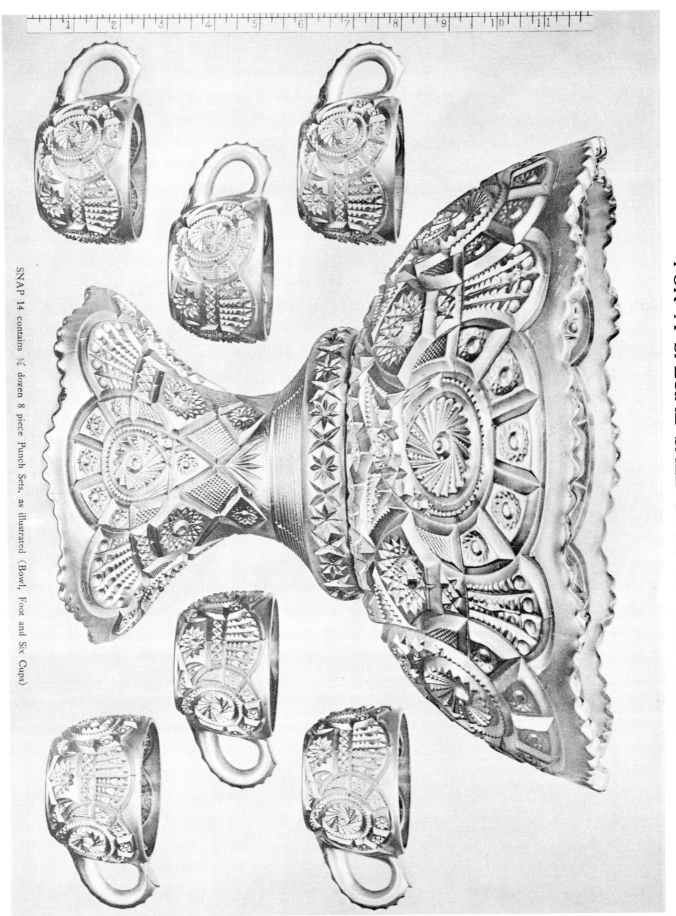

SNAP 14 contains ¾ dozen 8 piece Punch Sets, as illustrated (Bowl, Foot and Six Cups)

FOR A SPECIAL SALE LOOK UP THE PRICE!

136

Numerous new pieces of great beauty have been added to our line of moulded

NUCUT GLASS,

and a few of them are shown on this and the following pages.

Our special new catalog No. 101C will show this line complete, up to date.

If you are interested in popular priced glassware, you should write us for this catalog.

THE FACT OF THE MATTER IS THAT MANY PIECES OF OUR NUCUT GLASS ARE SIMPLY BEAUTIFUL, AND THEREFORE MERITORIOUS, TOTALLY ASIDE OF THE POPULAR PRICES AT WHICH THEY CAN BE SOLD.

No. 586A—12-oz. ice tea
Moulded star in cut and polished bottom
Packed 12 dozen in barrel
Per dozen, $1.00, any quantity

No. 586B—12½-oz. ice tea
Moulded star in cut and polished bottom
Packed 10 dozen in barrel
Per dozen, $1.00, any quantity

No. 586A—table tumbler
Moulded star in cut and polished bottom
Packed 17 dozen in barrel
Per dozen, $0.75, any quantity

No. 586B—table tumbler
Moulded star in cut and polished bottom
Packed 15 dozen in barrel
Per dozen, $0.75, any quantity

No. 586—½-gallon tankard—Nucut
Moulded star in cut and polished bottom
Packed 1½ dozen in barrel
Per dozen, $7.25, any quantity

FOR FULL LINE OF OUR FAMOUS NUCUT GLASS, SEE OUR CATALOG No. 101C.

No. 282C vase, crimped.
packed 1¾ dozen in barrel.

No. 2821 vase, handled.
packed 2 dozen in barrel.

No. 282 lemonade set, shown with No. 2829 glass tray.
packed ¾ dozen sets in barrel.
also sold
with No. 231 or No. 232 metal tray, packed 1 dozen sets in barrel.
or without tray, packed 1 dozen sets in barrel.

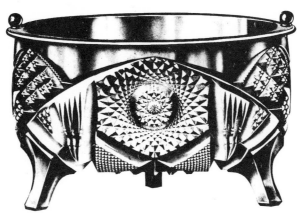

SIDE VIEW

showing high grade
lining.

*This is one of the
most wonderful pieces
of artistic mould work
ever produced.*

No. 587—8-inch fern dish and lining—Nucut
This is a brass lining, heavily nickel plated
Packed 2 dozen in barrel
Per dozen, complete, $10.50, any quantity

TOP VIEW

to show how bottom
is figured all over in
a deep design.

*Other moulded fern
dishes have a plain
bottom with a cheap
cut star.*

No. 587—8-inch fern dish—Nucut—no lining
Also useful as fruit or nut bowl
Packed 2¼ dozen in barrel
Per dozen, $5.50, any quantity

½ size cuts — For terms read inside front cover.

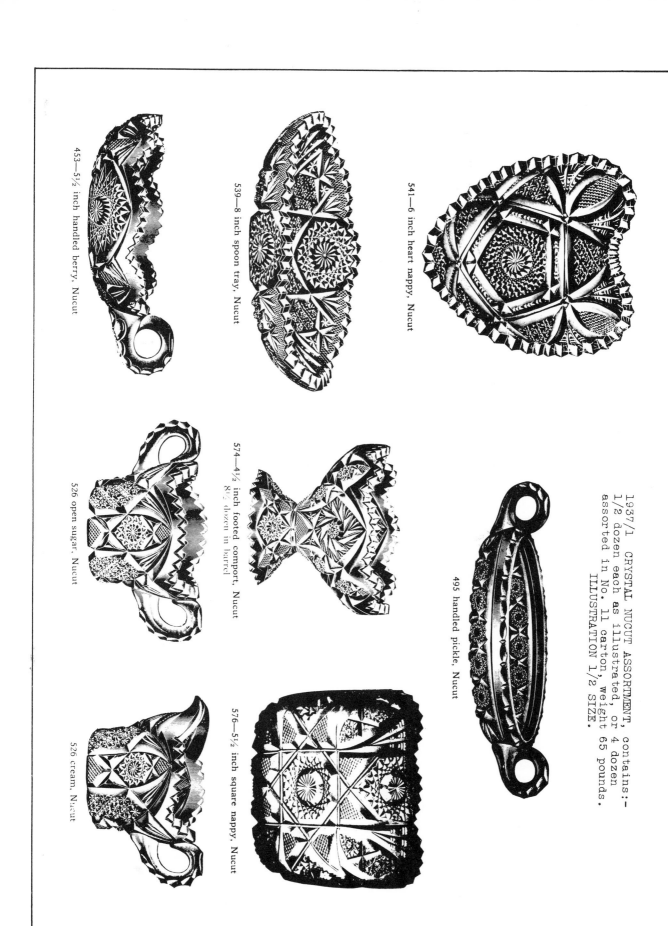

MOULDED Nucut GLASS

453—5½ inch handled berry, Nucut

539—8 inch spoon tray, Nucut

541—6 inch heart nappy, Nucut

526 open sugar, Nucut

574—4½ inch footed comport, Nucut
8½ dozen in barrel

526 cream, Nucut

576—5½ inch square nappy, Nucut

495 handled pickle, Nucut

1937/1 CRYSTAL NUCUT ASSORTMENT, contains:—
1/2 dozen each as illustrated, or 4 dozen
assorted in No. 11 carton, weight 65 pounds.
ILLUSTRATION 1/2 SIZE.

140

MOULDED  GLASS

1937/4 CRYSTAL NUCUT ASSORTMENT, contains:-
1/6 dozen each as illustrated; or one dozen
assorted in No. 11 carton, weight 65 pounds.
ILLUSTRATION 1/2 SIZE.

466—11 inch celery tray, Nucut

529—10 inch vase, Nucut

504—oval salad, Nucut

499/6A two-handled nappy, Nucut
round, diameter 6½ inches, not including handles

485/1 two handled comport, Nucut
round, diameter 7¼ inch, not including handles

517—7½ inch berry bowl, Nucut

141

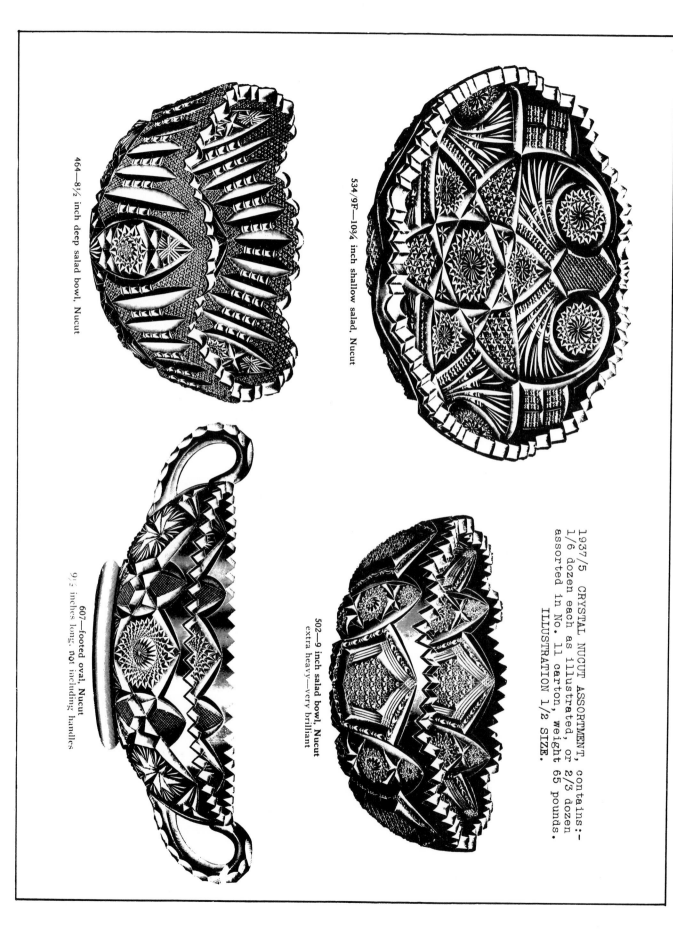

464—8½ inch deep salad bowl, Nucut

534/9F—10¾ inch shallow salad, Nucut

607—footed oval, Nucut
9½ inches long, not including handles

502—9 inch salad bowl, Nucut
extra heavy—very brilliant

MOULDED *Nucut* GLASS

1937/5 CRYSTAL NUCUT ASSORTMENT, contains:-
1/6 dozen each as illustrated, or 2/3 dozen
assorted in No. 11 carton, weight 65 pounds.
ILLUSTRATION 1/2 SIZE.

MOULDED NUCUT GLASS

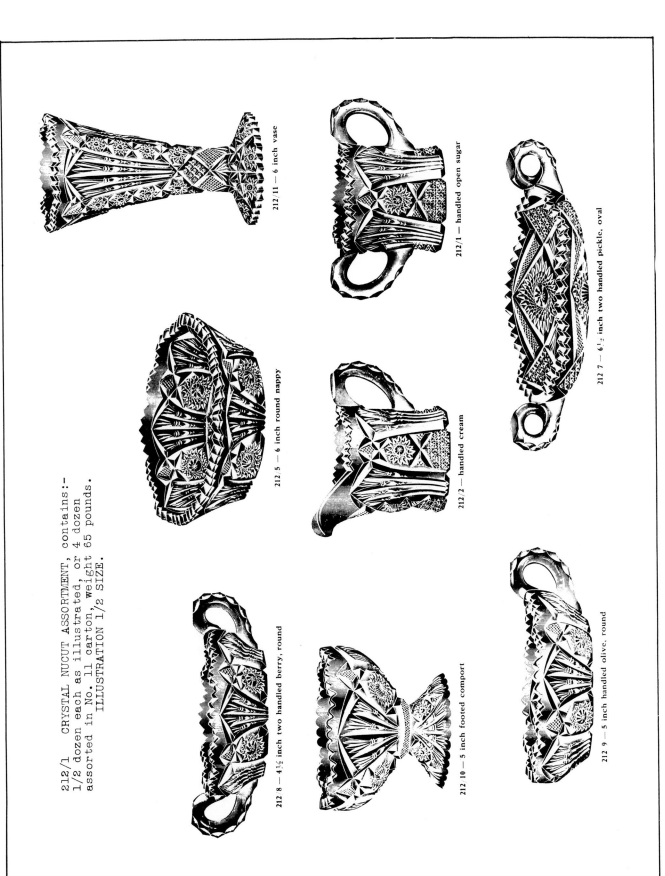

212/1 CRYSTAL NUCUT ASSORTMENT, contains:—
1/2 dozen each as illustrated, or 4 dozen
assorted in No. 11 carton, weight 65 pounds.
ILLUSTRATION 1/2 SIZE.

212/11 — 6 inch vase

212/1 — handled open sugar

212 7 — 6½ inch two handled pickle, oval

212.5 — 6 inch round nappy

212/2 — handled cream

212 8 — 4½ inch two handled berry, round

212.10 — 5 inch footed comport

212 9 — 5 inch handled olive, round

143

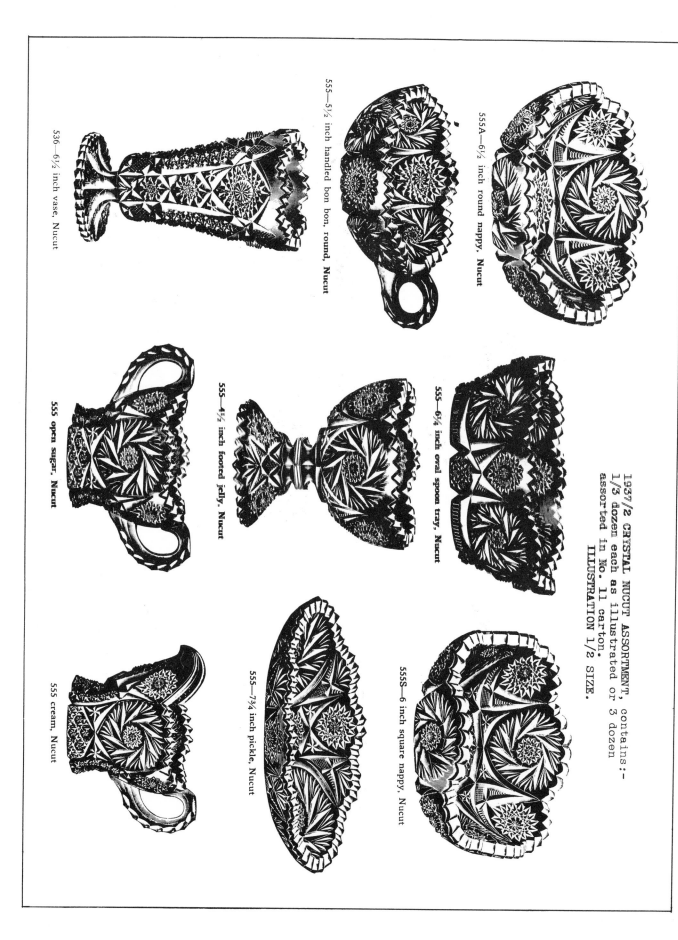

MOULDED *Nucut* GLASS

1937/2 CRYSTAL NUCUT ASSORTMENT, contains:-
1/3 dozen each as illustrated or 3 dozen
assorted in No. 11 carton.
ILLUSTRATION 1/2 SIZE.

555A—6½ inch round nappy, Nucut

555—5½ inch handled bon bon, round, Nucut

536—6½ inch vase, Nucut

555—6¼ inch oval spoon tray, Nucut

555—4½ inch footed jelly, Nucut

555 open sugar, Nucut

555S—6 inch square nappy, Nucut

555—7¾ inch pickle, Nucut

555 cream, Nucut

144

MOULDED Nucut GLASS

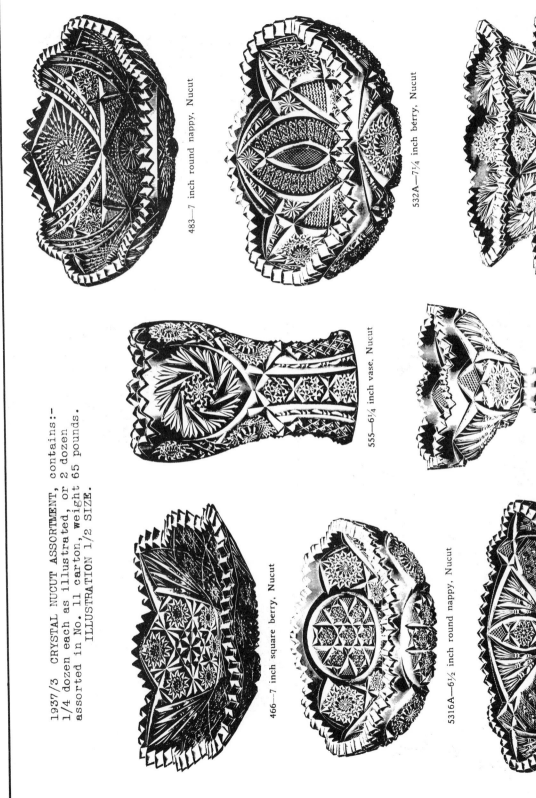

1937/3 CRYSTAL NUCUT ASSORTMENT, contains:—
1/4 dozen each as illustrated, or 2 dozen
assorted in No. 11 carton, weight 65 pounds.
ILLUSTRATION 1/2 SIZE.

483—7 inch round nappy, Nucut

532A—7¼ inch berry, Nucut

555 oval mayonnaise and plate set, Nucut

555—6¼ inch vase, Nucut

537—4½ inch footed jelly, Nucut

466—7 inch square berry, Nucut

5316A—6½ inch round nappy, Nucut

538—7½ inch oval dish, Nucut

Product of Imperial

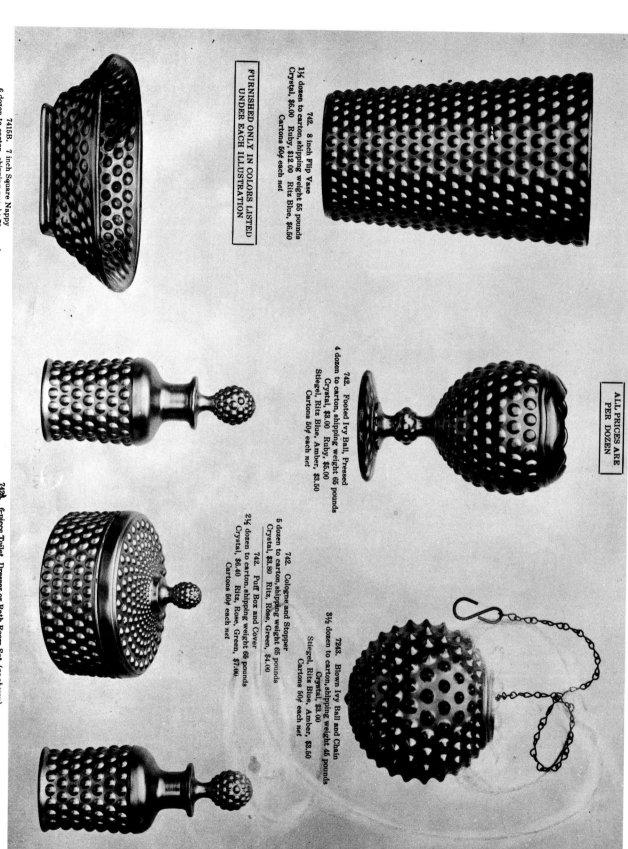

FURNISHED ONLY IN COLORS LISTED UNDER EACH ILLUSTRATION

ALL PRICES ARE PER DOZEN

742. 8 inch Flip Vase
1½ dozen to carton, shipping weight 55 pounds
Crystal, $6.00   Ruby, $12.00   Ritz Blue, $6.50
Cartons 50¢ each *net*

742. Footed Ivy Ball, Pressed
4 dozen to carton, shipping weight 65 pounds
Crystal, $3.00   Ruby, $5.00
Stiegel, Ritz Blue, Amber, $3.50
Cartons 50¢ each *net*

742. Cologne and Stopper
5 dozen to carton, shipping weight 65 pounds
Crystal, $3.80   Ritz, Rose, Green, $4.00
Cartons 50¢ each *net*

742. Puff Box and Cover
2½ dozen to carton, shipping weight 66 pounds
Crystal, $6.40   Ritz, Rose, Green, $7.00
Cartons 50¢ each *net*

7243. Blown Ivy Ball and Chain
3½ dozen to carton, shipping weight 45 pounds
Crystal, $3.00
Stiegel, Ritz Blue, Amber, $3.50
Cartons 50¢ each *net*

7415B.   7 inch Square Nappy
6 dozen to carton, shipping weight 70 pounds
Crystal, $1.60   Ruby, $3.50   Ritz Blue, $3.00
Cartons 50¢ each *net*

742.   6-piece Toilet, Dresser or Bath Room Set (*as shown*)
Each set in individual carton, 1 dozen sets to master carton, cartons 80¢ *net*
Shipping weight 65 pounds
Crystal, $14.00   Ritz Blue, Rose Pink, Imperial Green (color 81), $15.00

Illustrations ½ Size

146

CARTONS CHARGED AT NET PRICES

Early American Hobnail Pattern

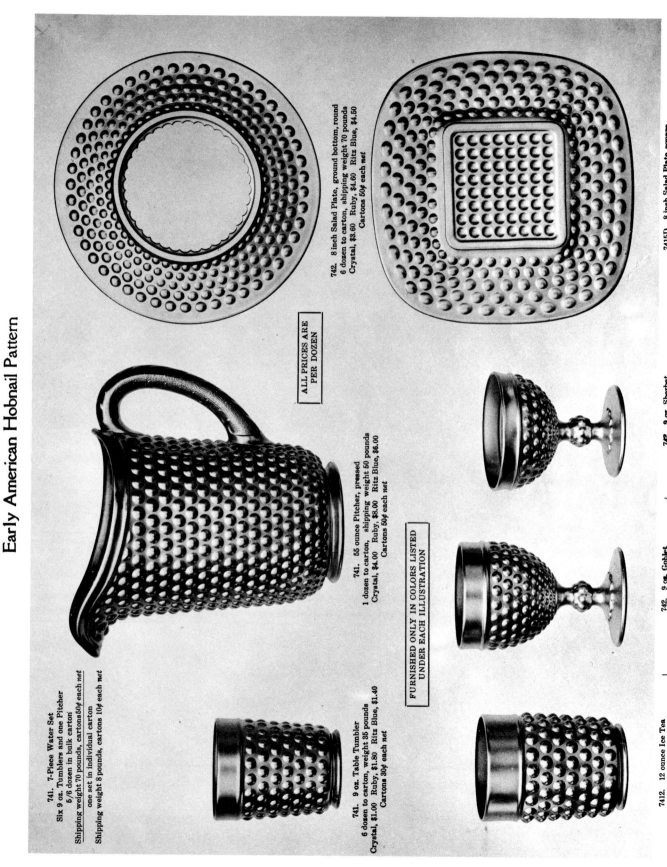

741. 7-Piece Water Set
Six 9 oz. Tumblers and one Pitcher
5/6 dozen in bulk carton
Shipping weight 70 pounds, cartons 50¢ each *net*
one set in individual carton
Shipping weight 8 pounds, cartons 10¢ each *net*

741. 9 oz. Table Tumbler
6 dozen to carton, weight 35 pounds
Crystal, $1.00 Ruby, $1.80 Ritz Blue, $1.40
Cartons 30¢ each *net*

ALL PRICES ARE PER DOZEN

741. 55 ounce Pitcher, pressed
1 dozen to carton, shipping weight 50 pounds
Crystal, $4.00 Ruby, $8.00 Ritz Blue, $6.00
Cartons 50¢ each *net*

FURNISHED ONLY IN COLORS LISTED UNDER EACH ILLUSTRATION

742. 8 inch Salad Plate, ground bottom, round
6 dozen to carton, shipping weight 70 pounds
Crystal, $3.60 Ruby, $4.60 Ritz Blue, $4.50
Cartons 50¢ each *net*

7415D. 8 inch Salad Plate, square
6 dozen to carton, shipping weight 70 pounds
Cryst.l, $1.60 Ruby, $3.50 Ritz Blue, $3.00
Cartons 50¢ each *net*

742. 9 oz. Sherbet
6 doz. to carton, shipping weight 45 pounds
Crystal, $1.60 Ruby, $3.50 Ritz Blue, $3.00
Cartons 35¢ each *net*

742. 9 oz. Goblet
6 dozen to carton, shipping weight 55 pounds
Crystal, $1.60 Ruby, $3.50 Ritz Blue, $3.00
Cartons 50¢ each *net*

7412. 12 ounce Ice Tea
6 dozen to carton, shipping weight 60 pounds
Crystal, $1.60 Ruby, $2.70 Ritz Blue, $2.00
Cartons 50¢ each *net*

Illustrations ½ Size

Product of Imperial

147

Each Piece Fire Polished By Hand

TRADITION PATTERN

OLD ENGLISH PATTERN

1655D. 8 inch Salad Plate
6 dozen in No. 1 carton
Weight 65 pounds

1655W. 7¾ inch Flared Nappy
6 dozen in No. 1 carton
Weight 65 pounds

16641½D. 7 inch Plate
8 dozen in No. 1 carton
Weight 65 pounds

166. Sherbet & Plate Set
6 dozen in No. 1 carton
Weight 65 pounds

16641½X. 6 inch Baked Apple
8 dozen in No. 1 carton
Weight 65 pounds

16641½A. 4½ inch Finger Bowl
8 dozen in No. 1 carton
Weight 65 pounds

166. 5 ounce Cocktail
6 dozen in No. 27 carton
Weight 35 pounds

166. 9 ounce Water
6 dozen in No. 26 carton
Weight 50 pounds

166. 12 ounce Iced Tea
6 dozen in No. 29 carton
Weight 55 pounds

165. 10 ounce Goblet
6 dozen in No. 51 carton
Weight 60 pounds

16541½A. 4½ inch Finger Bowl
8 dozen in No. 1 carton
Weight 65 pounds

16541½W. 6 inch Nappy
8 dozen in No. 1 carton
Weight 65 pounds

165. 6 ounce Sherbet
6 dozen in No. 52 carton
Weight 45 pounds

16541½X. 6 inch Baked Apple
8 dozen in No. 1 carton
Weight 65 pounds

165. 12 ounce Iced Tea
6 dozen in No. 29 carton
Weight 60 pounds

166. 4¼ inch Compote
6 dozen in No. 52 carton
Weight 45 pounds

X 184. 10 ounce Mug
6 dozen in No. 26 carton
Weight 60 pounds

1346A. 9 inch Comport or Pretzel Bowl
2½ dozen in No. 1 carton
Weight 65 pounds

1346N. 7 inch Flower Bowl
2½ dozen in No. 1 carton
Weight 65 pounds

1655F. 7 inch Shallow Nappy
6 dozen in No. 1 carton
Weight 65 pounds

165. Lipped Ice Pitcher
1 dozen in No. 4 carton
Weight 45 pounds

The Niagara (Open Stock) Pattern

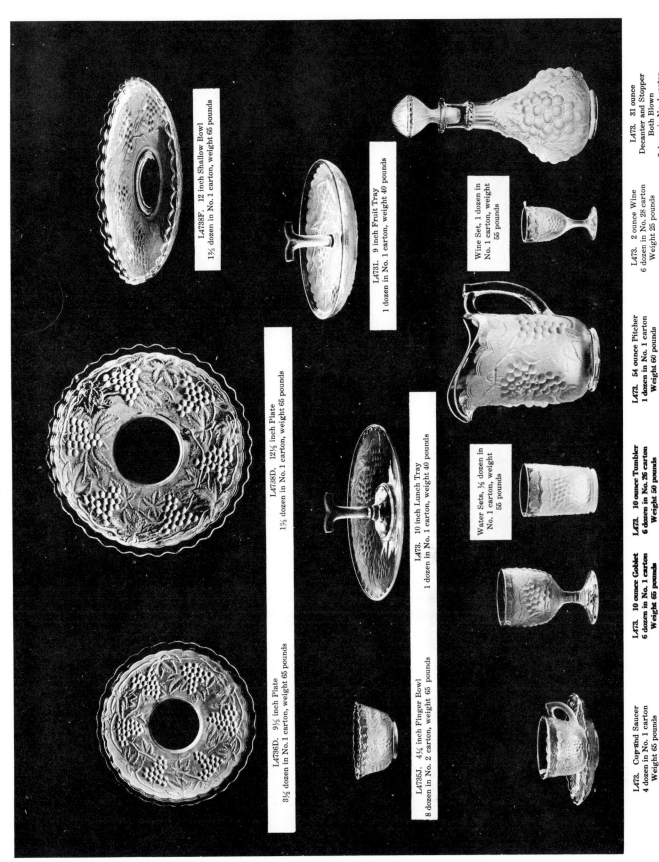

L4788F. 12 inch Shallow Bowl
1⅓ dozen in No. 1 carton, weight 65 pounds

L4738D. 12½ inch Plate
1⅓ dozen in No. 1 carton, weight 65 pounds

L4786D. 9½ inch Plate
3½ dozen in No. 1 carton, weight 65 pounds

L473I. 9 inch Fruit Tray
1 dozen in No. 1 carton, weight 40 pounds

L473. 10 inch Lunch Tray
1 dozen in No. 1 carton, weight 40 pounds

L4735J. 4¼ inch Finger Bowl
8 dozen in No. 2 carton, weight 65 pounds

L473. Cup and Saucer
4 dozen in No. 1 carton
Weight 65 pounds

L473. 10 ounce Goblet
6 dozen in No. 1 carton
Weight 65 pounds

L473. 10 ounce Tumbler
6 dozen in No. 26 carton
Weight 50 pounds

Water Sets, ½ dozen in
No. 1 carton, weight
55 pounds

Wine Set, 1 dozen in
No. 1 carton, weight
55 pounds

L473. 54 ounce Pitcher
1 dozen in No. 1 carton
Weight 60 pounds

L473. 2 ounce Wine
6 dozen in No. 28 carton
Weight 25 pounds

L473. 31 ounce
Decanter and Stopper
Both Blown
2 dozen in No. 1 carton
Weight 55 pounds

Illustrations ½ Size

Product of HAND MADE

149

The Niagara (Open Stock) Pattern

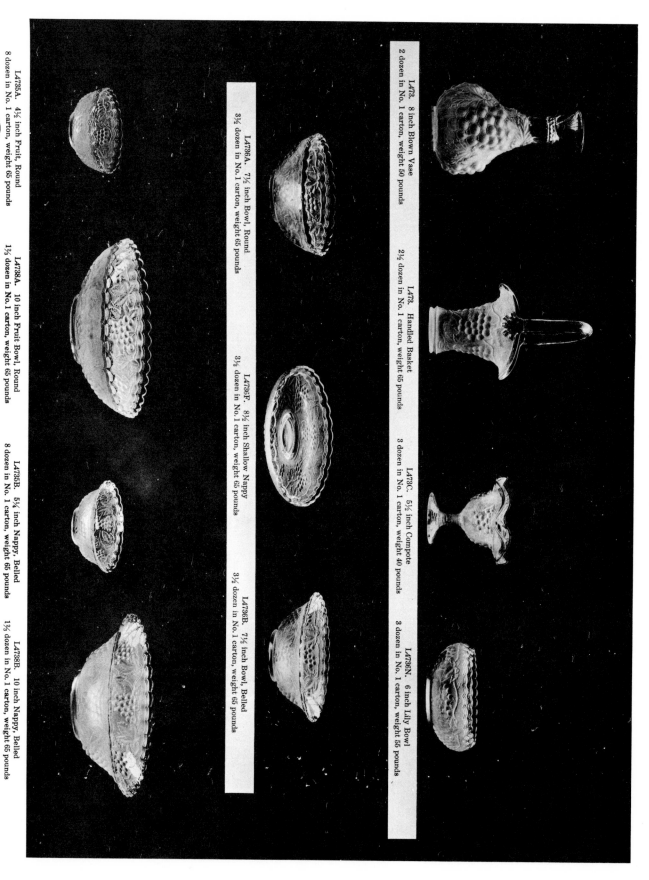

L473. 8 inch Blown Vase
2 dozen in No. 1 carton, weight 50 pounds

L473. Handled Basket
2½ dozen in No. 1 carton, weight 65 pounds

L473C. 5½ inch Compote
3 dozen in No. 1 carton, weight 40 pounds

L436N. 6 inch Lily Bowl
3 dozen in No. 1 carton, weight 55 pounds

L4736A. 7½ inch Bowl, Round
3½ dozen in No. 1 carton, weight 65 pounds

L4736F. 8½ inch Shallow Nappy
3½ dozen in No. 1 carton, weight 65 pounds

L4736B. 7½ inch Bowl, Belled
3½ dozen in No. 1 carton, weight 65 pounds

L4735A. 4½ inch Fruit, Round
8 dozen in No. 1 carton, weight 65 pounds

L4738A. 10 inch Fruit Bowl, Round
1½ dozen in No. 1 carton, weight 65 pounds

L4735B. 5¼ inch Nappy, Belled
8 dozen in No. 1 carton, weight 65 pounds

L4738B. 10 inch Nappy, Belled
1½ dozen in No. 1 carton, weight 65 pounds

Illustrations ¼ Size

Product of

HAND MADE

150

Imperial Pressed Plates and Trays

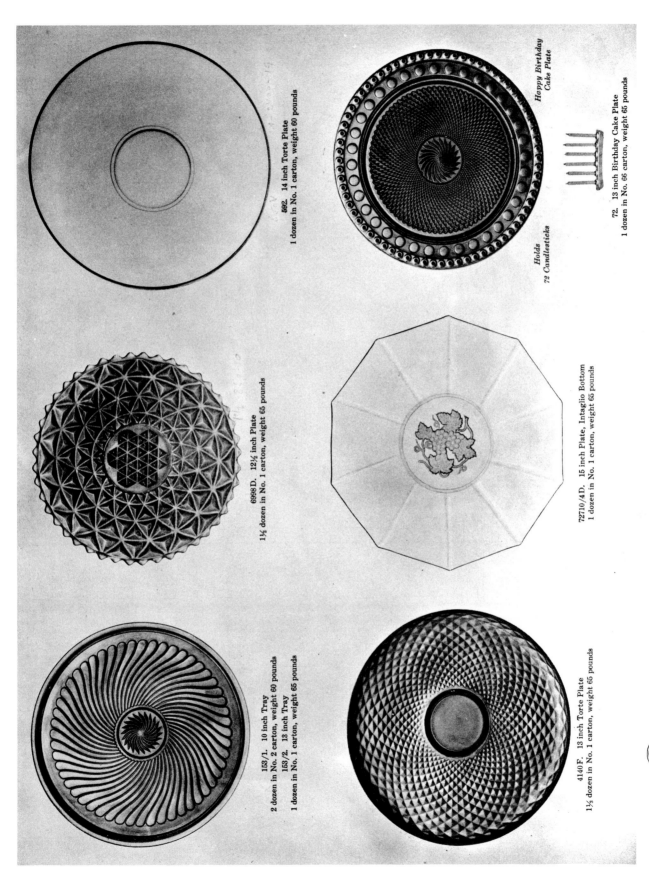

692. 14 inch Torte Plate
1 dozen in No. 1 carton, weight 60 pounds

Happy Birthday
Cake Plate

Holds
72 Candlesticks

72. 13 inch Birthday Cake Plate
1 dozen in No. 66 carton, weight 65 pounds

6998 D. 12½ inch Plate
1½ dozen in No. 1 carton, weight 65 pounds

72710/4D. 15 inch Plate, Intaglio Bottom
1 dozen in No. 1 carton, weight 65 pounds

Illustrations ¼ Size

153/1. 10 inch Tray
2 dozen in No. 2 carton, weight 60 pounds
153/2. 13 inch Tray
1 dozen in No. 1 carton, weight 65 pounds

4140 F. 13 inch Torte Plate
1½ dozen in No. 1 carton, weight 65 pounds

Product of

Illustrations ¼ Size

Metal Cover
Blown Jar
Pressed Plate

169. Marmalade Set
5 dozen in No. 1 carton, weight 65 pounds

785/3. 6-piece Cigarette Set
Cover hand-cut in center
2 dozen in No. 2 carton, weight 50 pounds

451 Ash Tray and 760 Tumbler are blown

451. 3¾ inch Ash Tray
30 dozen in No. 2 carton
Weight 65 pounds

760. 10 ounce Tumbler
6 dozen in No. 29 carton
Weight 55 pounds
Made in 5 sizes

142. 2-piece Canapé Set
5 dozen in No. 1 carton, weight 65 pounds

6 inch Pressed Plate
3¼ ounce Blown Cocktail

158. Canapé Set
4 dozen in No. 2 carton
Weight 55 pounds

85. 14 inch Plate, 1 dozen in No. 1 carton, weight 65 pounds

85158. 17-piece Cocktail or Hors d'Oeuvre Set (as shown). ⁹⁄₁₂ dozen in No. 1 carton, weight 65 pounds
85158. 13-piece Set (one plate and six canapé sets). ½ dozen in No. 1 carton, weight 55 pounds
85158. 9-piece Set (one plate and four canapé sets). ½ dozen in No. 2 carton, weight 50 pounds

Crystal Cocktail
used with all colors

1550. 7-piece Iced Tea Set, Blown
½ dozen in No. 1 carton, weight 55 pounds
Tumblers: 6 dozen in No. 29 carton, weight 55 pounds
Pitchers: 1 dozen in No. 1 carton, weight 40 pounds

1550. 80 ounce Ice Pitcher

165. 12 ounce Tumbler

152

The Mount Vernon Pattern

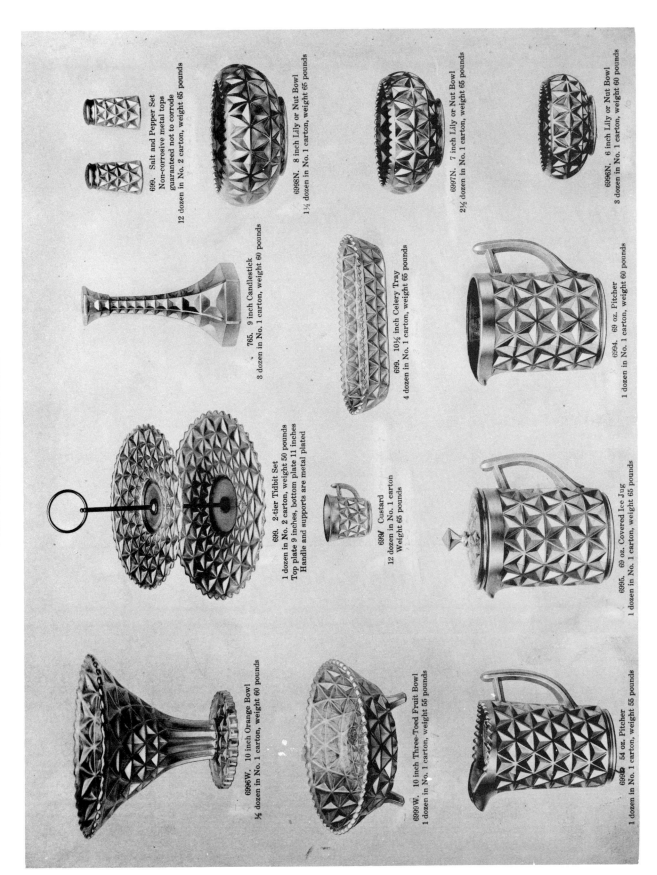

699. Salt and Pepper Set
Non-corrosive metal tops
guaranteed not to corrode
12 dozen in No. 2 carton, weight 65 pounds

6998N. 8 inch Lily or Nut Bowl
1½ dozen in No. 1 carton, weight 65 pounds

6997N. 7 inch Lily or Nut Bowl
2½ dozen in No. 1 carton, weight 65 pounds

6996N. 6 inch Lily or Nut Bowl
3 dozen in No. 1 carton, weight 60 pounds

765. 9 inch Candlestick
3 dozen in No. 1 carton, weight 60 pounds

699. 10½ inch Celery Tray
4 dozen in No. 1 carton, weight 65 pounds

6994. 69 oz. Pitcher
1 dozen in No. 1 carton, weight 60 pounds

699. 2-tier Tidbit Set
1 dozen in No. 2 carton, weight 50 pounds
Top plate 9 inches, bottom plate 11 inches
Handle and supports are metal plated

699. Custard
12 dozen in No. 1 carton
Weight 65 pounds

6995. 69 oz. Covered Ice Jug
1 dozen in No. 1 carton, weight 65 pounds

6996W. 10 inch Orange Bowl
½ dozen in No. 1 carton, weight 60 pounds

6999W. 10 inch Three-Toed Fruit Bowl
1 dozen in No. 1 carton, weight 55 pounds

6992. 54 oz. Pitcher
1 dozen in No. 1 carton, weight 55 pounds

Product of **HAND MADE**

The Mount Vernon Pattern

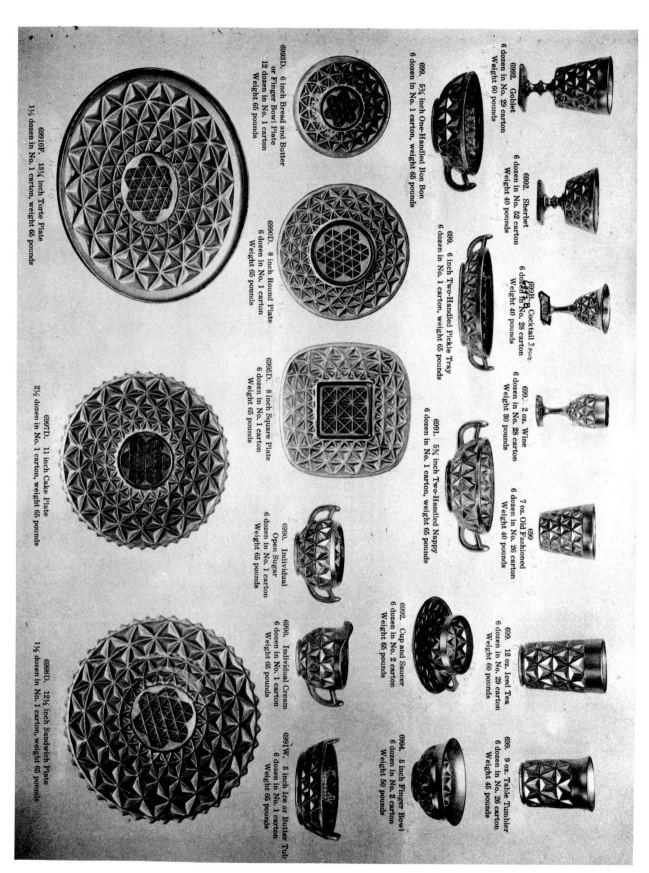

Illustrations ¼ Size

154

Imperial Hand Made Glassware

Also used for Cocktail Sets

Fish Plate

100. 1¼ oz. Boot Whiskey
6 dozen in No. 69 carton
Weight 20 pounds

142. 2-piece Canape Set
5 dozen in No. 1 carton
Weight 65 pounds

158. 2-piece Canape Set
4 dozen in No. 2 carton
Weight 55 pounds

160. 7 oz. Old Fashioned
and Muddler
6 dozen in No 2 carton
Weight 55 pounds

658. 6 oz. Old Fashioned
and Muddler
6 dozen in No. 2 carton
Weight 50 pounds

84. Blown Ice Tub
2 dozen in No. 1 carton
Weight 65 pounds

451. 3½ inch Ash Tray
30 dozen in No. 2 carton
Weight 60 pounds

355. 1¼ oz.
Liquor
6 dozen in
No. 69 carton
Weight
15 pounds

625. 26 oz. Decanter
1½ dozen in No. 1 carton
Weight 65 pounds

451. 9¼ inch Vase
5 dozen in No. 1 carton
Weight 40 pounds

3551. 18 oz. Decanter
4 dozen in No. 1 carton
Weight 50 pounds

756. 7 oz. Old Fashioned
and Muddler
6 dozen in No. 2 carton
Weight 55 pounds

699. 7 oz. Old Fashioned
and Muddler
6 dozen in No. 2 carton
Weight 55 pounds

×355. 12 oz. Tumbler
6 dozen in No. 29 carton
Weight 55 pounds

×355. 100 oz. Jug
¾ dozen in No. 1 carton
Weight 45 pounds

451. Decanter
1½ dozen in No. 1 carton
Weight 50 pounds

451 5½ oz. Tumbler
6 dozen in No. 27 carton
Weight 18 pounds

451J 9¾ oz. Tumbler
6 dozen in No. 26 carton
Weight 25 pounds

451. Cocktail Shaker
1½ dozen in No. 1 carton
Weight 40 pounds

4511 2½ oz. Liquor
6 dozen in No. 69 carton
Weight 15 pounds

451F Oyster
Cocktail
6 dozen in
No. 27 carton
Weight 25 lbs.

451. Goblet
4 dozen in
No. 70 carton
Weight 30 lbs.

451. Tall Sherbet
4 dozen in
No. 71 carton
Weight 30 lbs.

451. Low Sherbet
6 dozen in
No. 52 carton
Weight 28 lbs.

451. Cocktail
6 dozen in
No. 28 carton
Weight 25 lbs.

461. Wine
6 dozen in
No. 28 carton
Weight 22 lbs.

451. Cordial
6 dozen in
No. 27 carton
Weight 20 lbs.

451Q 12 oz. Ftd.
6 dozen in
No. 29 carton
Weight 35 lbs.

451J 12½ oz. Tumbler
6 dozen in No. 26 carton
Weight 35 pounds

451f 9 oz. Ftd.
6 dozen in
No. 29 carton
Weight 30 lbs.

323. 6 oz. Bitters and Tube
6 dozen in No. 29 carton
Weight 60 pounds

142. 3½ oz. Cocktail
6 dozen in No. 27 carton
Weight 30 pounds

142. Cocktail Shaker
1½ dozen in No. 1 carton
Weight 40 pounds

451. 7½ inch Vase
2 dozen in No. 1 carton
Weight 45 pounds

4512. 6 inch
Blown Rose Bowl
1½ dozen in No. 1 carton
Weight 40 pounds

144. Fruit or
Finger Bowl
6 dozen in No. 52 carton
Weight 28 lbs.

451. 5 oz. Ftd.
6 dozen in
No. 28 carton
Weight 28 lbs.

451
80 oz. Lipped Ice Pitcher
1 dozen in No. 1 carton
Weight 40 pounds

Imperial Hand Made Glassware

Product of

HAND MADE

Illustrations ¼ Size

155

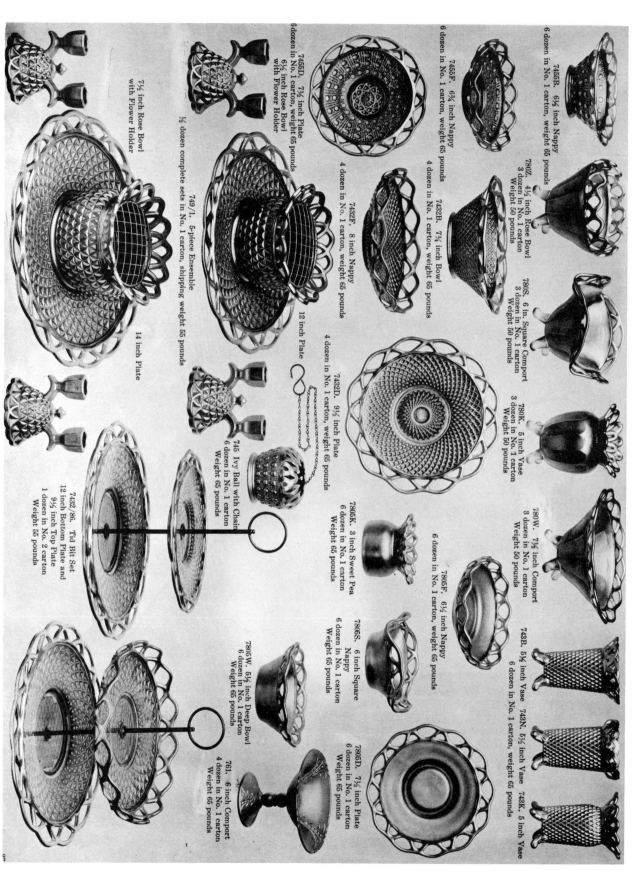

7455B. 6¼ inch Nappy
6 dozen in No. 1 carton, weight 65 pounds

7455F. 6¾ inch Nappy
6 dozen in No. 1 carton, weight 65 pounds

7455D. 7¼ inch Plate
6 dozen in No. 1 carton, weight 65 pounds

7½ inch Rose Bowl
with Flower Holder

749/2. 5-piece Ensemble
⅓ dozen in No. 1 Carton, shipping weight 50 pounds

6½ inch Rose Bowl
with Flower Holder

749/1. 5-piece Ensemble
½ dozen complete sets in No. 1 carton, shipping weight 55 pounds

14 inch Plate

780Z. 4½ inch Rose Bowl
3 dozen in No. 1 carton
Weight 50 pounds

7432B. 7¾ inch Bowl
4 dozen in No. 1 carton, weight 65 pounds

7½ inch Plate

12 inch Plate

745 Ivy Ball with Chain
6 dozen in No. 1 carton
Weight 65 pounds

7432/86. Tid Bit Set
12 inch Bottom Plate and
9½ inch Top Plate
1 dozen in No. 2 carton
Weight 55 pounds

780S. 6 in. Square Comport
3 dozen in No. 1 carton
Weight 50 pounds

780K. 5 inch Vase
3 dozen in No. 1 carton
Weight 50 pounds

7432F. 8 inch Nappy
4 dozen in No. 1 carton, weight 65 pounds

7432D. 9½ inch Plate
4 dozen in No. 1 carton, weight 65 pounds

7805K. 3 inch Sweet Pea
6 dozen in No. 1 carton
Weight 65 pounds

7805W. 5½ inch Deep Bowl
6 dozen in No. 1 carton
Weight 65 pounds

7432/87. Tid Bit Set
12 inch Bottom Plate and
11 inch Top Plate
dozen in No. 2 carton
Weight 60 pounds

Illustrations ½ Size

780W. 7½ inch Comport
3 dozen in No. 1 carton
Weight 50 pounds

7805F. 6½ inch Nappy
6 dozen in No. 1 carton, weight 65 pounds

7805S. 6 inch Square
Nappy
6 dozen in No. 1 carton
Weight 65 pounds

761. 6 inch Comport
4 dozen in No. 1 carton
Weight 65 pounds

743B. 5¾ inch Vase
6 dozen in No. 1 carton, weight 65 pounds

743N. 5½ inch Vase

743K. 5 inch Vase

7805D. 7½ inch Plate
6 dozen in No. 1 carton
Weight 65 pounds

156

Imperial Laced Edge Pattern

7499N. 8½ inch Flower Bowl
1 dozen in No. 1 carton, weight 50 pounds

7498N. 7½ inch Flower Bowl
2 dozen in No. 1 carton, weight 65 pounds

7498D. 12 inch Plate
2 dozen in No. 1 carton, weight 65 pounds

7498F. 11 inch Bowl
2 dozen in No. 1 carton, weight 65 pounds

Illustrations ¼ Size

7499F. 13 inch Fruit Bowl
1¼ dozen in No. 1 carton, weight 65 pounds

7498K. 7½ inch Rose
Bowl and Holder
1⅓ dozen in No. 1 carton
Weight 65 pounds

7498B. 10 inch Bowl
2½ dozen in No. 1 carton
Weight 65 pounds

Holders are made
of wire and well
coated.

770/2. 8 inch Blown Rose Bowl
⅔ dozen in No. 1 carton
Weight 40 pounds

7499B. 12 inch Orange Bowl
1¼ dozen in No. 1 carton, weight 65 pounds

7498R. 7½ inch Flower Bowl and Holder
1⅓ dozen in No. 1 carton, weight 55 pounds

7497E. 9½ inch Basket Bowl
2 dozen in No. 1 carton, weight 55 pounds

7497R. 6½ inch Flower Bowl and Holder
6 dozen in No. 1 carton
Weight 60 pounds

1346N. 7 inch Rose
Bowl and Holder
2 dozen in No. 1 carton
Weight 60 pounds

7499D. 14 inch Plate
1¼ dozen in No. 1 carton, weight 65 pounds

7497D. 11 inch Plate
2½ dozen in No. 1 carton, weight 65 pounds

X 7497K. 6½ inch Rose Bowl and Holder
2 dozen in No. 1 carton, weight 60 pounds

7497N. 6½ inch
Flower Bowl
2½ dozen in No. 1 carton
Weight 65 pounds

7497B. 9 inch Bowl
2½ dozen in No. 1 carton, weight 65 pounds

7497F. 9½ inch Bowl
2½ dozen in No. 1 carton, weight 65 pounds

Product of HAND MADE

157

Fancy Punch Sets

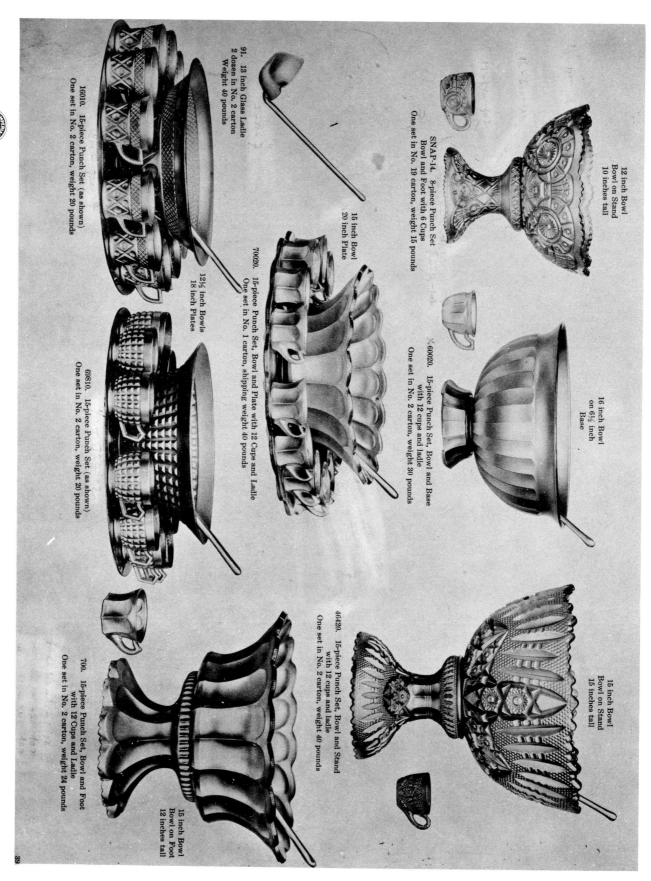

12 inch Bowl
Bowl on Stand
10 inches tall

SNAP-14. 8-piece Punch Set,
Bowl and Foot with 6 Cups
One set in No. 19 carton, weight 15 pounds

15 inch Bowl
20 inch Plate

91. 18 inch Glass Ladle
2 dozen in No. 2 carton
Weight 40 pounds

16010. 15-piece Punch Set (as shown)
One set in No. 2 carton, weight 20 pounds

12½ inch Bowls
18 inch Plates

70020. 15-piece Punch Set, Bowl and Plate with 12 Cups and Ladle
One set in No. 1 carton, shipping weight 40 pounds

69810. 15-piece Punch Set (as shown)
One set in No. 2 carton, weight 20 pounds

60020. 15-piece Punch Set, Bowl and Base
with 12 cups and ladle
One set in No. 2 carton, weight 30 pounds

16 inch Bowl
on 6½ inch
Base

16 inch Bowl
Bowl on Stand
15 inches tall

46420. 15-piece Punch Set, Bowl and Stand
with 12 cups and ladle
One set in No. 2 carton, weight 40 pounds

700. 15-piece Punch Set, Bowl and Foot
with 12 Cups and Ladle
One set in No. 2 carton, weight 24 pounds

15 inch Bowl
Bowl on Foot
12 inches tall

Illustrations ¼ Size

158

Imperial's Popular Console Sets

1537. 3-piece Oval Console Set
1 dozen in No. 1 carton, shipping weight 65 pounds

648B. 11 inch
Round Bowl

648B/169.
3-piece Console Set, 1 dozen in No. 1 carton
Weight 65 pounds
648B. 11 inch Bowl, 2 dozen in No. 1 carton, weight 65 pounds
169. Twin Candlestick, 6 dozen in No. 1 carton, weight 65 pounds

169

153B. 3-piece Round Console Set, 1 dozen in No. 1 carton, weight 65 pounds
153. Twin candlestick, 6 dozen in No. 1 carton, weight 65 pounds

7497F. 3-piece Console Set, 9½ inch Bowl
1¼ dozen in No. 1 carton, shipping weight 65 pounds

6567/169. 3-piece Console Set, 1¼ dozen in No. 1 carton, weight 65 pounds
6567. 9½ inch Bowl, 2½ dozen in No. 1 carton, weight 65 pounds

7499B. 3-piece Console Set, 12 inch Bowl
⅚ dozen in No. 1 carton, shipping weight 65 pounds

7499F. 3-piece Console Set, 13 inch Bowl
⅚ dozen in No. 1 carton, shipping weight 65 pounds

7498B. 3-piece Console Set, 10 inch Bowl
1 dozen in No. 1 carton, shipping weight 65 pounds

7498F. 3-piece Console Set, 11 inch Bowl
1 dozen in No. 1 carton, shipping weight 65 pounds

749B. 3-piece Console Set, 9 inch Bowl
1¼ dozen in No. 1 carton, weight 65 pounds
749. Twin Candlestick
6 dozen in No. 55 carton, weight 65 pounds

Product of HAND MADE

159

Square Feet

160. Goblet
6 dozen in No. 23 carton
Weight 55 pounds

160. Sherbet
6 dozen in No. 52 carton
Weight 40 pounds

160B. Cocktail
6 dozen in No. 28 carton
Weight 30 pounds

160. 12 ounce Ice Tea or Hiball
6 dozen in No. 29 carton
Weight 60 pounds

160. 6 ounce Ginger Ale
6 dozen in No. 28 carton
Weight 40 pounds

160. 7 ounce Old Fashion
6 dozen in No. 26 carton
Weight 40 pounds

160. Wine
6 dozen in No. 27 carton
Weight 30 pounds

160. Whiskey
6 dozen in No. 69 carton
Weight 30 pounds

1604½D. 7 inch Plate
8 dozen in No. 1 carton
Weight 65 pounds

160SD. 8 inch Salad Plate
4 dozen in No. 48 carton
Weight 55 pounds

1605. 3-piece Mayonnaise Set
3 dozen in No. 1 carton
Weight 65 pounds

1605W. 6¾ inch Flared Nappy
6 dozen in No. 1 carton
Weight 65 pounds

1604W. 4½ inch Fruit
12 dozen in No. 1 carton
Weight 60 pounds

160. Cup and Saucer
6 dozen in No. 1 carton
Weight 65 pounds

1601W. 3½ inch Individual Jelly
24 dozen in No. 1 carton
Weight 65 pounds

1605F. 7 inch Shallow Nappy
6 dozen in No. 1 carton
Weight 65 pounds

1604½X. 6 inch Baked Apple Nappy
8 dozen in No. 1 carton
Weight 65 pounds

1604½A. 4½ inch Finger Bowl
8 dozen in No. 1 carton
Weight 65 pounds

160. Decanter and Stopper
1½ dozen in No. 1 carton
Weight 65 pounds

160. Sugar and Cream Set
3 dozen in No. 1 carton
Weight 65 pounds

160F. 5¼ inch Compote
4 dozen in No. 1 carton. Weight 55 pounds

160X. 5¾ inch Compote
4 dozen in No. 1 carton. Weight 55 pounds

160R. 4½ inch Coaster
24 dozen in No. 1 carton
Weight 65 pounds

160U. 9½ inch Divided Relish
3 dozen in No. 1 carton. Weight 65 pounds

ALL CARTON CHARGES ARE NET

160. Handled Custard Cup
Crystal, Blue, Amber, $2.20
Ruby,   2.60
12 dozen to carton, shipping weight 70 pounds
Cartons 50¢ each *net*

1605W.   6¾ inch Fruit Bowl
Crystal, Blue, Amber, $3.00
Ruby,   3.50
6 dozen to carton, shipping weight 70 pounds
Cartons 50¢ each *net*

1605F. 7 inch Shallow Nappy
Crystal, Blue, Amber, $3.00
Ruby,   3.50
6 dozen to carton, shipping weight 70 pounds
Cartons 50¢ each *net*

1604½A.   4½ inch Finger Bowl
Crystal, Blue, Amber, $3.00
Ruby,   3.50
6 dozen to carton, shipping weight 50 pounds
Cartons 35¢ each *net*

1604W.   4½ inch Fruit Nappy
Crystal, Blue, Amber, $2.30
Ruby,   2.70
12 dozen to carton, shipping weight 60 pounds
Cartons 35¢ each *net*

ALL PRICES
ARE PER DOZEN

DESIGN
PATENTED

1604½X.   6 inch Fruit or Baked Apple
Crystal, Blue, Amber, $3.00
Ruby,   3.50
6 dozen to carton, shipping weight 50 pounds
Cartons 35¢ each *net*

1601.   4¼ inch Coaster, ground bottom
Crystal, Blue, Amber, $2.40
Ruby,   2.80
12 dozen to carton, shipping weight 60 pounds
Cartons 35¢ each *net*

160.   Handled Cup and Saucer
Crystal, Blue, Amber, $4.50
Ruby,   5.30
12 dozen to carton, shipping weight 70 pounds
Cartons 50¢ each *net*

EACH PIECE
HAND MADE
AND HIGHLY
FIRE POLISHED
BY HAND

Illustrations ½ Size

Product of Imperial

Product of

MAKE SALAD SETS
WITH SALAD PLATES
AND BUFFET OR
MAYONNAISE SETS

THEY SELL

1604½D. 7 inch Salad Plate
8 dozen in No. 18 carton
Weight 65 pounds

16010B. 12½ inch Fruit Bowl
1 dozen in No. 1 carton, weight 65 pounds

1608. 3-piece Mayonnaise Set
1 dozen in No. 1 carton, weight 65 pounds
1608V. 13½ inch Torte Plate, 1½ dozen
in No. 1 carton, weight 65 pounds

16010. 3-piece Buffet or Mayonnaise Set
5/6 dozen in No. 1 carton, weight 65 pounds
16010V. 16 inch Torte Plate, 1 dozen in No. 1 carton, weight 65 pounds

1605. 3-piece Mayonnaise Set
3 dozen in No. 1 carton, weight 65 pounds

16010R. 13 inch Center Bowl
1 dozen in No. 1 carton, weight 65 pounds

X 16010A. 11 inch Salad Bowl
1 dozen in No. 1 carton, weight 65 pounds

11 inch Bottom Tray
7½ inch Top Tray

X 698. 2-tier Tid Bit Set
1 dozen in No. 2 carton, weight 50 pounds

698./ 10½ inch Vase
1½ dozen in No. 1 carton
Weight 65 pounds

69810. 3-piece Buffet or Mayonnaise Set
5/6 dozen in No. 1 carton, shipping weight 65 pounds
69810V. 16 inch Plate, 1 dozen in No. 1 carton, weight 65 pounds

698. 2-piece Square Salad Set
7½ inch Square Bowl and 10½ inch Square Plate
1 dozen sets in No. 1 carton, weight 65 pounds

X 6985D. 7½ inch Salad Plate
8 dozen in No. 18 carton
Weight 65 pounds

1605D. 8 inch Salad Plate
4 dozen in No. 48 carton
Weight 55 pounds

Illustrations ¼ Size

162

Monticello Pattern

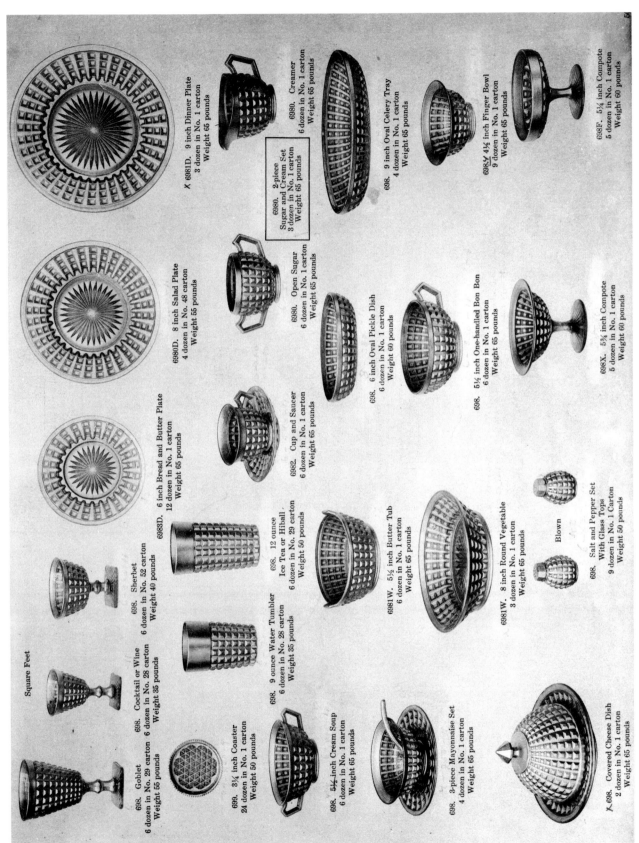

Square Feet

698. Goblet
6 dozen in No. 29 carton
Weight 55 pounds

698. Cocktail or Wine
6 dozen in No. 28 carton
Weight 35 pounds

698. Sherbet
6 dozen in No. 52 carton
Weight 40 pounds

699. 3¼ inch Coaster
24 dozen in No. 1 carton
Weight 50 pounds

698. 9 ounce Water Tumbler
6 dozen in No. 28 carton
Weight 35 pounds

6983D. 12 ounce
Ice Tea or Hiball
6 dozen in No. 29 carton
Weight 50 pounds

698. 5½ inch Cream Soup
6 dozen in No. 1 carton
Weight 65 pounds

698. 3-piece Mayonnaise Set
4 dozen in No. 1 carton
Weight 65 pounds

X 698. Covered Cheese Dish
2 dozen in No. 1 carton
Weight 65 pounds

6983D. 6 inch Bread and Butter Plate
12 dozen in No. 1 carton
Weight 65 pounds

6980D. 8 inch Salad Plate
4 dozen in No. 48 carton
Weight 55 pounds

X 6981D. 9 inch Dinner Plate
3 dozen in No. 1 carton
Weight 65 pounds

6982. Cup and Saucer
6 dozen in No. 1 carton
Weight 65 pounds

6980. Open Sugar
6 dozen in No. 1 carton
Weight 65 pounds

6980. Creamer
6 dozen in No. 1 carton
Weight 65 pounds

6980. 2-piece
Sugar and Cream Set
3 dozen in No. 1 carton
Weight 65 pounds

6981W. 5½ inch Butter Tub
6 dozen in No. 1 carton
Weight 65 pounds

698. 6 inch Oval Pickle Dish
6 dozen in No. 1 carton
Weight 60 pounds

6981W. 8 inch Round Vegetable
3 dozen in No. 1 carton
Weight 65 pounds

698. 9 inch Oval Celery Tray
4 dozen in No. 1 carton
Weight 65 pounds

698. 5½ inch One-handled Bon Bon
6 dozen in No. 1 carton
Weight 65 pounds

Blown

698. Salt and Pepper Set
With Glass Tops
9 dozen in No. 1 Carton
Weight 50 pounds

698½ 4½ inch Finger Bowl
9 dozen in No. 1 carton
Weight 65 pounds

698X. 5¾ inch Compote
5 dozen in No. 1 carton
Weight 60 pounds

698F. 5¼ inch Compote
5 dozen in No. 1 carton
Weight 60 pounds

Monticello Pattern

These four cupped shape pieces also used for nut bowls

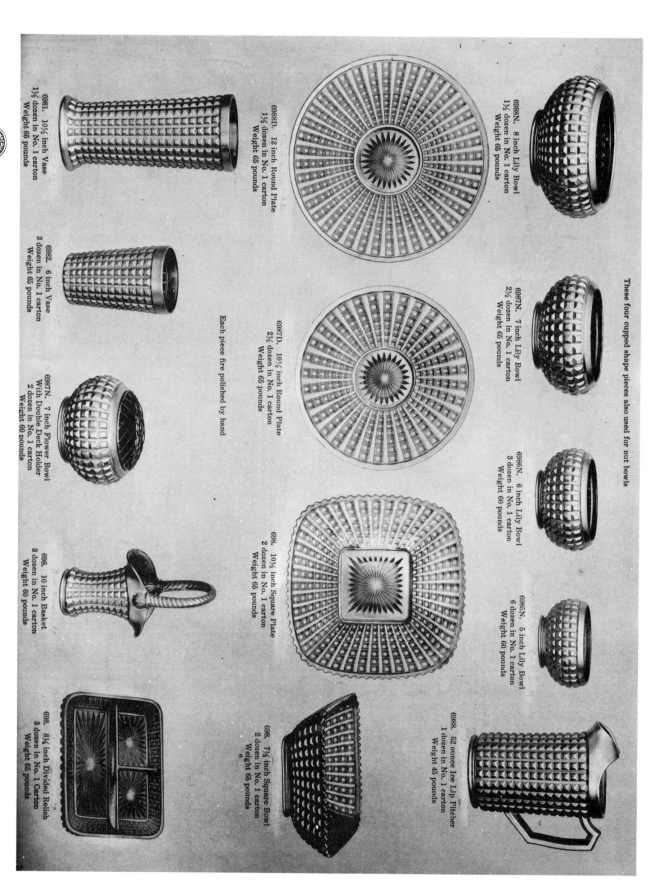

6988N. 8 inch Lily Bowl
1½ dozen in No. 1 carton
Weight 65 pounds

6987N. 7 inch Lily Bowl
2½ dozen in No. 1 carton
Weight 65 pounds

6986N. 6 inch Lily Bowl
3 dozen in No. 1 carton
Weight 60 pounds

6985N. 5 inch Lily Bowl
6 dozen in No. 1 carton
Weight 60 pounds

6988D. 12 inch Round Plate
1½ dozen in No. 1 carton
Weight 65 pounds

6987D. 10½ inch Round Plate
2½ dozen in No. 1 carton
Weight 65 pounds

Each piece fire polished by hand

698. 10½ inch Square Plate
2 dozen in No. 1 carton
Weight 65 pounds

6988. 52 ounce Ice Lip Pitcher
1 dozen in No. 1 carton
Weight 45 pounds

6981. 10½ inch Vase
1¼ dozen in No. 1 carton
Weight 65 pounds

6982. 6 inch Vase
3 dozen in No. 1 carton
Weight 65 pounds

6987N. 7 inch Flower Bowl
With Double Deck Holder
2 dozen in No. 1 carton
Weight 60 pounds

698. 10 inch Basket
3 dozen in No. 1 carton
Weight 60 pounds

698. 7½ inch Square Bowl
2 dozen in No. 1 carton
Weight 65 pounds

698. 8¼ inch Divided Relish
3 dozen in No. 1 Carton
Weight 65 pounds

No. 701 Reeded Pattern—Design Patented

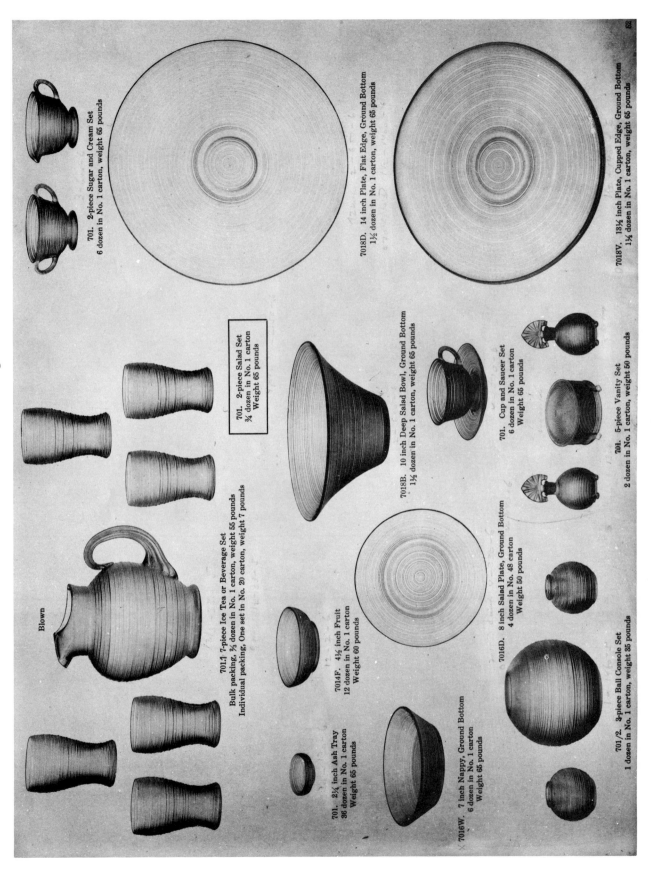

701. 2-piece Sugar and Cream Set
6 dozen in No. 1 carton, weight 65 pounds

7018D. 14 inch Plate, Flat Edge, Ground Bottom
1½ dozen in No. 1 carton, weight 65 pounds

7018V. 13½ inch Plate, Cupped Edge, Ground Bottom
1½ dozen in No. 1 carton, weight 65 pounds

701. 2-piece Salad Set
¾ dozen in No. 1 carton
Weight 65 pounds

7018B. 10 inch Deep Salad Bowl, Ground Bottom
1½ dozen in No. 1 carton, weight 65 pounds

701. Cup and Saucer Set
6 dozen in No. 1 carton
Weight 65 pounds

701. 5-piece Vanity Set
2 dozen in No. 1 carton, weight 50 pounds

Blown

701.1 7-piece Ice Tea or Beverage Set
Bulk packing, ⅝ dozen in No. 1 carton, weight 55 pounds
Individual packing, One set in No. 20 carton, weight 7 pounds

7014F. 4½ inch Fruit
12 dozen in No. 1 carton
Weight 60 pounds

7016D. 8 inch Salad Plate, Ground Bottom
4 dozen in No. 48 carton
Weight 50 pounds

701. 2¾ inch Ash Tray
36 dozen in No. 1 carton
Weight 65 pounds

7016W. 7 inch Nappy, Ground Bottom
6 dozen in No. 1 carton
Weight 65 pounds

701/2. 3-piece Ball Console Set
1 dozen in No. 1 carton, weight 85 pounds

Illustrations ¼ Size

Product of 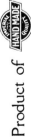 HAND MADE

165

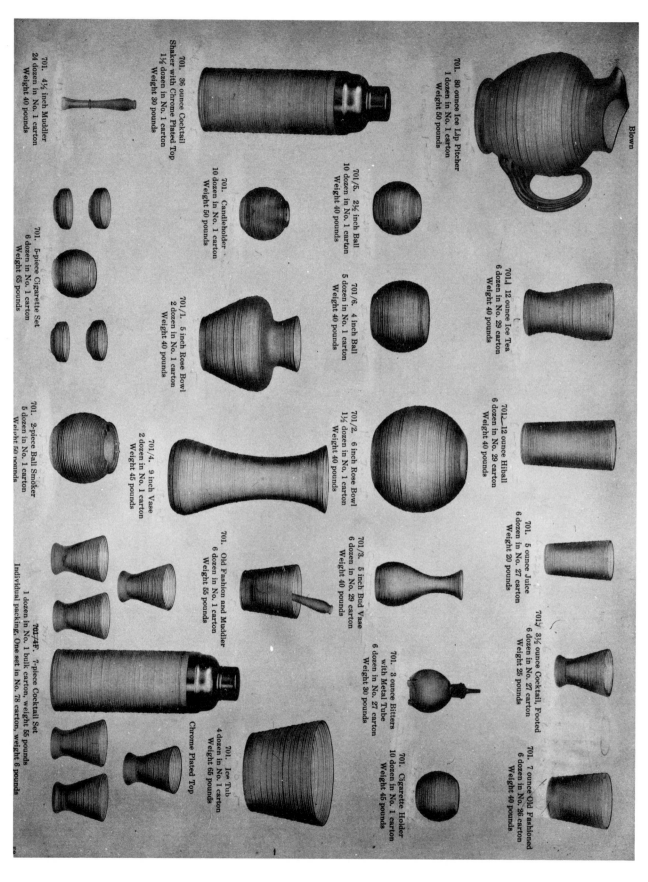

Blown

701. 80 ounce Ice Lip Pitcher
1 dozen in No. 1 carton
Weight 50 pounds

701. 36 ounce Cocktail
Shaker with Chrome Plated Top
1½ dozen in No. 1 carton
Weight 30 pounds

701. 4½ inch Muddler
24 dozen in No. 1 carton
Weight 40 pounds

701. 5-piece Cigarette Set
6 dozen in No. 1 carton
Weight 65 pounds

701. Candleholder
10 dozen in No. 1 carton
Weight 50 pounds

701/5. 2½ inch Ball
10 dozen in No. 1 carton
Weight 40 pounds

701/6. 4 inch Ball
5 dozen in No. 1 carton
Weight 40 pounds

701/1. 5 inch Rose Bowl
2 dozen in No. 1 carton
Weight 40 pounds

701. 2-piece Ball Smoker
1 dozen in No. 1 carton
Weight 50 pounds

701. 12 ounce Ice Tea
6 dozen in No. 29 carton
Weight 40 pounds

701. 12 ounce Hiball
6 dozen in No. 29 carton
Weight 40 pounds

701/2. 6 inch Rose Bowl
1½ dozen in No. 1 carton
Weight 40 pounds

701/4. 9 inch Vase
2 dozen in No. 1 carton
Weight 45 pounds

701. Old Fashion and Muddler
6 dozen in No. 1 carton
Weight 55 pounds

701/4F. 7-piece Cocktail Set
1 dozen in No. 1 bulk carton, weight 55 pounds
Individual packing. One set in No. 78 carton, weight 6 pounds

701. 5 ounce Juice
6 dozen in No. 27 carton
Weight 20 pounds

701/3. 5 inch Bud Vase
6 dozen in No. 29 carton
Weight 40 pounds

701. 3 ounce Bitters
with Metal Tube
6 dozen in No. 27 carton
Weight 30 pounds

701. 3½ ounce Cocktail, Footed
6 dozen in No. 27 carton
Weight 25 pounds

701. Cigarette Holder
10 dozen in No. 1 carton
Weight 45 pounds

701. 7 ounce Old Fashioned
6 dozen in No. 26 carton
Weight 40 pounds

701. Ice Tub
4 dozen in No. 1 carton
Weight 65 pounds

Chrome Plated Top

Imperial Empire Pattern

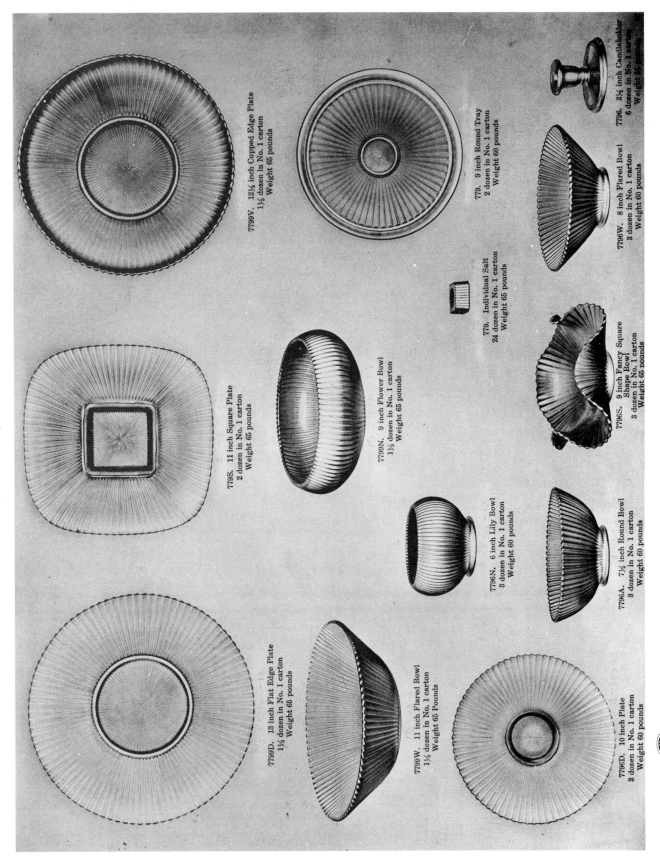

7799V. 12½ inch Cupped Edge Plate
1½ dozen in No. 1 carton
Weight 65 pounds

7799. 9 inch Round Tray
2 dozen in No. 1 carton
Weight 60 pounds

7796W. 8 inch Flared Bowl
3 dozen in No. 1 carton
Weight 60 pounds

7796. 2½ inch Candleholder
6 dozen in No. 1 carton
Weight 65 pounds

779. Individual Salt
24 dozen in No. 1 carton
Weight 65 pounds

7799S. 11 inch Square Plate
2 dozen in No. 1 carton
Weight 65 pounds

7799N. 9 inch Flower Bowl
1½ dozen in No. 1 carton
Weight 65 pounds

7796S. 9 inch Fancy Square
Shape Bowl
3 dozen in No. 1 carton
Weight 65 pounds

7796N. 6 inch Lily Bowl
3 dozen in No. 1 carton
Weight 60 pounds

7796A. 7½ inch Round Bowl
3 dozen in No. 1 carton
Weight 60 pounds

7799D. 13 inch Flat Edge Plate
1½ dozen in No. 1 carton
Weight 65 pounds

7799W. 11 inch Flared Bowl
1½ dozen in No. 1 carton
Weight 65 Pounds

7796D. 10 inch Plate
3 dozen in No. 1 carton
Weight 60 pounds

Product of AMERICA HAND MADE Quality

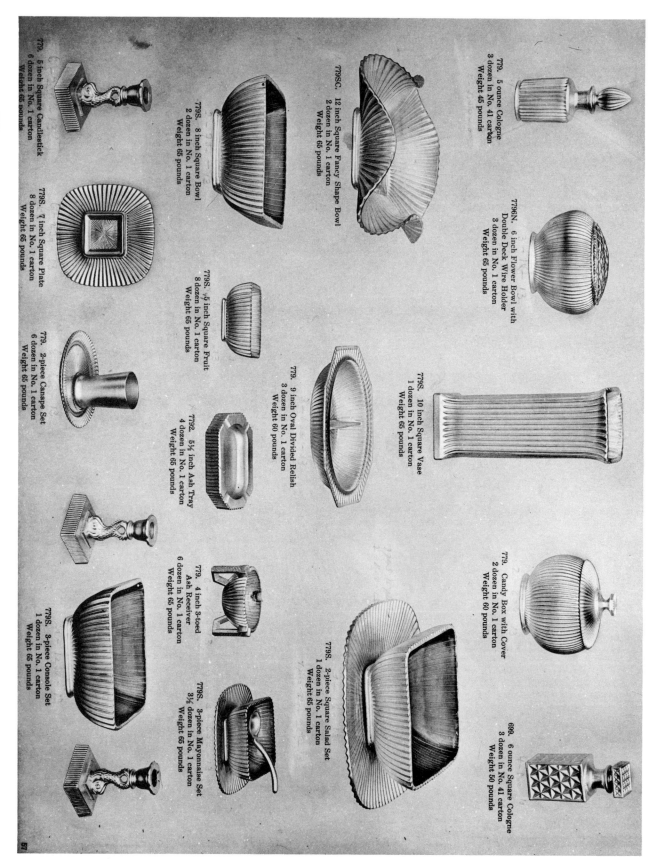

Imperial Empire Pattern

779. 5 ounce Cologne
3 dozen in No. 41 carton
Weight 45 pounds

779SC. 12 inch Square Fancy Shape Bowl
2 dozen in No. 1 carton
Weight 65 pounds

7796N. 6 inch Flower Bowl with
Double Deck Wire Holder
3 dozen in No. 1 carton
Weight 65 pounds

779S. 8 inch Square Bowl
2 dozen in No. 1 carton
Weight 65 pounds

779S. 5 inch Square Fruit
8 dozen in No. 1 carton
Weight 65 pounds

779. 9 inch Oval Divided Relish
3 dozen in No. 1 carton
Weight 60 pounds

779S. 10 inch Square Vase
1 dozen in No. 1 carton
Weight 65 pounds

779. 5 inch Square Candlestick
6 dozen in No. 1 carton
Weight 65 pounds

779S. 7 inch Square Plate
8 dozen in No. 1 carton
Weight 65 pounds

779. 2-piece Canape Set
6 dozen in No. 1 carton
Weight 65 pounds

7792. 5½ inch Ash Tray
4 dozen in No. 1 carton
Weight 65 pounds

779. 4 inch 3-toed
Ash Receiver
6 dozen in No. 1 carton
Weight 65 pounds

779. Candy Box with Cover
2 dozen in No. 1 carton
Weight 60 pounds

779S. 3-piece Console Set
1 dozen in No. 1 carton
Weight 65 pounds

779S. 3-piece Mayonnaise Set
3½ dozen in No. 1 carton
Weight 65 pounds

779S. 2-piece Square Salad Set
1 dozen in No. 1 carton
Weight 65 pounds

699. 6 ounce Square Cologne
3 dozen in No. 41 carton
Weight 50 pounds

57

Imperial Candlewick—Patented

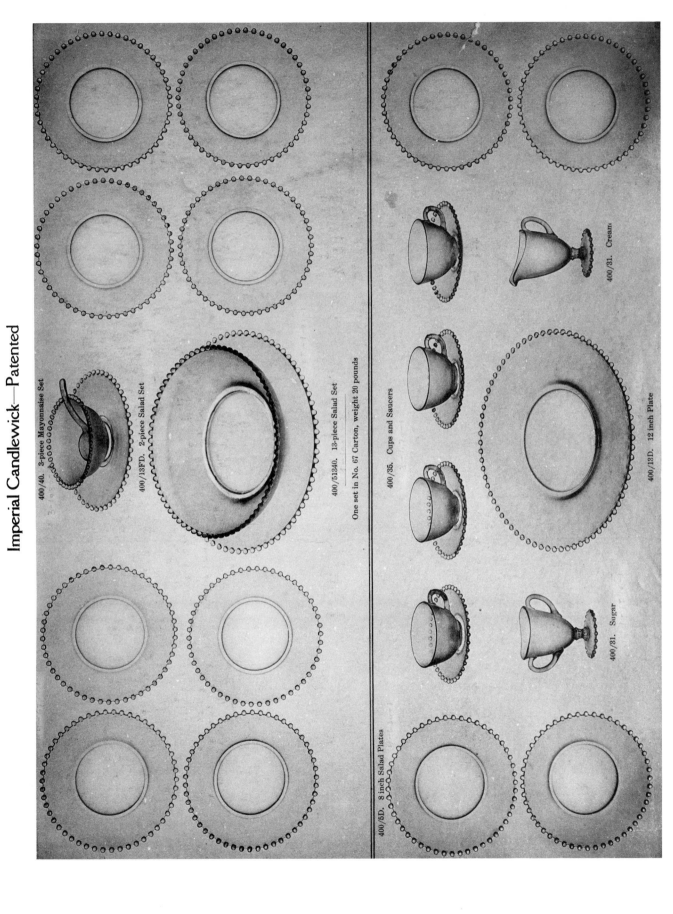

400/40. 3-piece Mayonnaise Set

400/13FD. 2-piece Salad Set

400/51340. 13-piece Salad Set

One set in No. 67 Carton, weight 20 pounds

400/5D. 8 inch Salad Plates

400/35. Cups and Saucers

400/31. Cream

400/31. Sugar

400/18D. 12 inch Plate

400/13. 15-piece Luncheon Set
One set in No. 7 Carton, weight 15 pounds

Product of

169

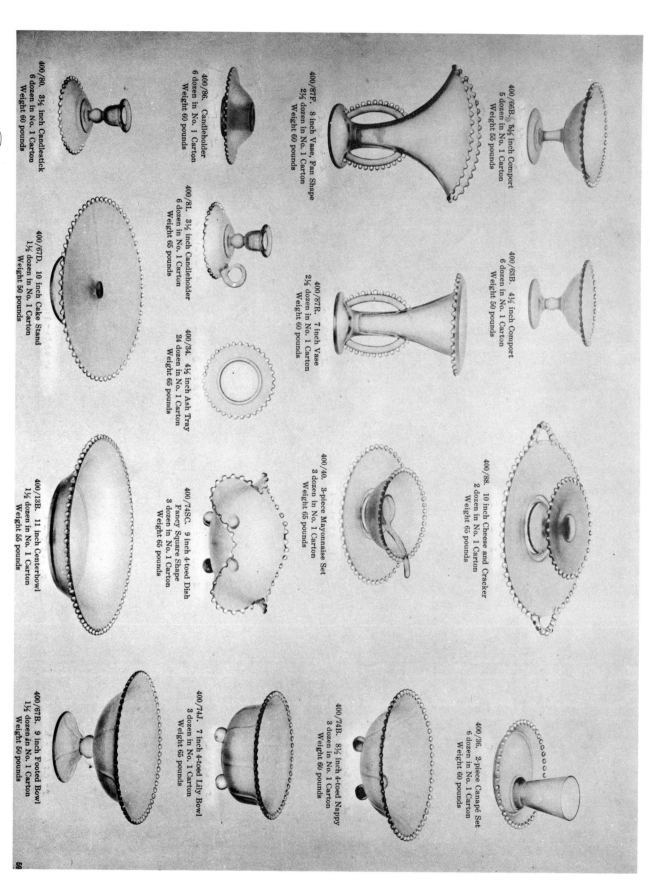

400/66B. 5½ inch Comport
5 dozen in No. 1 Carton
Weight 65 pounds

400/63B. 4½ inch Comport
6 dozen in No. 1 Carton
Weight 50 pounds

400/87FP. 8 inch Vase, Fan Shape
2½ dozen in No. 1 Carton
Weight 60 pounds

400/86. Candleholder
6 dozen in No. 1 Carton
Weight 60 pounds

400/80. 3½ inch Candlestick
6 dozen in No. 1 Carton
Weight 60 pounds

400/87R. 7 inch Vase
2½ dozen in No. 1 Carton
Weight 60 pounds

400/81. 3½ inch Candleholder
6 dozen in No. 1 Carton
Weight 65 pounds

400/67D. 10 inch Cake Stand
1½ dozen in No. 1 Carton
Weight 50 pounds

400/34. 4½ inch Ash Tray
24 dozen in No. 1 Carton
Weight 65 pounds

400/88. 10 inch Cheese and Cracker
2 dozen in No. 1 Carton
Weight 65 pounds

400/40. 3-piece Mayonnaise Set
3 dozen in No. 1 Carton
Weight 65 pounds

400/74SC. 9 inch 4-toed Dish
Fancy Square Shape
3 dozen in No. 1 Carton
Weight 65 pounds

400/13B. 11 inch Centerbowl
1½ dozen in No. 1 Carton
Weight 55 pounds

400/36. 2-piece Canapé Set
6 dozen in No. 1 Carton
Weight 60 pounds

400/74B. 8½ inch 4-toed Nappy
3 dozen in No. 1 Carton
Weight 60 pounds

400/74J. 7 inch 4-toed Lily Bowl
3 dozen in No. 1 Carton
Weight 65 pounds

400/67B. 9 inch Footed Bowl
1½ dozen in No. 1 Carton
Weight 50 pounds

Octagon and Square Luncheon Sets—Hand Made

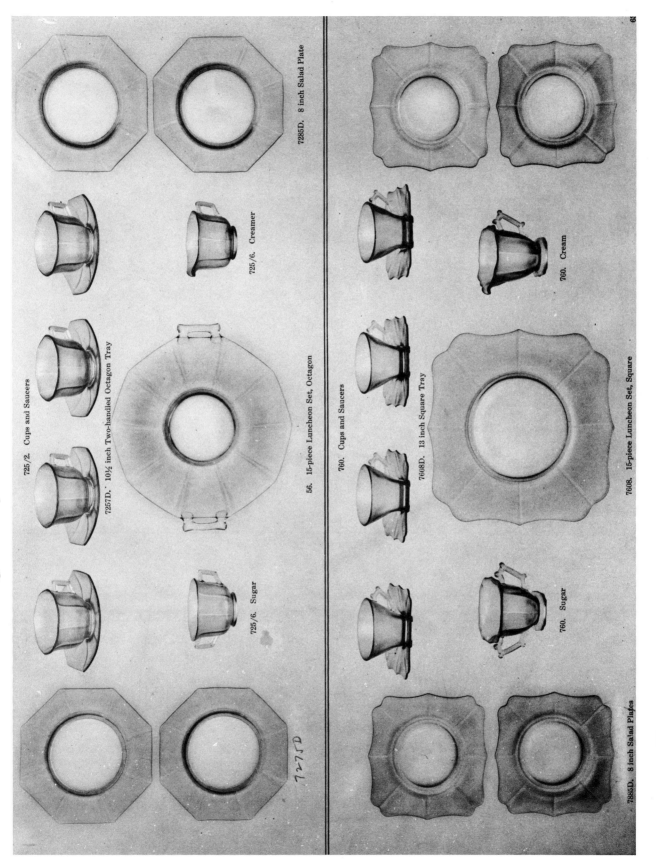

7285D. 8 inch Salad Plate

725/6. Creamer

725/2. Cups and Saucers

7257D. 10½ inch Two-handled Octagon Tray

56. 15-piece Luncheon Set, Octagon

725/6. Sugar

7285D. 8 inch Salad Plates

760. Cream

760. Cups and Saucers

7608D. 13 inch Square Tray

7608. 15-piece Luncheon Set, Square

760. Sugar

7885D. 8 inch Salad Plates

 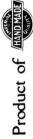

Product of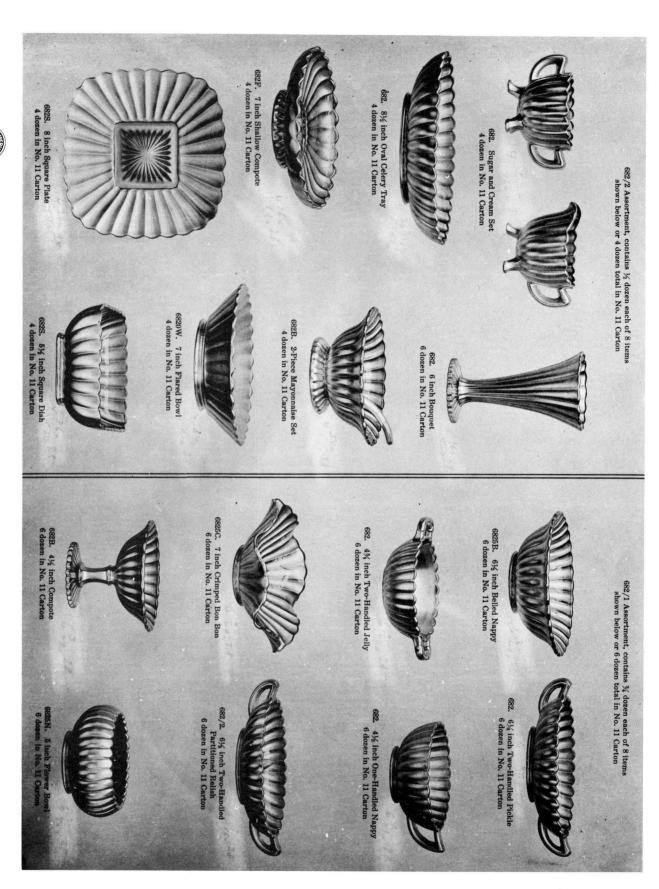

682/2 Assortment, contains ½ dozen each of 8 items
shown below or 4 dozen total in No. 11 Carton

682. Sugar and Cream Set
4 dozen in No. 11 Carton

682. 8¼ inch Oval Celery Tray
4 dozen in No. 11 Carton

682F. 7 inch Shallow Compote
4 dozen in No. 11 Carton

682S. 8 inch Square Plate
4 dozen in No. 11 Carton

682S. 5½ inch Square Dish
4 dozen in No. 11 Carton

682W. 7 inch Flared Bowl
4 dozen in No. 11 Carton

682B. 2-Piece Mayonnaise Set
4 dozen in No. 11 Carton

682. 6 inch Bouquet
6 dozen in No. 11 Carton

682/1 Assortment, contains ¾ dozen each of 8 items
shown below or 6 dozen total in No. 11 Carton

682B. 6¼ inch Belled Nappy
6 dozen in No. 11 Carton

682. 4½ inch Two-Handled Jelly
6 dozen in No. 11 Carton

682CC. 7 inch Crimped Bon Bon
6 dozen in No. 11 Carton

682B. 4½ inch Compote
6 dozen in No. 11 Carton

682N. 5 inch Flower Bowl
6 dozen in No. 11 Carton

682/2. 6½ inch Two-Handled
Partitioned Relish
6 dozen in No. 11 Carton

682. 4½ inch One-Handled Nappy
6 dozen in No. 11 Carton

682. 6¼ inch Two-Handled Pickle
6 dozen in No. 11 Carton

No. 6828D 15-Piece Luncheon Set, One Set in No. 4 Carton, weight 15 pounds

6620D. 8 inch Salad Plate

682. Cup and Saucer

6828D. 12 inch Cake Plate

682. Sugar and Cream Set

163B. 3 piece Console Set
1 dozen in No. 11 Carton, weight 60 pounds

6823D. 6 inch Plate
12 dozen in No. 11 Carton
Weight 65 pounds

6827D. 10½ inch Plate
2½ dozen in No. 11 Carton
Weight 65 pounds

6827B. 8½ inch Salad Bowl
2½ dozen in No. 11 Carton
Weight 65 pounds

6828B. 10 inch Salad Bowl
1¼ dozen in No. 11 Carton
Weight 65 pounds

Illustrations ¼ Size

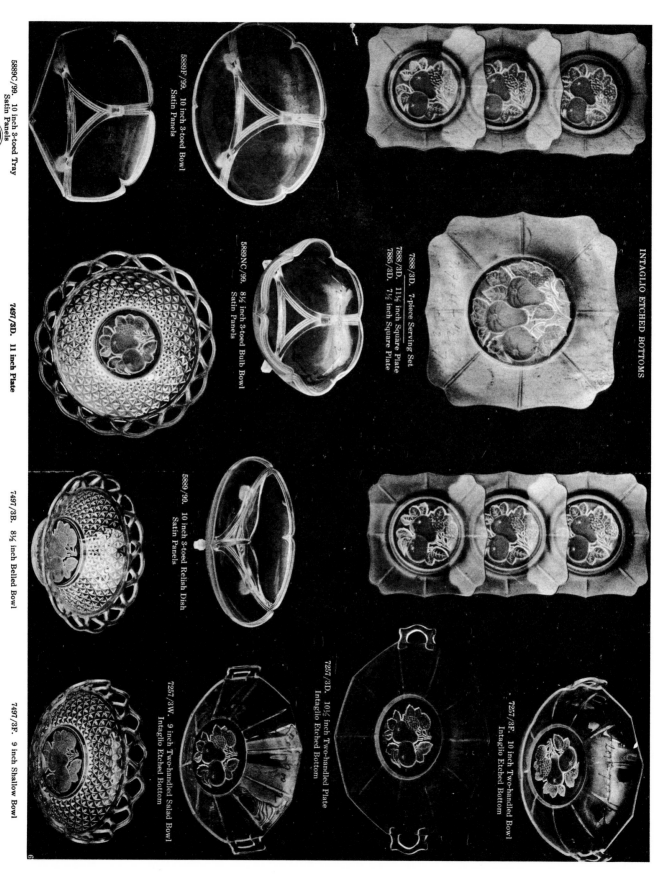

Product of [IMPERIAL HAND MADE QUALITY]

5889C/99. 10 inch 3-toed Tray
Satin Panels

5889F/99. 10 inch 3-toed Bowl
Satin Panels

5889NC/99. 8½ inch 3-toed Bulb Bowl
Satin Panels

7888/3D. 7-piece Serving Set
7888/3D. 11½ inch Square Plate
7885/3D. 7½ inch Square Plate

INTAGLIO ETCHED BOTTOMS

7497/3D. 11 inch Plate

7497/3B. 8½ inch Belled Bowl

5889/99. 10 inch 3-toed Relish Dish
Satin Panels

LACED EDGE PIECES WITH INTAGLIO ETCHED FRUIT BOTTOMS

7497/3F. 9 inch Shallow Bowl

7257/3W. 9 inch Two-handled Salad Bowl
Intaglio Etched Bottom

7257/3D. 10½ inch Two-handled Plate
Intaglio Etched Bottom

7257/3F. 10 inch Two-handled Bowl
Intaglio Etched Bottom

Illustrations ¾ Size

174

Imperial Intaglio Design in Bottom of Each Piece

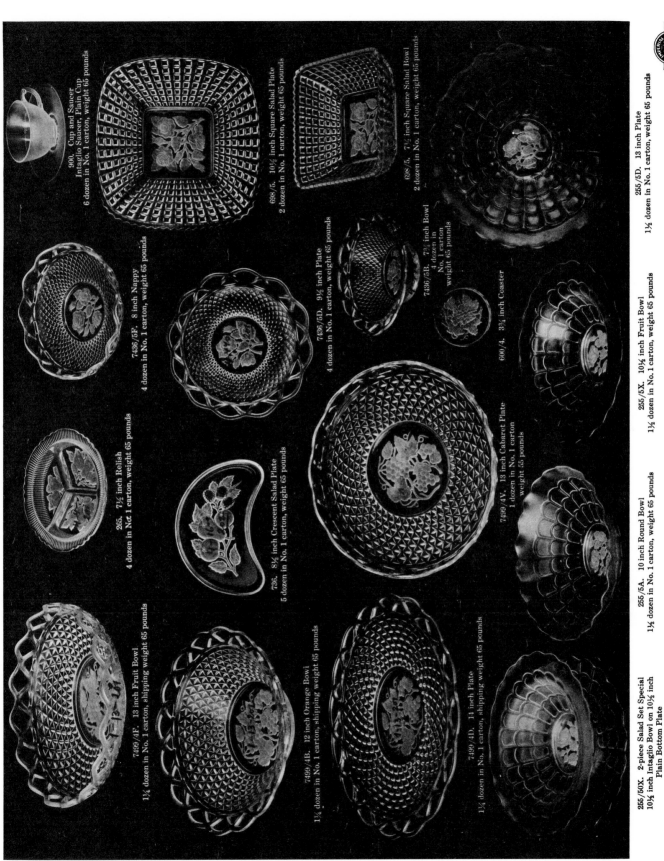

900. Cup and Saucer
Intaglio Saucer, Plain Cup
6 dozen in No. 1 carton, weight 65 pounds

698/5. 10½ inch Square Salad Plate
2 dozen in No. 1 carton, weight 65 pounds

698/5. 7½ inch Square Salad Bowl
2 dozen in No. 1 carton, weight 65 pounds

255/5D. 18 inch Plate
1½ dozen in No. 1 carton, weight 65 pounds

7436/5F. 8 inch Nappy
4 dozen in No. 1 carton, weight 65 pounds

7436/5B. 7½ inch Bowl
4 dozen in
No. 1 carton
weight 65 pounds

7436/5D. 9½ inch Plate
4 dozen in No. 1 carton, weight 65 pounds

255/5X. 10½ inch Fruit Bowl
1½ dozen in No. 1 carton, weight 65 pounds

265. 7½ inch Relish
4 dozen in No. 1 carton, weight 65 pounds

600/4. 3¾ inch Coaster

736. 8½ inch Crescent Salad Plate
5 dozen in No. 1 carton, weight 65 pounds

7499/4V. 13 inch Cabaret Plate
1 dozen in No. 1 carton
weight 55 pounds

255/5A. 10 inch Round Bowl
1½ dozen in No. 1 carton, weight 65 pounds

7499/4F. 13 inch Fruit Bowl
1½ dozen in No. 1 carton, shipping weight 65 pounds

7499/4B. 12 inch Orange Bowl
1¼ dozen in No. 1 carton, shipping weight 65 pounds

7499/4D. 14 inch Plate
1½ dozen in No. 1 carton, shipping weight 65 pounds

255/50X. 2-piece Salad Set Special
10½ inch Intaglio Bowl on 10½ inch
Plain Bottom Plate
1 dozen in No. 1 carton, shipping weight 65 pounds
Illustrations ¼ Size

Product of

175

Imperial Intaglio Design (On Crystal Glass Only)

785. 3¼ inch Ash Tray
Per dozen, $3.00
12 dozen in carton, shipping weight 40 pounds
Cartons 35¢ each *net*

785. 4½ inch Covered Cigarette Box
Per dozen, $12.00
6 dozen in carton, shipping weight 65 pounds
Cartons 35¢ each *net*

INTAGLIO

Exquisite mould designing which has evoked praise from our largest customers. The dog and ball, and the fruit, are finished in Satin effect and form a highly pleasing contrast in color with the highly polished Crystal background. These are the initial items in a large line that is certain to develop in the near future.

Made in two sizes

900. 7¼ inch Shallow Nappy
Per dozen, $7.50
4 dozen in carton, shipping weight 50 pounds
Cartons 35¢ each *net*

Illustrating 13 inch size

900. 13 inch Shallow Fruit Bowl
Per dozen, $60.00
1 dozen in carton, shipping weight 60 pounds
Cartons 50¢ each *net*

Round Plate shown at right, *made in two sizes*

900. 8 inch Salad Plate
Per dozen, $7.50
4 dozen to carton, shipping weight 50 pounds
Cartons 35¢ each *net*

900. 14 inch Torte or Chop Plate
Per dozen, $60.00
1 dozen to carton, shipping weight 60 pounds
Cartons 50¢ each *net*

Illustrating 8 inch size

800. 8 inch Salad Plate
Per dozen, $7.50
4 dozen to carton, shipping weight 50 pounds
Cartons 35¢ each *net*

Illustrations ½ Size

900. 8 inch Salad Plate
Made in two sizes

CARTONS EXTRA AT NET PRICES

Intaglio with Lalique Border

L7255/4B. 7¼ inch Two-handled Nappy
6 dozen in No. 1 carton, weight 65 pounds

L7255/4. 3-piece Mayonnaise Set
3 dozen in No. 1 carton, weight 65 pounds

L7258/4W. 9 inch Two-handled Bowl
2½ dozen in No. 1 carton, weight 65 pounds

L7258/4F. 10 inch Two-handled Bowl
2½ dozen in No. 1 carton, weight 65 pounds

L7255/4D. 7¼ inch Two-handled Plate
6 dozen in No. 1 carton, weight 65 pounds

L7258/4D. 10½ inch Two-handled Plate
2½ dozen in No. 1 carton, weight 65 pounds

L7275/4F. 7 inch Nappy
6 dozen in No. 1 carton, weight 65 pounds

L72710/4A. 12 inch Fruit Bowl
1 dozen in No. 1 carton, weight 65 pounds

L72710/4D. 15 inch Torte Plate
1 dozen in No. 1 carton, weight 65 pounds

L7275/4D. 8 inch Salad Plate
6 dozen in No. 1 carton, weight 65 pounds

Illustrations ¼ Size

Product of

177

Intaglio with Lalique Border, except 748, 7480 and 783 Relish, which have plain border

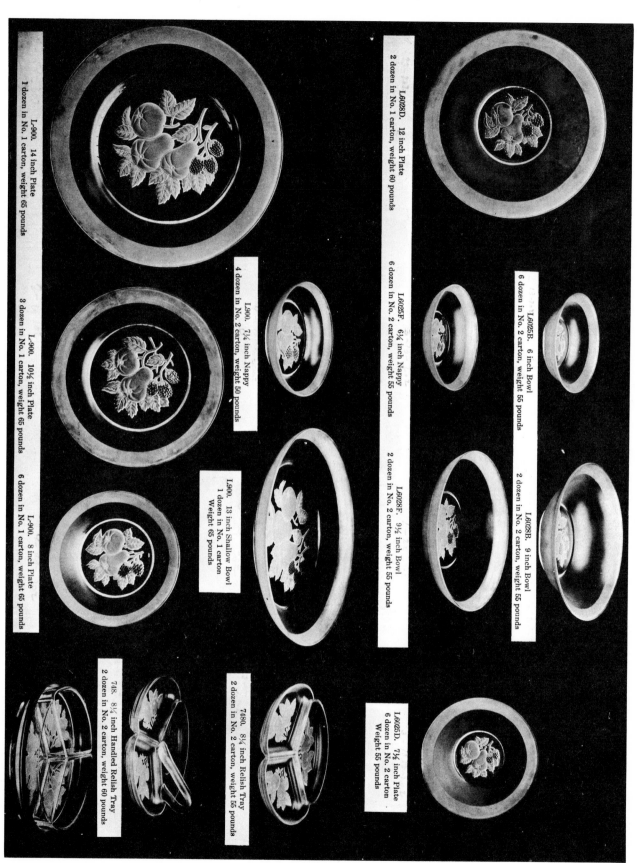

L.6028D. 12 inch Plate
2 dozen in No. 1 carton, weight 60 pounds

L.6028B. 6 inch Bowl
6 dozen in No. 2 carton, weight 55 pounds

L.6025B. 6 inch Bowl
6 dozen in No. 2 carton, weight 55 pounds

L.6025F. 6¾ inch Nappy
6 dozen in No. 2 carton, weight 55 pounds

L.900. 7¼ inch Nappy
4 dozen in No. 2 carton, weight 50 pounds

L-900. 14 inch Plate
1 dozen in No. 1 carton, weight 65 pounds

L.6028B. 9 inch Bowl
2 dozen in No. 2 carton, weight 55 pounds

L.6028F. 9¾ inch Bowl
2 dozen in No. 2 carton, weight 55 pounds

L900. 13 inch Shallow Bowl
1 dozen in No. 1 carton
Weight 65 pounds

L-900. 10½ inch Plate
3 dozen in No. 1 carton, weight 65 pounds

L-900. 8 inch Plate
6 dozen in No. 1 carton, weight 65 pounds

L.6025D. 7½ inch Plate
6 dozen in No. 2 carton
Weight 55 pounds

748. 8¼ inch Handled Relish Tray
2 dozen in No. 2 carton, weight 60 pounds

7480. 8¼ inch Relish Tray
2 dozen in No. 2 carton, weight 55 pounds

783. 4-piece Relish Set
1 dozen in No. 1 carton, weight 65 pounds

Illustrations ¼ Size

Fine Rock Crystal Cuttings By Crown

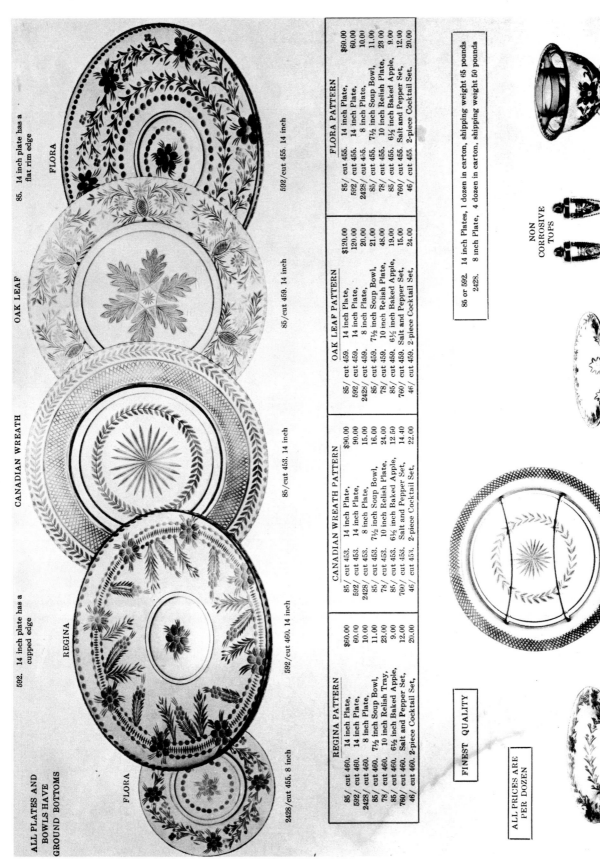

ALL PLATES AND
BOWLS HAVE
GROUND BOTTOMS

592. 14 inch plate has a
cupped edge

OAK LEAF

85. 14 inch plate has a
flat rim edge

FLORA

CANADIAN WREATH

REGINA

FLORA

592/cut 460. 14 inch

2428/cut 455. 8 inch

85/cut 460. 14 inch

592/cut 455. 14 inch

85/cut 459. 14 inch

REGINA PATTERN		
85/ cut 460.	14 inch Plate,	$60.00
592/ cut 460.	14 inch Plate,	60.00
2428/ cut 460.	8 inch Plate,	10.00
85/ cut 460.	7½ inch Soup Bowl,	11.00
78/ cut 460.	10 inch Relish Tray,	23.00
85/ cut 460.	6½ inch Baked Apple,	9.00
760/ cut 460.	Salt and Pepper Set,	12.00
46/ cut 460.	2-piece Cocktail Set,	20.00

CANADIAN WREATH PATTERN		
85/ cut 453.	14 inch Plate,	$90.00
592/ cut 453.	14 inch Plate,	90.00
2428/ cut 453.	8 inch Plate,	15.00
85/ cut 453.	7½ inch Soup Bowl,	16.00
78/ cut 453.	10 inch Relish Plate,	24.00
85/ cut 453.	6½ inch Baked Apple,	12.50
760/ cut 453.	Salt and Pepper Set,	14.40
46/ cut 453.	2-piece Cocktail Set,	22.00

OAK LEAF PATTERN		
85/ cut 459.	14 inch Plate,	$120.00
592/ cut 459.	14 inch Plate,	90.00
2428/ cut 459.	8 inch Plate,	20.00
85/ cut 459.	7½ inch Soup Bowl,	21.00
78/ cut 459.	10 inch Relish Plate,	48.00
85/ cut 459.	6½ inch Baked Apple,	19.00
760/ cut 459.	Salt and Pepper Set,	15.00
46/ cut 459.	2-piece Cocktail Set,	24.00

FLORA PATTERN		
85/ cut 455.	14 inch Plate,	$60.00
592/ cut 455.	14 inch Plate,	60.00
2428/ cut 455.	8 inch Plate,	10.00
85/ cut 455.	7½ inch Soup Bowl,	11.00
78/ cut 455.	10 inch Relish Plate,	23.00
85/ cut 455.	6½ inch Baked Apple,	9.00
760/ cut 455.	Salt and Pepper Set,	12.00
46/ cut 455.	2-piece Cocktail Set,	20.00

FINEST QUALITY

ALL PRICES ARE
PER DOZEN

85/ cut 455. 7½ inch Soup
4 dozen in carton
Shipping weight 65 pounds

78/ cut 453. 10 inch Relish
2 dozen in carton
Shipping weight 65 pounds

NON
CORROSIVE
TOPS

85 or 592. 14 inch Plates, 1 dozen in carton, shipping weight 65 pounds
2428. 8 inch Plate, 4 dozen in carton, shipping weight 50 pounds

85/ cut 459. 6½ inch Baked Apple
6 dozen in carton
Shipping weight 65 pounds

Illustrations ½ Size

760/ cut 460. Salt and Pepper Set
10 dozen in carton
Shipping weight 65 pounds

46/ cut 455. 2-piece Cocktail Set *supreme*
3½ dozen in carton
Shipping weight 65 pounds

CARTONS 35¢ AND 50¢ EACH NET

Product of Crown

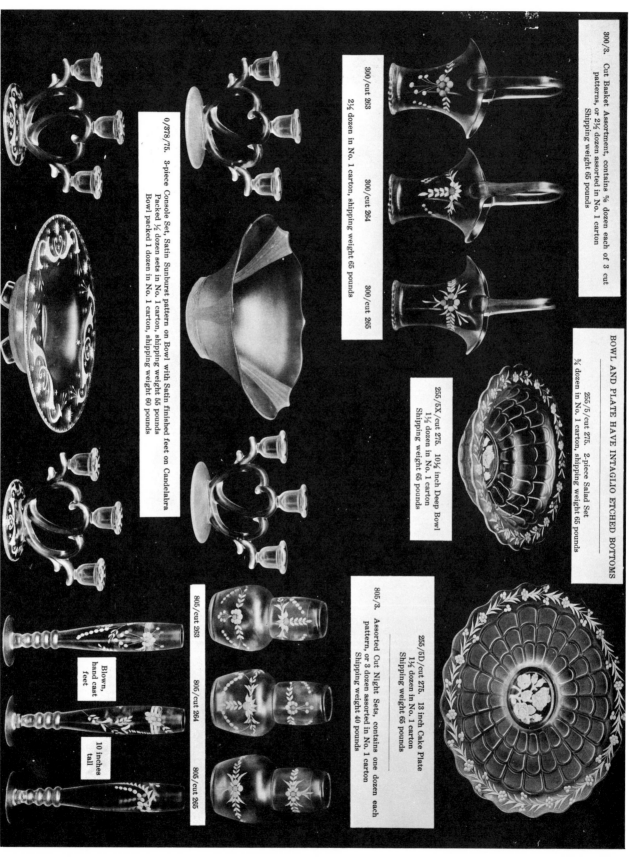

300./3. Cut Basket Assortment, contains ⁵⁄₆ dozen each of 3 cut patterns, or 2½ dozen assorted in No. 1 carton
Shipping weight 65 pounds

300/cut 263   300/cut 264   300/cut 265
2½ dozen in No. 1 carton, shipping weight 65 pounds

BOWL AND PLATE HAVE INTAGLIO ETCHED BOTTOMS
255./5/cut 275. 2-piece Salad Set
½ dozen in No. 1 carton, shipping weight 65 pounds

255./5X/cut 275. 10¼ inch Deep Bowl
1½ dozen in No. 1 carton
Shipping weight 65 pounds

0/378./75. 3-piece Console Set, Satin Sunburst pattern on Bowl with Satin finished feet on Candelabra
Packed ½ dozen sets in No. 1 carton, shipping weight 55 pounds
Bowl packed 1 dozen in No. 1 carton, shipping weight 60 pounds

75BX/42. 3-piece Console Set, Decorated Satin Scroll with Hand Cut Stars
Packed ½ dozen sets in No. 1 carton, shipping weight 55 pounds

451/cut 129   451/cut 128   451/cut 125
451./3. Assorted Bud Vases, contains 2 dozen each pattern, or 6 dozen assorted in No. 1 carton, shipping weight 45 pounds

Blown, hand cast feet

10 inches tall

805/cut 263   805/cut 264   805/cut 265

805./3. Assorted Cut Night Sets, contains one dozen each pattern, or 3 dozen assorted in No. 1 carton
Shipping weight 40 pounds

255./5D/cut 275. 13 inch Cake Plate
1½ dozen in No. 1 carton
Shipping weight 65 pounds

Illustrations ½ Size

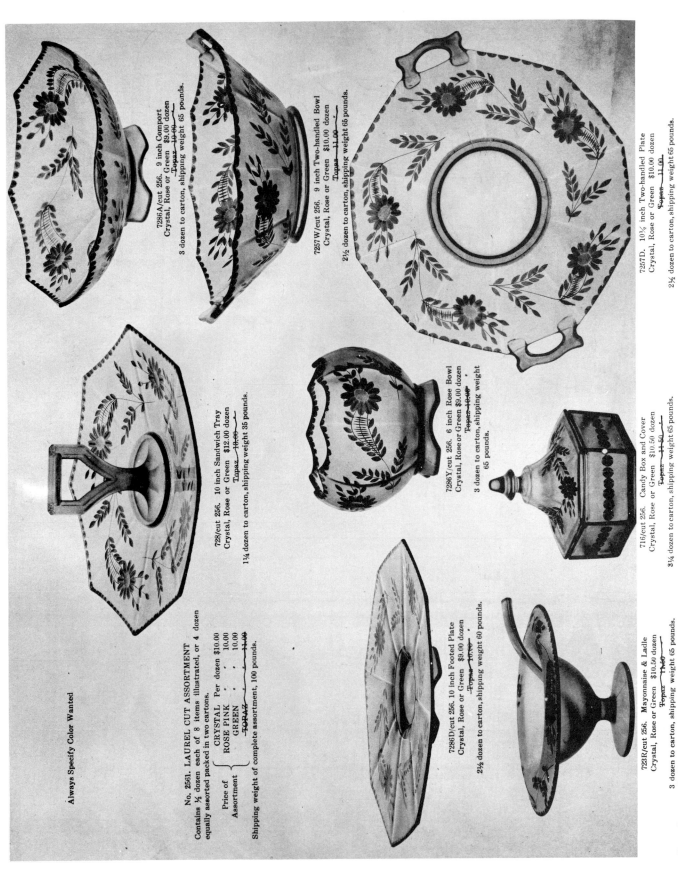

7286A/cut 256.   9 inch Comport
Crystal, Rose or Green $9.00 dozen
Topaz   10.00
3 dozen to carton, shipping weight 65 pounds.

7257W/cut 256.   9 inch Two-handled Bowl
Crystal, Rose or Green $10.00 dozen
Topaz   11.00
2½ dozen to carton, shipping weight 66 pounds.

7257D.   10½ inch Two-handled Plate
Crystal, Rose or Green $10.00 dozen
Topaz   11.00
2½ dozen to carton, shipping weight 65 pounds.

CARTONS CHARGED EXTRA 50c EACH NET

Always Specify Color Wanted

No. 2561. LAUREL CUT ASSORTMENT
Contains ½ dozen each of 8 items illustrated, or 4 dozen
equally assorted packed in two cartons.

Price of	CRYSTAL Per dozen	$10.00
Assortment	ROSE PINK	10.00
	GREEN	10.00
	TOPAZ	11.00

Shipping weight of complete assortment, 100 pounds.

728/cut 256.   10 inch Sandwich Tray
Crystal, Rose or Green $12.00 dozen
Topaz   13.00
1¼ dozen to carton, shipping weight 35 pounds.

7286Y/cut 256.   6 inch Rose Bowl
Crystal, Rose or Green $9.00 dozen
Topaz   10.00
3 dozen to carton, shipping weight
65 pounds.

716/cut 256.   Candy Box and Cover
Crystal, Rose or Green $10.50 dozen
Topaz   11.50
3¼ dozen to carton, shipping weight 65 pounds.

Illustrations three-sevenths size

7286D/cut 256. 10 inch Footed Plate
Crystal, Rose or Green $9.00 dozen
Topaz   10.00
2½ dozen to carton, shipping weight 60 pounds.

728R/cut 256.   Mayonnaise & Ladle
Crystal, Rose or Green $10.50 dozen
Topaz   11.50
3 dozen to carton, shipping weight 65 pounds.

Product of Crown

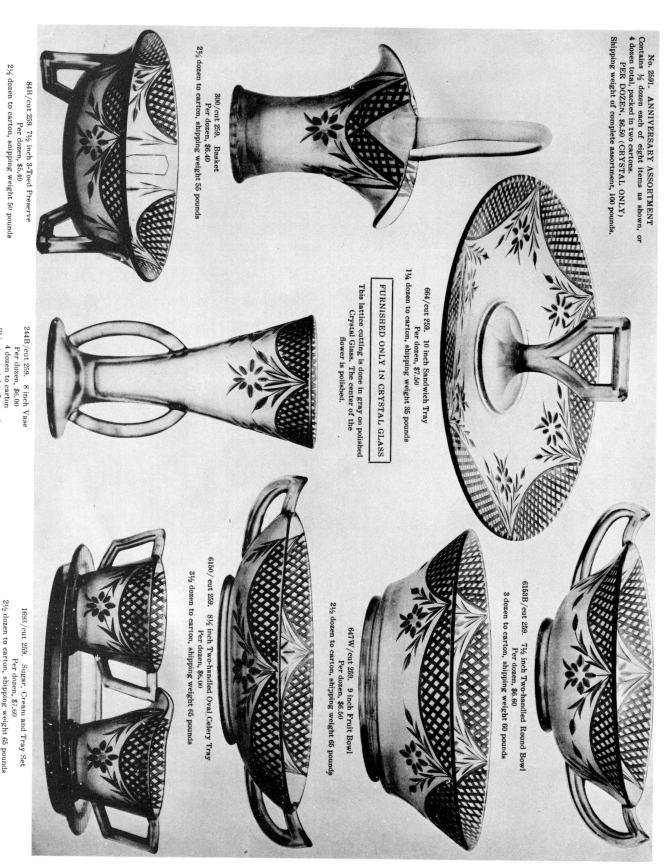

No. 2591. ANNIVERSARY ASSORTMENT
Contains ½ dozen each of eight items as shown, or
4 dozen total, packed in two cartons.
PER DOZEN, $6.50 (CRYSTAL ONLY)
Shipping weight of complete assortment, 100 pounds.

300/cut 259. Basket
Per dozen, $6.40
2⅔ dozen to carton, shipping weight 55 pounds

84B/cut 259. 7½ inch 3-Toed Preserve
Per dozen, $5.40
2½ dozen to carton, shipping weight 50 pounds

664/cut 259. 10 inch Sandwich Tray
Per dozen, $7.50
1¼ dozen to carton, shipping weight 35 pounds

FURNISHED ONLY IN CRYSTAL GLASS

This lattice cutting is done in gray on polished
Crystal Glass. The center of the
flower is polished.

244B/cut 259. 8 inch Vase
Per dozen, $6.00
4 dozen to carton
Shipping weight 65 pounds

6153B/cut 259. 7½ inch Two-handled Round Bowl
Per dozen, $6.60
3 dozen to carton, shipping weight 60 pounds

647W/cut 259. 9 inch Fruit Bowl
Per dozen, $6.50
2½ dozen to carton, shipping weight 65 pounds

6150/cut 259. 8¼ inch Two-handled Oval Celery Tray
Per dozen, $6.00
3½ dozen to carton, shipping weight 65 pounds

1693/cut 259. Sugar, Cream and Tray Set
Per dozen, $7.60
2½ dozen to carton, shipping weight 65 pounds

Illustrations ½ Size

CARTONS CHARGED EXTRA 50c EACH NET

182

No. 259   Anniversary Hand-Cut Pattern (Open Stock)

One-half dozen, seven or nine piece sets in 50¢ bulk
carton, shipping weight 50 pounds, or one seven or nine
piece set in 15¢ individual carton, shipping weight 7 lbs.
Carton charges are net

451 BLOWN GEORGIAN SHAPE

451/cut 259. Ice Pitcher
Per dozen, $10.80
1 dozen to carton, shipping weight 40 pounds
Cartons 50¢ each extra

451/cut 259. 12½ ounce
Per dozen, $3.20
6 dozen to carton, weight 35 lbs.
Cartons 50¢ each extra

451/cut 259. 9¾ ounce
Per dozen, $2.80
6 dozen to carton, weight 25lbs.
Cartons 30¢ each extra

451/cut 259. 5½ ounce
Per dozen, $2.40
6 dozen to carton, weight 16 lbs.
Cartons 25¢ each extra

250/cut 259. Cocktail
Per dozen, $3.90
6 dozen to carton, weight 25 pounds
Cartons 90¢ each extra

250/cut 259. Saucer Champagne
Per dozen, $3.90
6 dozen to carton, weight 35 pounds
Cartons 90¢ each extra

250/cut 259. Goblet
Per dozen, $3.90
6 dozen to carton, weight 40 pounds
Cartons 90¢ each extra

24271½/cut 259. 7½ inch Salad Plate
Ground Bottom. Per dozen, $5.50
6 dozen to carton, shipping weight 65 pounds
Cartons 50¢ each extra

Illustrations ½ Size

ALL CARTON CHARGES ARE NET

Product of Imperial

183

Product of Crown

ALL GRAY CUTTING WITH POLISHED
CENTERS IN FLOWERS.

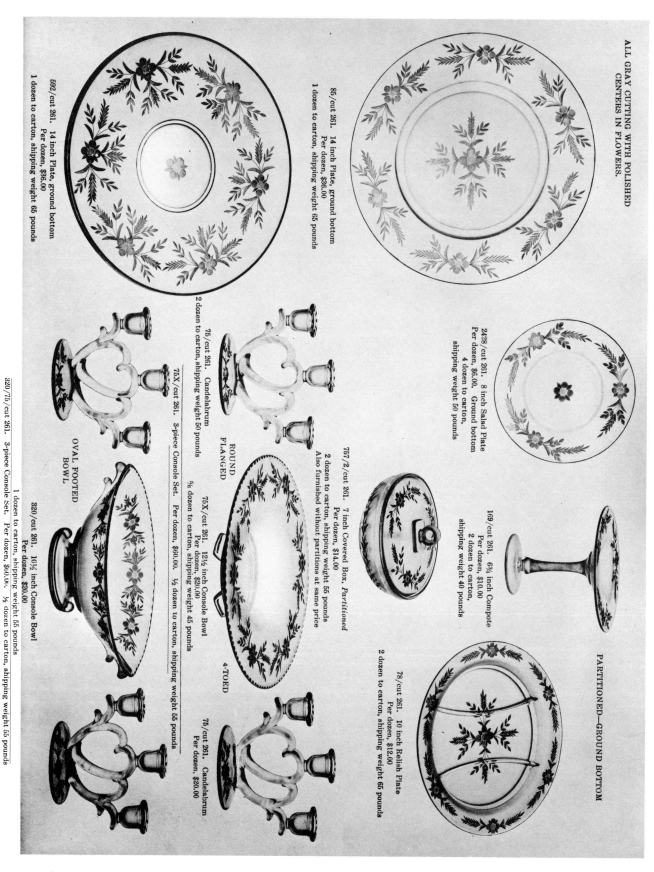

692/cut 261.   14 inch Plate, ground bottom
Per dozen, $36.00
1 dozen to carton, shipping weight 65 pounds

85/cut 261.   14 inch Plate, ground bottom
Per dozen, $36.00
1 dozen to carton, shipping weight 65 pounds

2428/cut 261.   8 inch Salad Plate
Per dozen, $6.00.   Ground bottom
4 dozen to carton,
shipping weight 50 pounds

169/cut 261.   6¾ inch Compote
Per dozen, $10.00
2 dozen to carton,
shipping weight 40 pounds

PARTITIONED—GROUND BOTTOM

78/cut 261.   10 inch Relish Plate
Per dozen, $12.00
2 dozen to carton, shipping weight 65 pounds

75/cut 261.   Candelabrum
2 dozen to carton, shipping weight 50 pounds

75X/cut 261.   3-piece Console Set.   Per dozen, $60.00.   ½ dozen to carton, shipping weight 55 pounds

75X/cut 261.   12½ inch Console Bowl
Per dozen, $20.00
⅚ dozen to carton, shipping weight 45 pounds

ROUND
FLANGED
4-TOED

757/2/cut 261.   7 inch Covered Box, Partitioned
Per dozen, $14.00
2 dozen to carton, shipping weight 55 pounds
Also furnished without partitions at same price

OVAL FOOTED
BOWL.

320/cut 261.   10½ inch Console Bowl
Per dozen, $20.00
1 dozen to carton, shipping weight 55 pounds

75/cut 261.   Candelabrum
Per dozen, $20.00

320/75/cut 261.   3-piece Console Set.   Per dozen, $60.00.   ½ dozen to carton, shipping weight 55 pounds

Illustrations ½ Size

CARTONS EXTRA 50¢ EACH NET

184

Corona (No. 269) and Primrose (No. 270) Cut Patterns

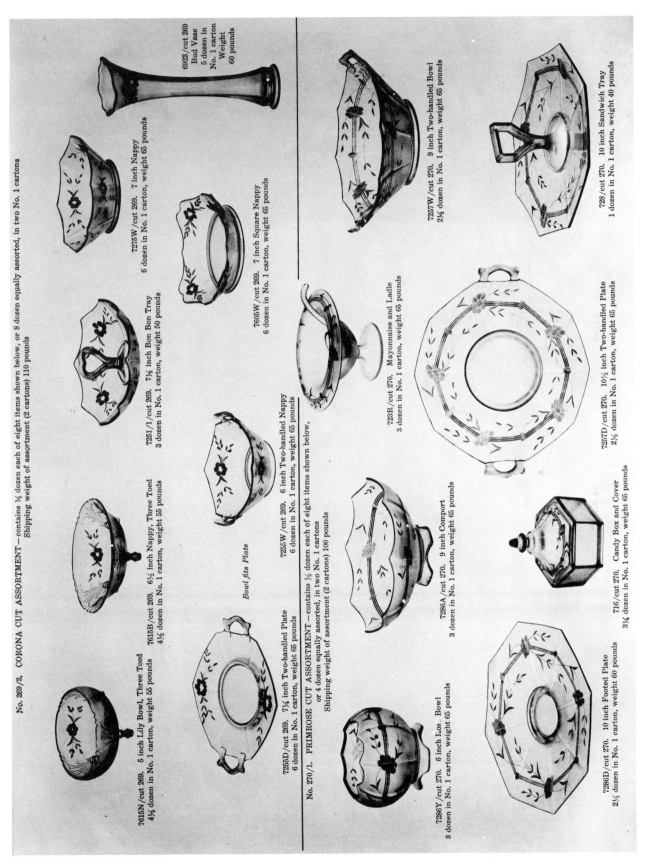

No. 269/2. CORONA CUT ASSORTMENT — contains ½ dozen each of eight items shown below, or 8 dozen equally assorted, in two No. 1 cartons
Shipping weight of assortment (2 cartons) 110 pounds

6923/cut 269
Bud Vase
5 dozen in
No. 1 carton
Weight
60 pounds

7275W/cut 269. 7 inch Nappy
6 dozen in No. 1 carton, weight 65 pounds

7615N/cut 269. 5 inch Lily Bowl, Three Toed
4½ dozen in No. 1 carton, weight 65 pounds

7615B/cut 269. 6½ inch Nappy, Three Toed
4½ dozen in No. 1 carton, weight 55 pounds

7251/1/cut 269. 7½ inch Bon Bon Tray
3 dozen in No. 1 carton, weight 50 pounds

7605W/cut 269. 7 inch Square Nappy
6 dozen in No. 1 carton, weight 65 pounds

Bowl fits Plate

7255W/cut 269. 6 inch Two-handled Nappy
6 dozen in No. 1 carton, weight 65 pounds

7255D/cut 269. 7¼ inch Two-handled Plate
6 dozen in No. 1 carton, weight 65 pounds

No. 270/1. PRIMROSE CUT ASSORTMENT — contains ½ dozen each of eight items shown below,
or 4 dozen equally assorted, in two No. 1 cartons
Shipping weight of assortment (2 cartons) 100 pounds

7257W/cut 270. 9 inch Two-handled Bowl
2½ dozen in No. 1 carton, weight 65 pounds

728/cut 270. 10 inch Sandwich Tray
1 dozen in No. 1 carton, weight 40 pounds

723R/cut 270. Mayonnaise and Ladle
3 dozen in No. 1 carton, weight 65 pounds

7257D/cut 270. 10½ inch Two-handled Plate
2½ dozen in No. 1 carton, weight 65 pounds

7286A/cut 270. 9 inch Comport
3 dozen in No. 1 carton, weight 65 pounds

716/cut 270. Candy Box and Cover
3¼ dozen in No. 1 carton, weight 65 pounds

7286Y/cut 270. 6 inch Rose Bowl
3 dozen in No. 1 carton, weight 65 pounds

7286D/cut 270. 10 inch Footed Plate
2½ dozen in No. 1 carton, weight 60 pounds

Illustrations ¼ Size

Product of Crown

185

No. 280 Danube All Gray Cut Pattern

450/499/cut 280. 3-piece Mayonnaise Set
3 dozen in No. 2 Carton
Shipping weight 40 lbs.

7280/cut 280. 8 inch Plate
4 dozen in No. 48 carton
Shipping weight 55 pounds

499/cut 280. 6 inch Plate
12 dozen in No. 1 carton
Shipping weight 55 pounds

320/75/cut 280. 10½ inch Console Bowl

320/75/cut 280. 3-piece Console Set
Set consists of one 10½ inch Oval Bowl and two Candelabrum shown at right, packed ½ dozen sets in No. 1
carton, shipping weight 55 pounds

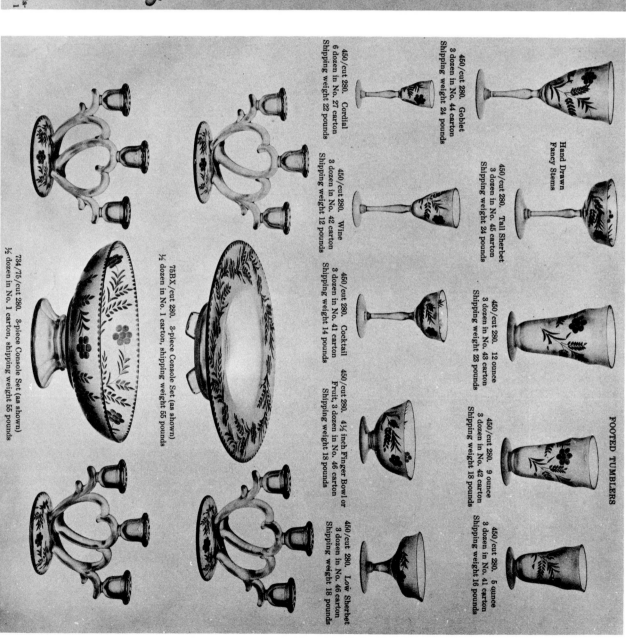

Hand Drawn
Fancy Stems

450/cut 280. Tall Sherbet
3 dozen in No. 45 carton
Shipping weight 24 pounds

450/cut 280. Goblet
3 dozen in No. 44 carton
Shipping weight 24 pounds

450/cut 280. Wine
3 dozen in No. 42 carton
Shipping weight 12 pounds

450/cut 280. Cordial
6 dozen in No. 27 carton
Shipping weight 22 pounds

450/cut 280. Cocktail
3 dozen in No. 41 carton
Shipping weight 14 pounds

FOOTED TUMBLERS

450/cut 280. 12 ounce
3 dozen in No. 43 carton
Shipping weight 28 pounds

450/cut 280. 9 ounce
3 dozen in No. 42 carton
Shipping weight 18 pounds

450/cut 280. 5 ounce
3 dozen in No. 41 carton
Shipping weight 16 pounds

450/cut 280. 4½ inch Finger Bowl or
Fruit, 3 dozen in No. 46 carton
Shipping weight 18 pounds

450/cut 280. Low Sherbet
3 dozen in No. 46 carton
Shipping weight 18 pounds

76BX/cut 280. 3-piece Console Set (as shown)
½ dozen in No. 1 carton, shipping weight 55 pounds

734/75/cut 280. 3-piece Console Set (as shown)
½ dozen in No. 1 carton, shipping weight 55 pounds

No. 280 Danube All Gray Hand Cut Pattern

280/1. Danube Cut Assortment, contains one piece each of 15 items as shown or 1¼ dozen packed in No. 1 carton, shipping weight 50 pounds

7257W/cut 280. 9 inch Two-handled Bowl
2½ dozen in No. carton
Shipping weight 65 pounds

760/2/ cut 280. 10¾ inch Lunch Tray
1 dozen in No. 1 carton
Shipping weight 40 pounds

7723/cut 280. Sugar, Cream and Tray Set
3 dozen in No. 1 carton
Shipping weight 65 pounds

724/2/ cut 280. 6¼ inch Covered Dish
2 dozen in No. 1 carton
Shipping weight 65 pounds

728/cut 280. 9½ inch Relish Tray
3 dozen in No. 1 carton
Shipping weight 65 pounds

727/cut 280. 11 inch Cheese and Cracker Set
2 dozen in No. 1 carton
Shipping weight 65 pounds

78/1/cut 280. 10 inch Relish Plate
2 dozen in No. 1 carton
Shipping weight 65 pounds

7257D/cut 280. 10½ inch Two-handled plate
2½ dozen in No. 1 carton
Shipping weight 65 pounds

7287D/cut 280. 12 inch Footed Cake Plate
1½ dozen in No. 1 carton
Shipping weight 50 pounds

727/1/cut 280. 11 inch Celery Tray
4 dozen in No. 1 carton
Shipping weight 65 pounds

7287A/cut 280. 10½ inch Comport
1½ dozen in No. 1 carton
Shipping weight 50 pounds

7255W/cut 280. 3-piece Mayonnaise set
3 dozen in No. 1 carton
Shipping weight 65 pounds

378/cut 280. 11 inch Deep Bowl
1 dozen in No. 1 carton
Shipping weight 60 pounds

592/cut 280. 14 inch Supper Plate
1 dozen in No. 1 carton
Shipping weight 65 pounds

761/cut 280. 11 inch Relish Dish
2 dozen in No. 1 carton
Shipping weight 65 pounds

Illustrations ¼ Size

Product of Crown

187

No. 451 Ringing Rock Crystal Monticello Pattern (Open Stock)

Both plates furnished
in three sizes

ALL BOTTOMS
ARE GROUND

ILLUSTRATING

7½ inch round shape
8 inch octagon shape
PLATES

2426/cut 451.   6 inch.   Per dozen, $9.00
10 dozen to carton, shipping weight, 65 pounds
2427½/cut 451.   7½ inch.   Per dozen, $9.50
6 dozen to carton, shipping weight 65 pounds
24210/cut 451.   10½ inch.   Per dozen, $20.00
3 dozen to carton, shipping weight 65 pounds

NON-CORROSIVE SILVER PLATED TOPS

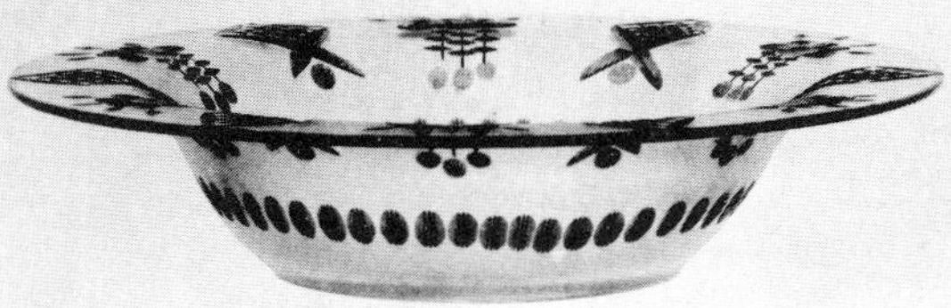

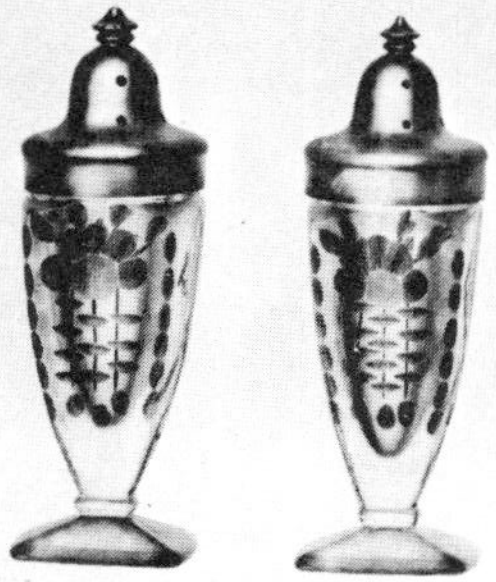

MADE IN TWO SIZES

85/cut 451.   7½ inch Belled Nappy
Per dozen, $10.80
6 dozen to carton, shipping weight 65 pounds
85/cut 451.   6¼ inch Baked Apple Nappy
Per dozen, $9.00
6 dozen to carton, shipping weight 60 pounds
BOTH SIZES HAVE GROUND BOTTOMS
Illustration shows 7½ inch Belled Nappy

72/1/cut 451.   6 inch.   Per dozen, $9.00
10 dozen to carton, shipping weight 65 pounds
72/4/cut 451.   8 inch.   Per dozen, $9.50
6 dozen to carton, shipping weight 65 pounds
72/8/cut 451.   15 inch.   Per dozen, $80.00
1 dozen to carton, shipping weight 65 pounds

760/cut 451.   Salt and Pepper Set
Per dozen sets, $12.00
10 dozen to carton, shipping weight 65 pounds

35/cut 451.   Ice Cube Set
Per dozen, $32.00
2 dozen to carton, shipping weight 65 pounds

Product of Crown

Illustrations ½ Size

CARTONS CHARGED EXTRA 50c EACH NET

188

No. 4511. MONTICELLO ASSORTMENT
Contains ⅓ dozen each of 8 items illustrated, or 4 dozen packed in two cartons.
PER DOZEN $12.50
Shipping weight of complete assortment, 100 pounds.

Always Specify Color Wanted

727/9/cut 451. 3 Piece Mayonnaise Set
Per dozen $15.00. 4 dozen to carton
Shipping weight, 60 pounds

7251/1/cut 451. 7½ inch Bon Bon Tray
Per dozen $11.00. 3 dozen to carton
Shipping weight, 50 pounds

760/cut 451. Sugar and Cream Set
Per dozen $14.00. 3¼ dozen to carton
Shipping weight, 50 pounds

7286W/cut 451. 8½ inch Comport
Per dozen $10.50 2½ dozen to carton
Shipping weight, 60 pounds

727/cut 451. 8 inch Vase
Per dozen $12.00. 3 dozen to carton
Shipping weight, 65 pounds

7286Y/cut 451. 6 inch Rose Bowl
Per dozen $10.50. 3 dozen to carton
Shipping weight, 65 pounds

724/2/cut 451. 6¼ inch Covered Dish, partitioned
Per dozen $15.00. 2 dozen to carton
Shipping weight, 65 pounds

727/1/cut 451. 11 inch Celery Tray, ground bottom
Per dozen $12.00. 4 dozen to carton
Shipping weight, 65 pounds

CARTONS CHARGED EXTRA 50c EACH NET

Illustrations ½ Size

Product of Crown

189

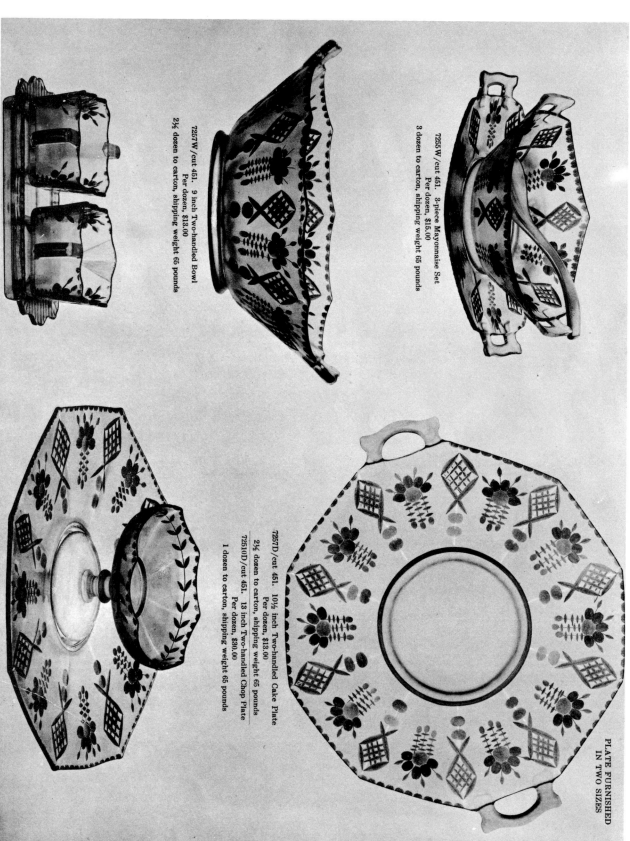

7255W/cut 451.   3-piece Mayonnaise Set
Per dozen, $15.00
3 dozen to carton, shipping weight 65 pounds

7257W/cut 451.   9 inch Two-handled Bowl
Per dozen, $13.00
2½ dozen to carton, shipping weight 65 pounds

7723/cut 451.   Sugar, Cream and Tray Set
Per dozen, $15.00
3 dozen to carton, shipping weight 65 pounds

Illustrations ½ Size

PLATE FURNISHED
IN TWO SIZES

7257D/cut 451.   10½ inch Two-handled Cake Plate
Per dozen, $13.00
2½ dozen to carton, shipping weight 65 pounds
72510D/cut 451.   13 inch Two-handled Chop Plate
Per dozen, $30.00
1 dozen to carton, shipping weight 65 pounds

727/cut 451.   11 inch Cracker and Cheese Set
Per dozen, $16.00
2 dozen to carton, shipping weight 65 pounds
CARTONS CHARGED EXTRA 50c EACH NET

Product of Crown

190

Product of Crown

FINE ROCK CRYSTAL CONSOLE SETS
Six sets to carton, shipping weight 50 pounds

734W/cut 451.   3-piece, per set, $5.00

Illustrations ½ Size

OVAL SHAPE

OVAL SHAPE

320/1/cut 451.   3-piece (Low Candleholders as shown) per set, $5.00
320/2/cut 451.   3-piece (8¼ inch Tall Candlesticks) per set, $5.00

CARTONS CHARGED EXTRA 50c EACH NET

Latest style
in Candleholders

Candleholder has socket
in center to hold
candlestick erect.

7287A/cut 451.   10½ inch Comport, per dozen, $14.00
1½ dozen to carton, shipping weight 50 pounds
7287A/cut 451.   3-piece, per set, $2.40

No. 451 Ringing Rock Crystal Monticello Pattern (Open Stock)

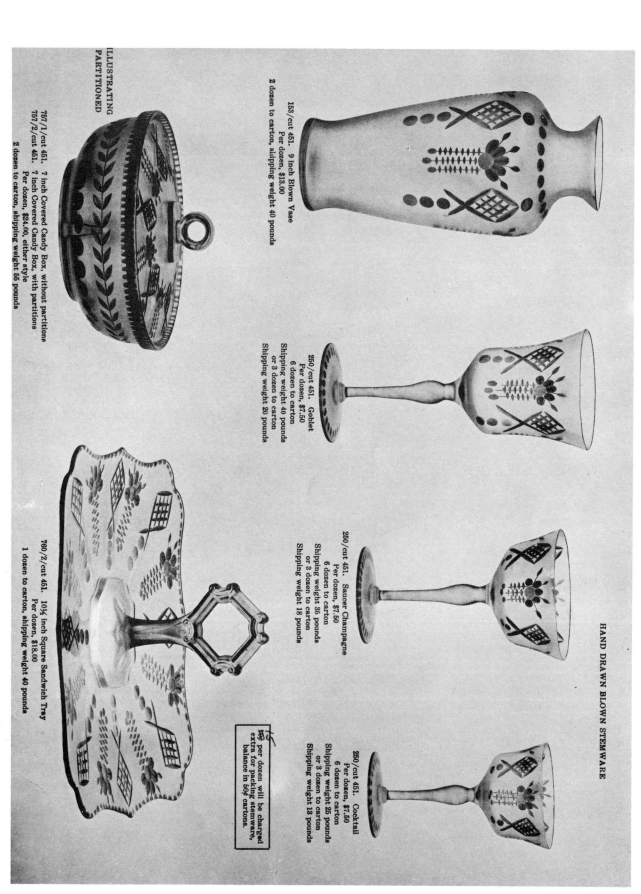

HAND DRAWN BLOWN STEMWARE

ILLUSTRATING
PARTITIONED

757/1/cut 451. 7 inch Covered Candy Box, without partitions
757/2/cut 451. 7 inch Covered Candy Box, with partitions
Per dozen, $24.00, either style
2 dozen to carton, shipping weight 55 pounds

152/cut 451. 9 inch Blown Vase
Per dozen, $18.00
2 dozen to carton, shipping weight 40 pounds

250/cut 451. Goblet
Per dozen, $7.50
6 dozen to carton
or 3 dozen to carton
Shipping weight 40 pounds
Shipping weight 20 pounds

250/cut 451. Saucer Champagne
Per dozen, $7.50
6 dozen to carton
or 3 dozen to carton
Shipping weight 35 pounds
Shipping weight 18 pounds

250/cut 451. Cocktail
Per dozen, $7.50
6 dozen to carton
or 3 dozen to carton
Shipping weight 25 pounds
Shipping weight 18 pounds

50¢ per dozen will be charged
extra for packing stemware,
balance in 50¢ cartons.

760/2/cut 451. 10½ inch Square Sandwich Tray
Per dozen, $18.00
1 dozen to carton, shipping weight 40 pounds

Rock Crystal Ice Tea or Beverage Sets (Georgian Shape)

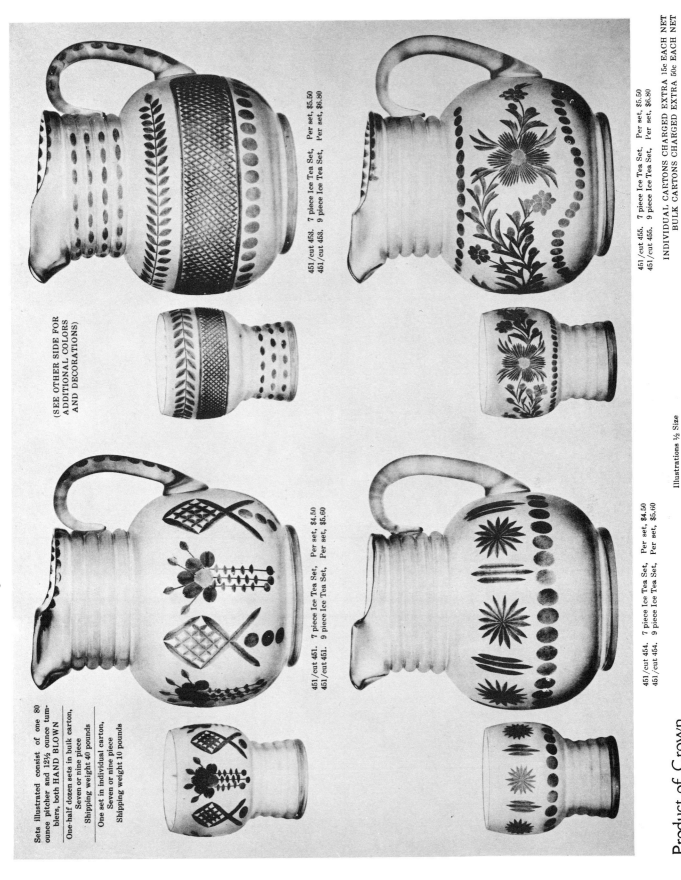

(SEE OTHER SIDE FOR
ADDITIONAL COLORS
AND DECORATIONS)

451/cut 453.   7 piece Ice Tea Set,   Per set, $5.50
451/cut 453.   9 piece Ice Tea Set,   Per set, $6.80

451/cut 455,   7 piece Ice Tea Set,   Per set, $5.50
451/cut 455,   9 piece Ice Tea Set,   Per set, $6.80

INDIVIDUAL CARTONS CHARGED EXTRA 15c EACH NET
BULK CARTONS CHARGED EXTRA 50c EACH NET

Illustrations ½ Size

Sets illustrated consist of one 80
ounce pitcher and 12½ ounce tumblers, both HAND BLOWN

One-half dozen sets in bulk carton,
Seven or nine piece
Shipping weight 40 pounds

One set in individual carton,
Seven or nine piece
Shipping weight 10 pounds

451/cut 451.   7 piece Ice Tea Set,   Per set, $4.50
451/cut 451.   9 piece Ice Tea Set,   Per set, $5.60

451/cut 454.   7 piece Ice Tea Set,   Per set, $4.50
451/cut 454.   9 piece Ice Tea Set,   Per set, $5.60

Product of Crown

193

Product of Crown

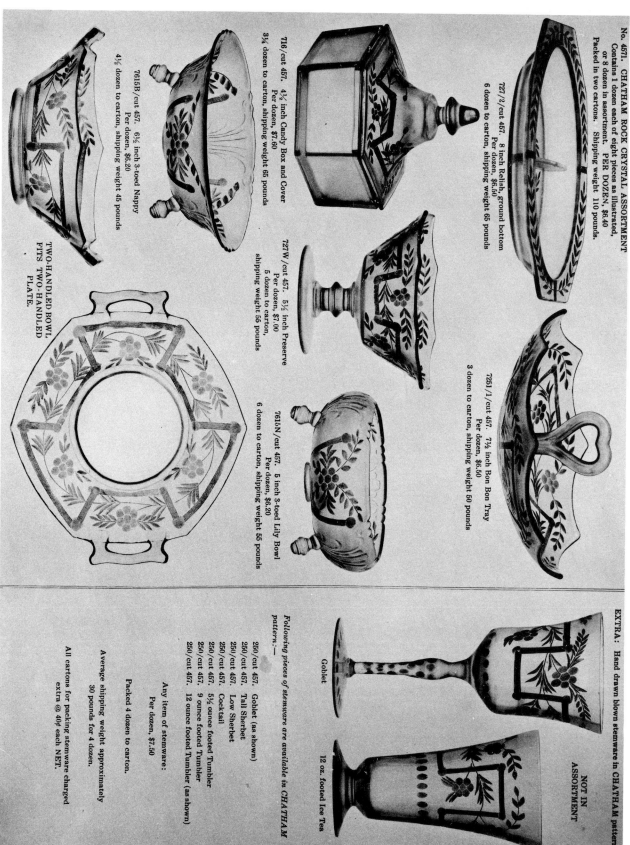

No. 457L. CHATHAM ROCK CRYSTAL ASSORTMENT
Contains 1 dozen each of eight pieces as illustrated, or 8 dozen in assortment. PER DOZEN, $6.40
Packed in two cartons. Shipping weight 110 pounds.

727/2/cut 457. 8 inch Relish, ground bottom
Per dozen, $6.50
6 dozen to carton, shipping weight 65 pounds

716/cut 457. 4½ inch Candy Box and Cover
Per dozen, $7.60
3½ dozen to carton, shipping weight 65 pounds

7615B/cut 457. 6¾ inch 3-toed Nappy
Per dozen, $5.20
4½ dozen to carton, shipping weight 45 pounds

727W/cut 457. 5½ inch Preserve
Per dozen, $7.00
5 dozen to carton, shipping weight 55 pounds

7615N/cut 457. 5 inch 3-toed Lily Bowl
Per dozen, $5.20
6 dozen to carton, shipping weight 55 pounds

7251/1/cut 457. 7½ inch Bon Bon Tray
Per dozen, $6.50
3 dozen to carton, shipping weight 50 pounds

7255W/cut 457. 6 inch Two-handled Bowl
Per dozen, $5.60
6 dozen to carton, shipping weight 65 pounds

7255D/cut 457. 7¼ inch Two-handled Plate
Per dozen, $5.60
6 dozen to carton, shipping weight 65 pounds

Illustrations ½ Size

TWO-HANDLED BOWL
FITS TWO-HANDLED
PLATE.

EXTRA: Hand drawn blown stemware in CHATHAM pattern.

NOT IN
ASSORTMENT

Following pieces of stemware are available in CHATHAM pattern.—

250/cut 457.	Goblet (as shown)
250/cut 457.	Tall Sherbet
250/cut 457.	Low Sherbet
250/cut 457.	Cocktail
250/cut 457.	5½ ounce footed Tumbler
250/cut 457.	9 ounce footed Tumbler
250/cut 457.	12 ounce footed Tumbler (as shown)

Any item of stemware:
Per dozen, $7.50

Packed 4 dozen to carton.

Average shipping weight approximately
30 pounds for 4 dozen.

All cartons for packing stemware charged
extra @ 40¢ each NET.

Goblet

12 oz. footed Ice Tea

CARTONS CHARGED EXTRA 50¢ EACH NET

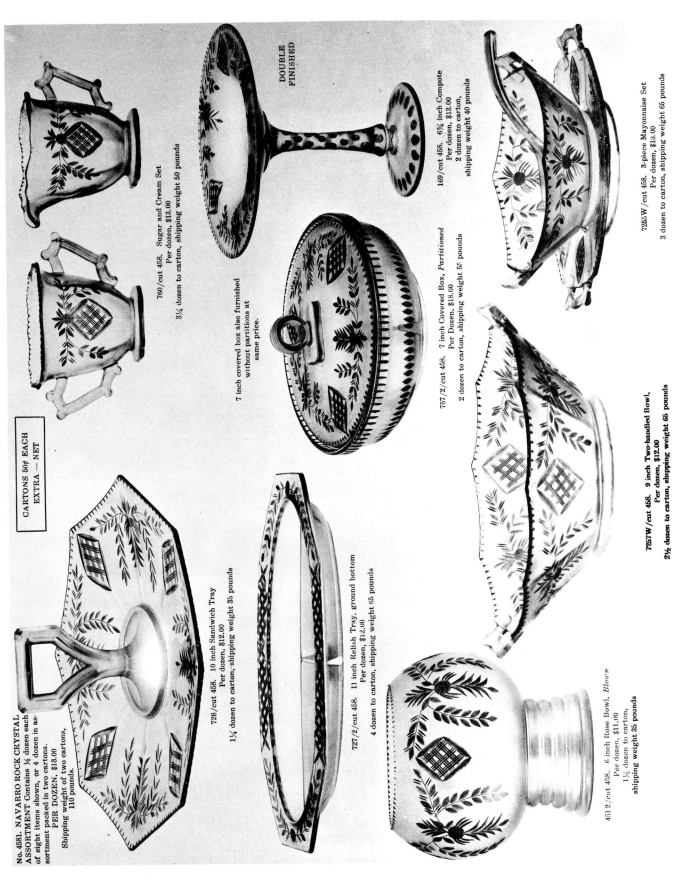

DOUBLE FINISHED

No. 458L. NAVARRO ROCK CRYSTAL
ASSORTMENT Contains ½ dozen each
of eight items shown, or 4 dozen in assortment packed in two cartons.
PER DOZEN, $13.00
Shipping weight of two cartons,
110 pounds.

CARTONS 50¢ EACH
EXTRA — NET

760/cut 458.   Sugar and Cream Set
Per dozen, $13.00
3¼ dozen to carton, shipping weight 50 pounds

7 inch covered box also furnished
without partitions at
same price.

169/cut 458.   6¾ inch Compote
Per dozen, $13.00
2 dozen to carton,
shipping weight 40 pounds

7265W/cut 458.   3-piece Mayonnaise Set
Per dozen, $13.00
3 dozen to carton, shipping weight 65 pounds

757/2/cut 458.   7 inch Covered Box, Partitioned
Per Dozen, $18.00
2 dozen to carton, shipping weight 55 pounds

728/cut 458.   10 inch Sandwich Tray
Per dozen, $12.00
1½ dozen to carton, shipping weight 35 pounds

727/2/cut 458.   11 inch Relish Tray, ground bottom
Per dozen, $12.00
4 dozen to carton, shipping weight 65 pounds

7257W/cut 458.   9 inch Two-handled Bowl,
Per dozen, $12.00
2½ dozen to carton, shipping weight 65 pounds

451 2/cut 458.   6 inch Rose Bowl, Blown
Per dozen, $11.00
1½ dozen to carton,
shipping weight 35 pounds

Illustrations ½ Size

Product of Crown

No. 465   Viking Rock Crystal Pattern

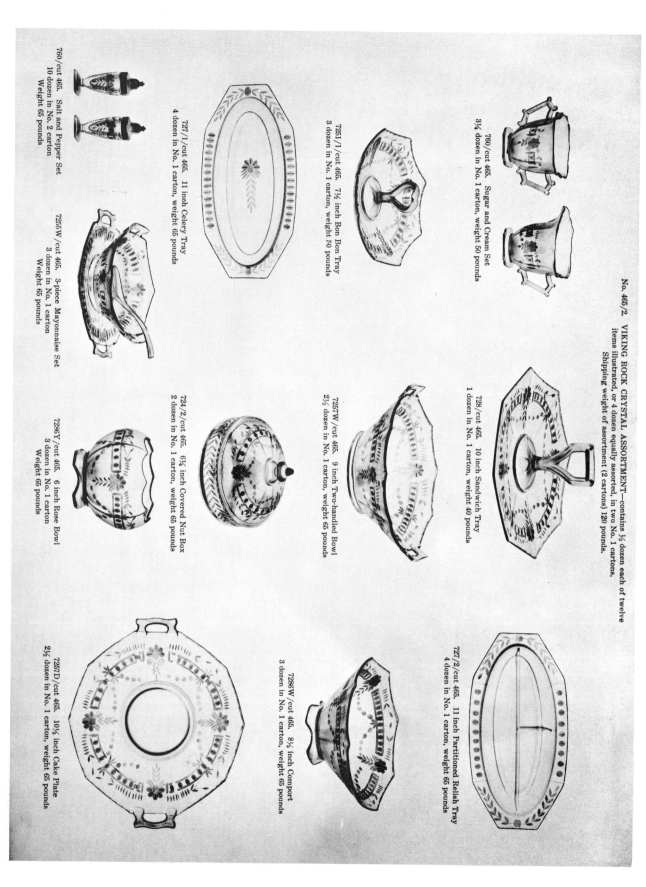

No. 465/2. VIKING ROCK CRYSTAL ASSORTMENT—contains ⅓ dozen each of twelve items illustrated, or 4 dozen equally assorted, in two No. 1 cartons. Shipping weight of assortment (2 cartons) 120 pounds.

760/cut 465.   Sugar and Cream Set
3¾ dozen in No. 1 carton, weight 50 pounds

7251/1/cut 465.   7½ inch Bon Bon Tray
3 dozen in No. 1 carton, weight 50 pounds

727/1/cut 465.   11 inch Celery Tray
4 dozen in No. 1 carton, weight 65 pounds

7255W/cut 465.   3-piece Mayonnaise Set
3 dozen in No. 1 carton
Weight 65 pounds

760/cut 465.   Salt and Pepper Set
10 dozen in No. 2 carton
Weight 65 pounds

728/cut 465.   10 inch Sandwich Tray
1 dozen in No. 1 carton, weight 40 pounds

7257W/cut 465.   9 inch Two-handled Bowl
2½ dozen in No. 1 carton, weight 65 pounds

724/2/cut 465.   6¼ inch Covered Nut Box
2 dozen in No. 1 carton, weight 65 pounds

7286Y/cut 465.   6 inch Rose Bowl
3 dozen in No. 1 carton
Weight 65 pounds

727/2/cut 465.   11 inch Partitioned Relish Tray
4 dozen in No. 1 carton, weight 65 pounds

7286W/cut 465.   8½ inch Comport
3 dozen in No. 1 carton, weight 65 pounds

7251D/cut 465.   10½ inch Cake Plate
2½ dozen in No. 1 carton, weight 65 pounds

No. 465   Viking Rock Crystal Pattern

No. 465/3.   VIKING ROCK CRYSTAL ASSORTMENT—contains ½ dozen each of nine items illustrated, or 3 dozen equally assorted, in two No. 1 cartons. Shipping weight of assortment (2 cartons) 100 pounds.

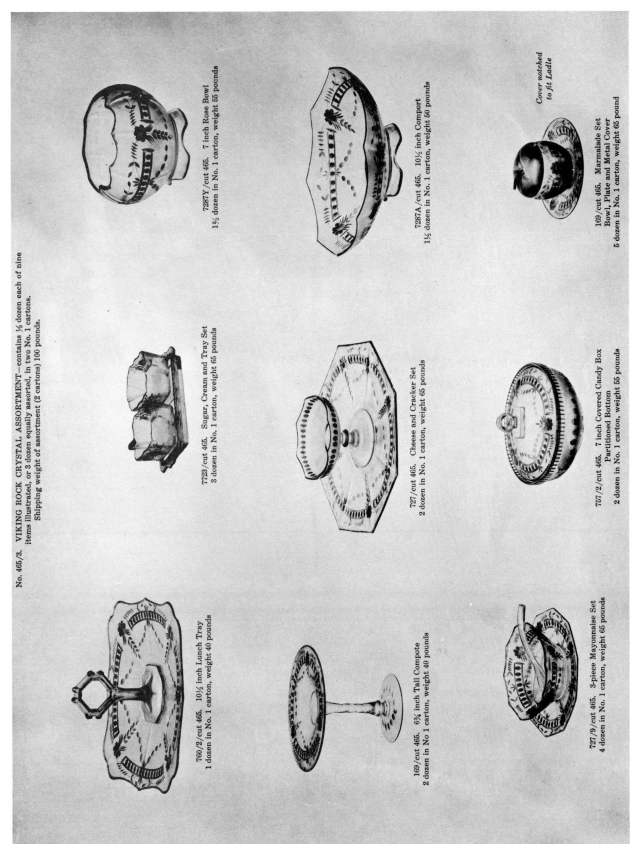

7287Y/cut 465.   7 inch Rose Bowl
1½ dozen in No. 1 carton, weight 55 pounds

7287A/cut 465.   10½ inch Comport
1½ dozen in No. 1 carton, weight 50 pounds

Cover notched to fit Ladle

169/cut 465.   Marmalade Set
Bowl, Plate and Metal Cover
5 dozen in No. 1 carton, weight 65 pound

7723/cut 465.   Sugar, Cream and Tray Set
3 dozen in No. 1 carton, weight 65 pounds

727/cut 465.   Cheese and Cracker Set
2 dozen in No. 1 carton, weight 65 pounds

757/2/cut 465.   7 inch Covered Candy Box
Partitioned Bottom
2 dozen in No. 1 carton, weight 55 pounds

760/2/cut 465.   10½ inch Lunch Tray
1 dozen in No. 1 carton, weight 40 pounds

169/cut 465.   6¾ inch Tall Compote
2 dozen in No 1 carton, weight 40 pounds

727/9/cut 465.   3-piece Mayonnaise Set
4 dozen in No. 1 carton, weight 65 pounds

Illustrations ¼ Size

Product of Crown

197

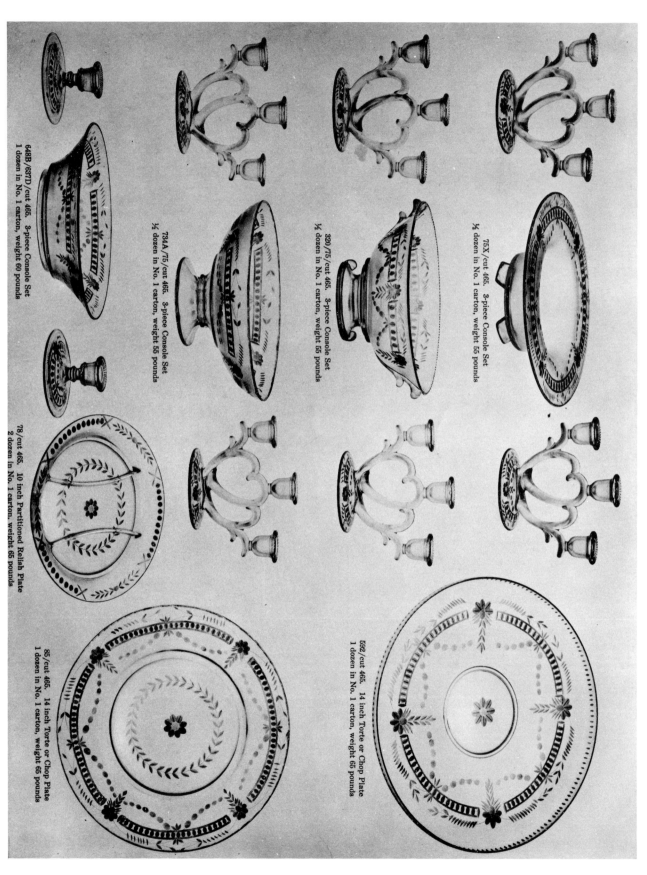

648B/63TD/cut 465. 3-piece Console Set
1 dozen in No. 1 carton, weight 60 pounds

794A/715/cut 465. 3-piece Console Set
½ dozen in No. 1 carton, weight 55 pounds

320/75/cut 465. 3-piece Console Set
½ dozen in No. 1 carton, weight 55 pounds

75X/cut 465. 3-piece Console Set
½ dozen in No. 1 carton, weight 55 pounds

78/cut 465. 10 inch Partitioned Relish Plate
2 dozen in No. 1 carton, weight 65 pounds

85/cut 465. 14 inch Torte or Chop Plate
1 dozen in No. 1 carton, weight 65 pounds

592/cut 465. 14 inch Torte or Chop Plate
1 dozen in No. 1 carton, weight 65 pounds

Illustrations ¼ Size

198

No. 600   Hand-Cut Pattern on Genuine Ruby Glass Only

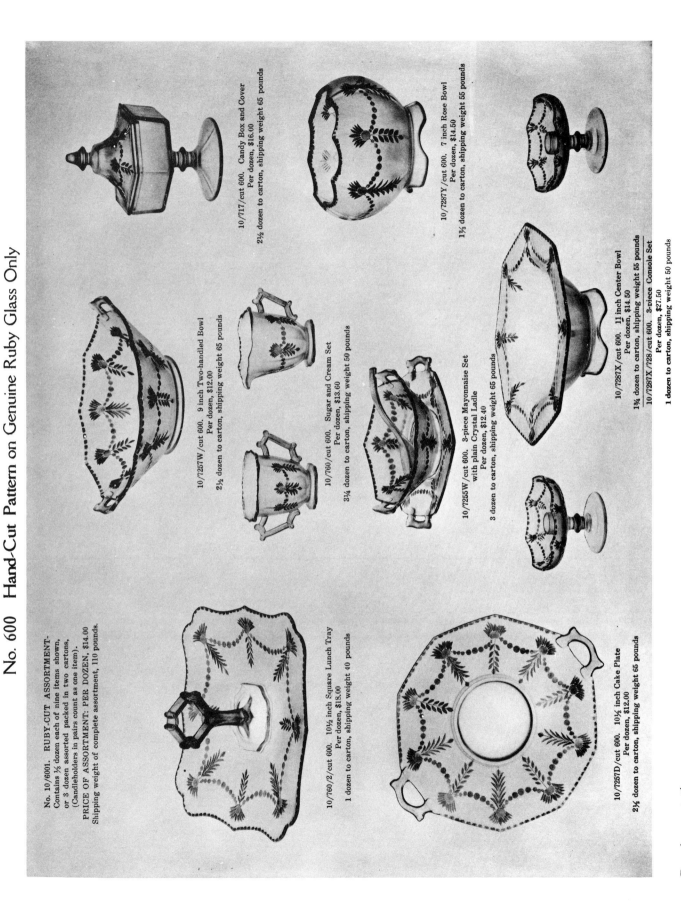

No. 10/600I. RUBY-CUT ASSORTMENT—
Contains ⅓ dozen each of nine items shown,
or 3 dozen assorted packed in two cartons.
(Candleholders in pairs count as one item).
PRICE OF ASSORTMENT: PER DOZEN, $14.00.
Shipping weight of complete assortment, 110 pounds.

10/717/cut 600.   Candy Box and Cover
Per dozen, $16.00
2½ dozen to carton, shipping weight 65 pounds

10/7287Y/cut 600.   7 inch Rose Bowl
Per dozen, $14.50
1⅝ dozen to carton, shipping weight 55 pounds

10/7257W/cut 600.   9 inch Two-handled Bowl
Per dozen, $12.00
2½ dozen to carton, shipping weight 65 pounds

10/760/cut 600.   Sugar and Cream Set
Per dozen, $13.60
3¼ dozen to carton, shipping weight 50 pounds

10/7255W/cut 600.   3-piece Mayonnaise Set
with plain Crystal Ladle
Per dozen, $12.40
3 dozen to carton, shipping weight 65 pounds

10/7287X/cut 600.   11 inch Center Bowl
Per dozen, $14.50
1⅝ dozen to carton, shipping weight 55 pounds
10/7287X/728/cut 600.   3-piece Console Set
Per dozen, $27.50
1 dozen to carton, shipping weight 50 pounds

10/760/2/cut 600.   10½ inch Square Lunch Tray
Per dozen, $18.00
1 dozen to carton, shipping weight 40 pounds

10/7257D/cut 600.   10½ inch Cake Plate
Per dozen, $12.00
2½ dozen to carton, shipping weight 65 pounds

CARTONS CHARGED EXTRA 50¢ EACH NET

Illustrations ⅗ Size

Product of Crown

199

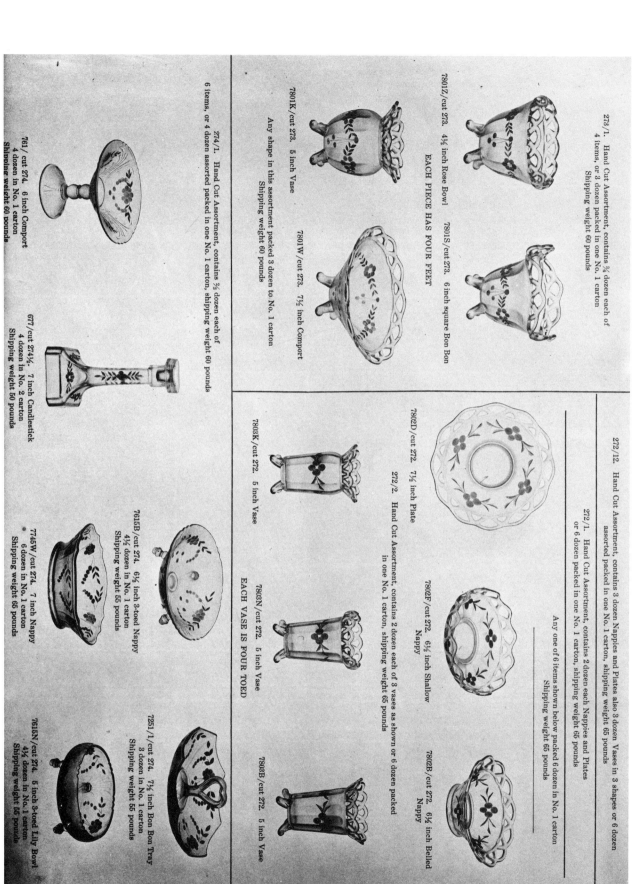

New Hand Cut Patterns

273/1. Hand Cut Assortment, contains ¾ dozen each of 4 items, or 3 dozen packed in one No. 1 carton
Shipping weight 60 pounds

7801Z/cut 273. 4½ inch Rose Bowl

7801S/cut 273. 6 inch square Bon Bon

EACH PIECE HAS FOUR FEET

7801K/cut 273. 5 inch Vase

7801W/cut 273. 7½ inch Comport

Any shape in this assortment packed 3 dozen to No. 1 carton
Shipping weight 60 pounds

274/1. Hand Cut Assortment, contains ⅔ dozen each of 6 items, or 4 dozen assorted packed in one No. 1 carton, shipping weight 60 pounds

761/cut 274. 6 inch Comport
4 dozen in No. 1 carton
Shipping weight 60 pounds

677/cut 274½. 7 inch Candlestick
4 dozen in No. 2 carton
Shipping weight 50 pounds

7615B/cut 274. 6½ inch 3-toed Nappy
4½ dozen in No. 1 carton
Shipping weight 55 pounds

7746W/cut 274. 7 inch Nappy
6 dozen in No. 1 carton
Shipping weight 65 pounds

272/12. Hand Cut Assortment, contains 3 dozen Nappies and Plates also 3 dozen Vases in 3 shapes or 6 dozen assorted packed in one No. 1 carton, shipping weight 65 pounds

272/1. Hand Cut Assortment, contains 2 dozen each Nappies and Plates or 6 dozen packed in one No. 1 carton, shipping weight 65 pounds

Any one of 6 items shown below packed 6 dozen in No. 1 carton
Shipping weight 65 pounds

7802D/cut 272. 7½ inch Plate

272/2. Hand Cut Assortment, contains 2 dozen each of 3 vases as shown or 6 dozen packed in one No. 1 carton, shipping weight 65 pounds

7802F/cut 272. 6½ inch Shallow Nappy

7802B/cut 272. 6½ inch Belled Nappy

7803K/cut 272. 5 inch Vase

7803N/cut 272. 5 inch Vase

EACH VASE IS FOUR TOED

7803B/cut 272. 5 inch Vase

7251/1/cut 274. 7½ inch Bon Bon Tray
3 dozen in No. 1 carton
Shipping weight 55 pounds

7615N/cut 274. 6 inch 3-toed Lily Bowl
4½ dozen in No. 1 carton
Shipping weight 65 pounds

New Imperial Novelties

FOUR-TOED LACE EDGED VASES

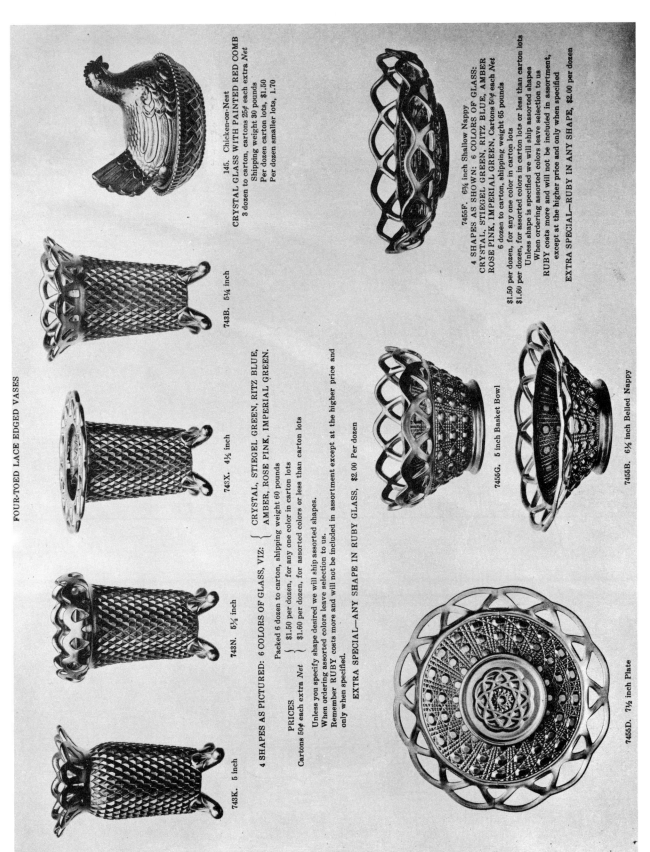

743K. 5 inch

743N. 5⅛ inch

743X. 4½ inch

743B. 5¼ inch

4 SHAPES AS PICTURED: 6 COLORS OF GLASS, VIZ: { CRYSTAL, STIEGEL GREEN, RITZ BLUE, AMBER, ROSE PINK, IMPERIAL GREEN.

Packed 6 dozen to carton, shipping weight 60 pounds

PRICES { $1.50 per dozen, for any one color in carton lots
Cartons 50¢ each extra Net { $1.60 per dozen, for assorted colors or less than carton lots

Unless you specify shape desired we will ship assorted shapes.
When ordering assorted colors leave selection to us.
Remember RUBY costs more and will not be included in assortment except at the higher price and only when specified.

EXTRA SPECIAL—ANY SHAPE IN RUBY GLASS, $2.00 Per dozen

145. Chicken-on-Nest
CRYSTAL GLASS WITH PAINTED RED COMB
3 dozen to carton, cartons 25¢ each extra Net
Shipping weight 30 pounds
Per dozen carton lots, $1.50
Per dozen smaller lots, 1.70

7455F. 6¾ inch Shallow Nappy
4 SHAPES AS SHOWN: 6 COLORS OF GLASS:
CRYSTAL, STIEGEL GREEN, RITZ BLUE, AMBER
ROSE PINK, IMPERIAL GREEN, Cartons 5½¢ each Net
6 dozen to carton, shipping weight 65 pounds
$1.50 per dozen, for any one color in carton lots
$1.60 per dozen, for assorted colors in carton lots or less than carton lots
Unless shape is specified we will ship assorted shapes
When ordering assorted colors leave selection to us
RUBY costs more and will not be included in assortment,
except at the higher price and only when specified
EXTRA SPECIAL—RUBY IN ANY SHAPE, $2.00 per dozen

7455G. 5 inch Basket Bowl

7455B. 6½ inch Belled Nappy

7455D. 7½ inch Plate

Illustrations ½ Size

 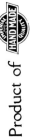

201

Hand Made, Hand Decorated Tumblers, Well Melted Edges

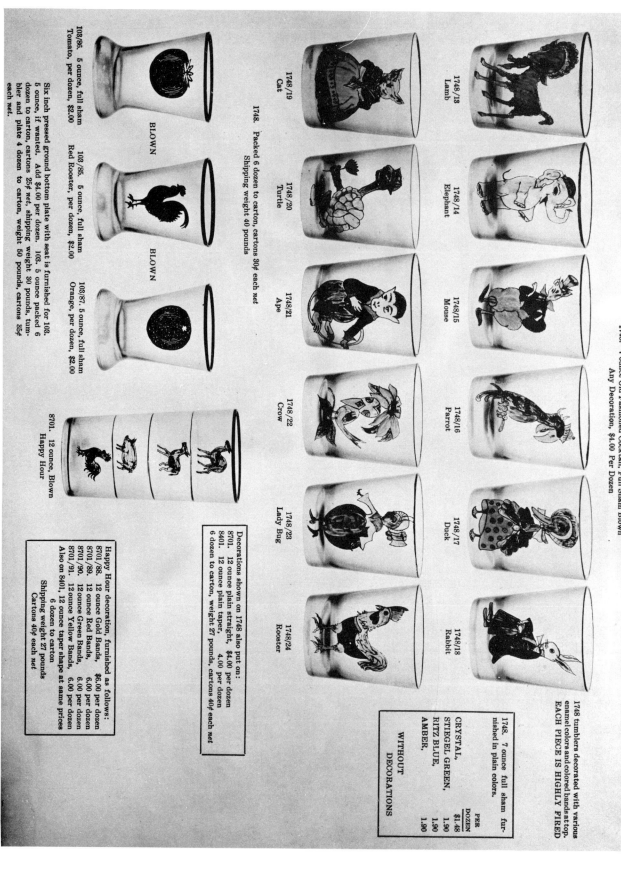

1748. 7 ounce Old Fashioned Cocktail, Full Sham Blown
Any Decoration, $4.00 Per Dozen

1748 tumblers decorated with various enamel colors and colored bands at top.
EACH PIECE IS HIGHLY FIRED

1748/13 Lamb

1748/14 Elephant

1748/15 Mouse

1748/16 Parrot

1748/17 Duck

1748/18 Rabbit

1748/19 Cat

1748/20 Turtle

1748/21 Ape

1748/22 Crow

1748/23 Lady Bug

1748/24 Rooster

1748. Packed 6 dozen to carton, cartons 30¢ each *net*
Shipping weight 40 pounds

1748. 7 ounce full sham furnished in plain colors.

	PER DOZEN
CRYSTAL,	$1.48
STIEGEL GREEN,	1.90
RITZ BLUE,	1.90
AMBER,	1.90
WITHOUT DECORATIONS	

BLOWN

BLOWN

BLOWN

103/86. 5 ounce, full sham Tomato, per dozen, $2.00

103/85. 5 ounce, full sham Red Rooster, per dozen, $2.00

103/87. 5 ounce, full sham Orange, per dozen, $2.00

Six inch pressed ground bottom plate with seat is furnished for 103. 5 ounce, if wanted. Add $4.00 per dozen. 103. 5 ounce packed 6 dozen to carton, cartons 25¢ *net*, shipping weight 30 pounds, tumbler and plate 4 dozen to carton, shipping weight 50 pounds, cartons 35¢ each *net*.

8701. 12 ounce, Blown Happy Hour

Decorations shown on 1748 also put on:
8701. 12 ounce plain straight, $4.00 per dozen
8401. 12 ounce plain taper, 4.00 per dozen
6 dozen to carton, weight 27 pounds, cartons 40¢ each *net*

Happy Hour decoration, furnished as follows:
8701/88. 12 ounce Gold Bands, $6.00 per dozen
8701/89. 12 ounce Red Bands, 6.00 per dozen
8701/90. 12 ounce Green Bands, 6.00 per dozen
8701/91. 12 ounce Yellow Bands, 6.00 per dozen
Also on 8401, 12 ounce taper shape at same prices
6 dozen to carton
Shipping weight 27 pounds
Cartons 40¢ each *net*

Illustrations ½ Size

Georgian Shape

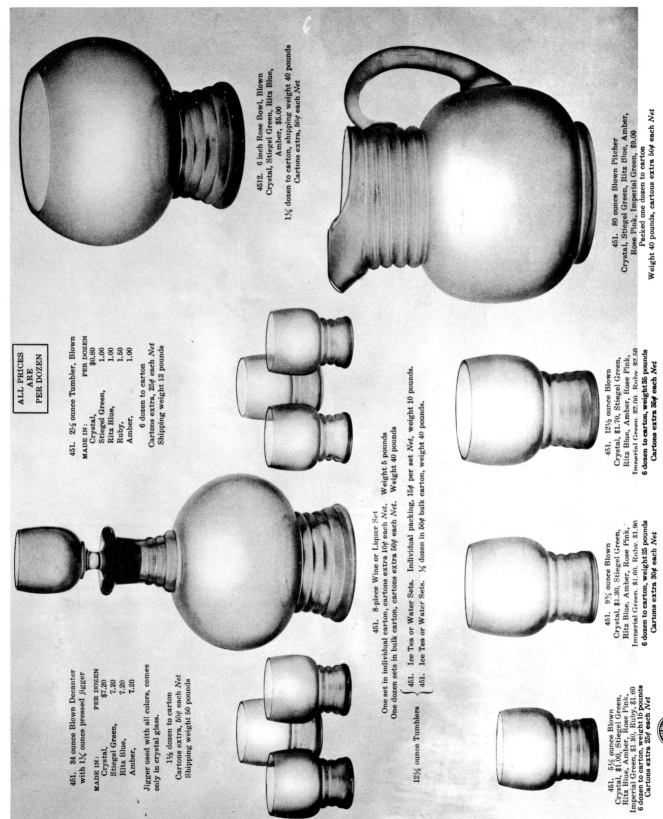

Illustrations ½ Size

ALL PRICES ARE PER DOZEN

451. 34 ounce Blown Decanter with 1¼ ounce pressed Jigger

MADE IN:	PER DOZEN
Crystal,	$7.20
Stiegel Green,	7.20
Ritz Blue,	7.20
Amber,	7.20

Jigger used with all colors, comes only in crystal glass.

1½ dozen to carton
Cartons extra, 50¢ each *Net*
Shipping weight 50 pounds

451. 2½ ounce Tumbler, Blown

MADE IN:	PER DOZEN
Crystal,	$0.80
Stiegel Green,	1.00
Ritz Blue,	1.00
Ruby,	1.50
Amber,	1.00

6 dozen to carton
Cartons extra, 25¢ each *Net*
Shipping weight 13 pounds

4512. 6 inch Rose Bowl, Blown
Crystal, Stiegel Green, Ritz Blue, Amber, $5.00
1½ dozen to carton, shipping weight 40 pounds
Cartons extra, 50¢ each *Net*

451. 80 ounce Blown Pitcher
Crystal, Stiegel Green, Ritz Blue, Amber, Rose Pink, Imperial Green, $9.00
Packed one dozen to carton
Weight 40 pounds, cartons extra 50¢ each *Net*

451. 8-piece Wine or Liquor Set. Weight 5 pounds
One set in individual carton, cartons extra 10¢ each *Net*.
One dozen sets in bulk carton, cartons extra 50¢ each *Net*. Weight 40 pounds

{ 451. Ice Tea or Water Sets. Individual packing, 15¢ per set *Net*, weight 10 pounds.
451. Ice Tea or Water Sets. ½ dozen in 50¢ bulk carton, weight 40 pounds.

12½ ounce Tumblers

451. 12½ ounce Blown
Crystal, $1.70, Stiegel Green, Ritz Blue, Amber, Rose Pink, Imperial Green $2.00, Ruby $2.50
6 dozen to carton, weight 36 pounds
Cartons extra 35¢ each *Net*

451. 9¾ ounce Blown
Crystal, $1.30, Stiegel Green, Ritz Blue, Amber, Rose Pink, Imperial Green, $1.60, Ruby, $1.90
6 dozen to carton, weight 25 pounds
Cartons extra 30¢ each *Net*

451. 5½ ounce Blown
Crystal, $1.00, Stiegel Green, Ritz Blue, Amber, Rose Pink, Imperial Green, $1.30, Ruby, $1.60
6 dozen to carton, weight 16 pounds
Cartons extra 25¢ each *Net*

HOLDER MADE TO FIT
STANDARD PACK OF CIGARETTES
OR PLAYING CARDS
PLATINUM TRIMMED ON
TOP EDGE

CALIENTE   HOB-NAIL

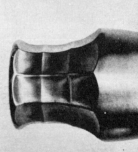

147. Swan

Furnished in six colors:

Crystal
Stiegel Green
Ritz Blue } Per dozen in carton lots of six dozen and one color, $1.50

Amber
Rose Pink
Imperial Green } Per dozen, assorted colors also less than carton lots, $1.60

Packed six dozen to carton
Shipping weight 60 pounds
Cartons extra 60¢ each Net

60. Honey Pot or Preserve Jar with cover

Capacity 7 ounces liquid measurement

Crystal, Stiegel Green, Ritz Blue Amber

Packed 4 dozen to carton
Shipping weight 60 pounds
Cartons 35¢ each extra Net
Per dozen, carton lots, $2.50
Per dozen, smaller lots, $2.70

739. Holder

Packed 6 dozen to carton
Shipping weight 35 pounds
Cartons 36¢ each extra Net

MADE IN:	CARTON LOTS	SMALLER LOTS
Crystal,	$2.40	$2.50
Stiegel Green,	2.40	2.50
Ritz Blue,	2.40	2.50
Amber,	2.40	2.50
Rose Pink,	2.40	2.50
Imperial Green,	2.40	2.50
Price for assorted colors same as small lots		

7112. 9 ounce Tumbler

6 dozen to carton
Shipping weight 50 pounds
Cartons 30¢ each extra Net

MADE IN:	CARTON LOTS	SMALLER LOTS
Crystal,	$1.20	$1.30
Ritz Blue,	1.40	1.50
Amber,	1.40	1.50
Rose Pink,	1.40	1.50
Imperial Green,	1.40	1.50
Ruby,	1.60	1.80
Price for assorted colors same as smaller lots		

741. 9 ounce Tumbler

6 dozen to carton
Shipping weight 40 pounds
Cartons 30¢ each extra Net

MADE IN:	CARTON LOTS	SMALLER LOTS
Crystal,	$1.00	$1.10
Ritz Blue,	1.40	1.50
Amber,	1.40	1.50
Rose Pink,	1.40	1.50
Imperial Green,	1.40	1.50
Ruby,	1.60	1.80
Price for assorted colors same as smaller lots		

153. Twin Candleholder

Made in 6 colors of glass:

CRYSTAL,	
STIEGEL GREEN,	color 3
RITZ BLUE,	color 6
AMBER,	color 40
ROSE PINK,	color 64
IMPERIAL GREEN,	color 81

153B. 10 inch Belled Console or Fruit Bowl

Furnished in same colors as candleholder
Per dozen, carton lots of 1½ dozen in one color, $6.00
Per dozen, assorted colors or less than carton lots, $6.60
Shipping weight 60 pounds, cartons 60¢ each extra Net

163B. 3-piece Console Set, one Bowl with 2 Candleholders

Furnished in same colors as candleholder
Per dozen, carton lots of 1 dozen sets in one color, $9.20
Per dozen, assorted colors or less than carton lots, $9.80

153. Twin Candleholder

Furnished in same colors as candleholder
6 dozen to carton, shipping weight 65 pounds
Cartons 50¢ each extra Net
Per dozen, carton lots of 6 dozen one color, $1.60
Per dozen, assorted colors or less than carton lots, $1.70
In colors as listed at left
Shipping weight 60 pounds, cartons 50¢ each extra Net
Individual carton packing 10¢ each extra Net

Hand Cut Patterns on Hand Made Blanks

5887V /cut 177.   10 inch Two-handled Tray

5887F /cut 177.   9½ inch Two-handled Bowl

5887D /cut 177.   10½ inch Two-handled Plate

5887B /cut 177.   9 inch Two-handled

5887W /cut 177.   9 inch Two-handled Bowl

5887H /cut 177.   10½ inch Two-handled Muffin

5889 /cut 204.   10 inch 3-toed Relish Dish

5889F /cut 204.   10 inch 3-toed Bowl

5888C /cut 204
7 inch 3-toed Tray

5885B /cut 204
6½ inch 3-toed Bon Bon

5886F /cut 204
7 inch 3-toed Bowl

5886A /cut 204
5½ inch 3-toed Nappy

5886 /cut 204
6½ inch 3-toed Relish

5886N /cut 204
5 inch 3-toed Lily Bowl

5889NC /cut 204.   8½ inch 3-toed Bulb Bowl

5889C /cut 204.   10 inch 3-toed Tray

Product of

205

Hand Made Imperial Glass Extra Highly Fire Polished

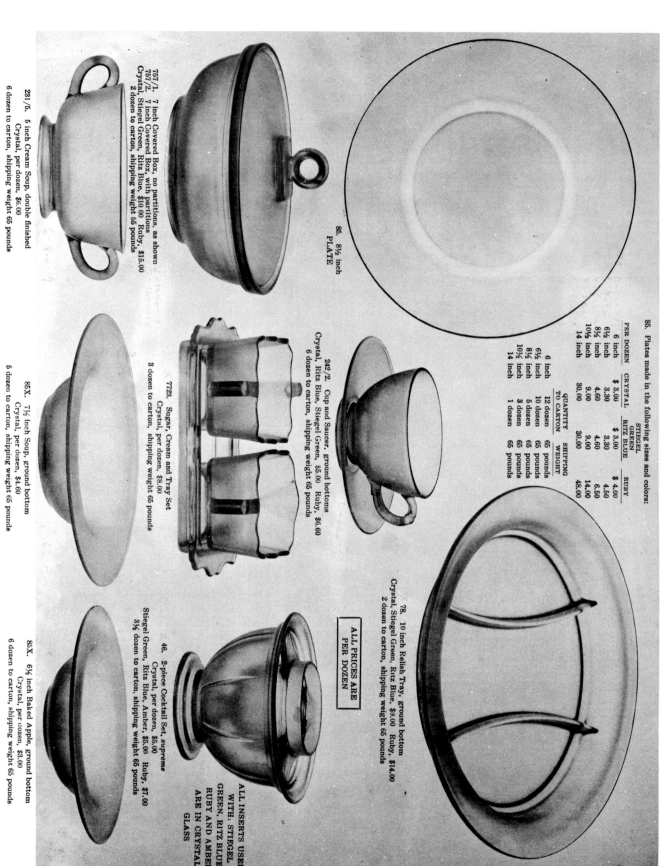

Product of Imperial

231/5. 5 inch Cream Soup, double finished
Crystal, per dozen, $6.00
6 dozen to carton, shipping weight 65 pounds

757/1. 7 inch Covered Box, no partitions, as shown
757/2. 7 inch Covered Box, with partitions
Crystal, Stiegel Green, Ritz Blue, $10.00 Ruby, $15.00
2 dozen to carton, shipping weight 65 pounds

86. 8½ inch
PLATE

85. Plates made in the following sizes and colors:

PER DOZEN	CRYSTAL	STIEGEL GREEN RITZ BLUE	RUBY
6 inch	$ 3.00	$ 3.00	$ 4.00
6½ inch	3.30	3.30	4.60
8½ inch	4.60	4.60	6.50
10½ inch	9.00	9.00	14.00
14 inch	30.00	30.00	48.00

	QUANTITY TO CARTON	SHIPPING WEIGHT
6 inch	12 dozen	65 pounds
6½ inch	10 dozen	65 pounds
8½ inch	5 dozen	65 pounds
10½ inch	3 dozen	65 pounds
14 inch	1 dozen	65 pounds

242/2. Cup and Saucer, ground bottoms
Crystal, Ritz Blue, Stiegel Green, $5.00 Ruby, $6.60
6 dozen to carton, shipping weight 65 pounds

7723. Sugar, Cream and Tray Set
Crystal, per dozen, $8.00
3 dozen to carton, shipping weight 65 pounds

85X. 7½ inch Soup, ground bottom
Crystal, per dozen, $4.60
5 dozen to carton, shipping weight 65 pounds

78. 10 inch Relish Tray, ground bottom
Crystal, Stiegel Green, Ritz Blue, $9.00 Ruby, $14.00
2 dozen to carton, shipping weight 65 pounds

ALL PRICES ARE PER DOZEN

46. 2-piece Cocktail Set, supreme
Crystal, per dozen, $5.00
Stiegel Green, Ritz Blue, Amber, $5.00 Ruby, $7.00
3½ dozen to carton, shipping weight 65 pounds

ALL INSERTS USED WITH: STIEGEL GREEN, RITZ BLUE, RUBY AND AMBER ARE IN CRYSTAL GLASS

85X. 6½ inch Baked Apple, ground bottom
Crystal, per dozen, $3.00
6 dozen to carton, shipping weight 65 pounds

Illustrations ½ Size

CARTONS CHARGED EXTRA AT NET PRICES 50¢ EACH

206

Hand Made Imperial Glass

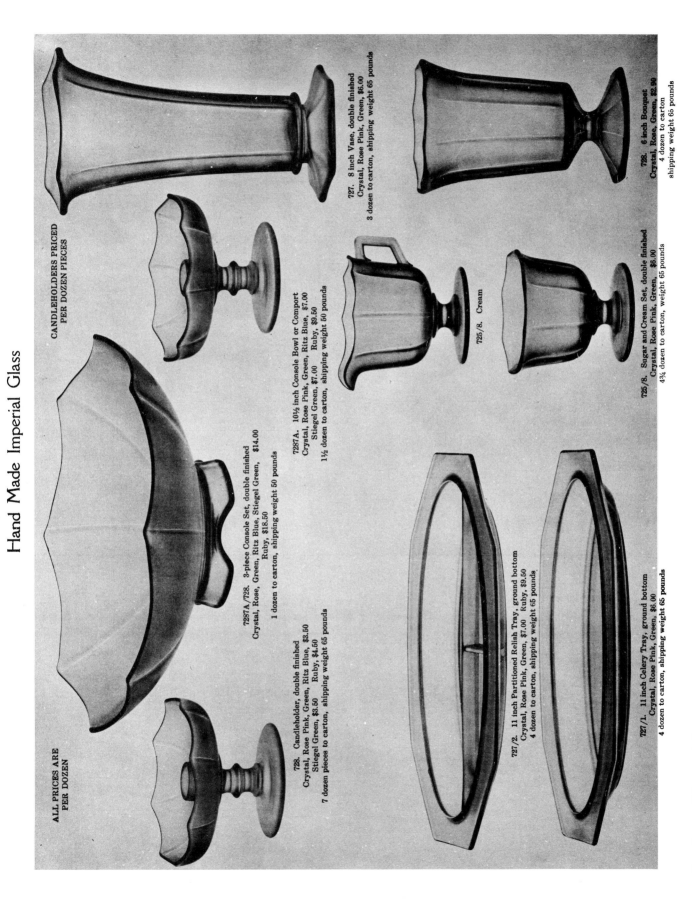

**CANDLEHOLDERS PRICED
PER DOZEN PIECES**

7287A/728. 3-piece Console Set, double finished
Crystal, Rose, Green, Ritz Blue, Stiegel Green, $14.00
Ruby, $18.50
1 dozen to carton, shipping weight 50 pounds

728. Candleholder, double finished
Crystal, Rose Pink, Green, Ritz Blue, $3.50
Stiegel Green, $3.50   Ruby, $4.50
7 dozen pieces to carton, shipping weight 65 pounds

7287A. 10½ inch Console Bowl or Comport
Crystal, Rose Pink, Green, Ritz Blue, $7.00
Stiegel Green, $7.00   Ruby, $9.50
1½ dozen to carton, shipping weight 50 pounds

727. 8 inch Vase, double finished
Crystal, Rose Pink, Green, $6.00
3 dozen to carton, shipping weight 65 pounds

725/8. Cream

725/8. Sugar and Cream Set, double finished
Crystal, Rose Pink, Green, $6.00
4¾ dozen to carton, weight 65 pounds

728. 6 inch Bouquet
Crystal, Rose, Green, $2.90
4 dozen to carton
shipping weight 66 pounds

727/1. 11 inch Celery Tray, ground bottom
Crystal, Rose Pink, Green, $6.00
4 dozen to carton, shipping weight 65 pounds

727/2. 11 inch Partitioned Relish Tray, ground bottom
Crystal, Rose Pink, Green, $7.00   Ruby, $9.50
4 dozen to carton, shipping weight 65 pounds

Illustrations ½ Size

Product of Imperial

Fine Quality Imperial Glassware

EACH PIECE ILLUSTRATED ON THIS PAGE IS DOUBLE FINISHED. ALL ITEMS FURNISHED ONLY IN COLORS LISTED UNDER EACH ILLUSTRATION.

169. 6¾ inch High Stem Compote
CRYSTAL, Per dozen, $7.00
STIEGEL GREEN, Per dozen, 7.00
RITZ BLUE, Per dozen, 7.00
AMBER, Per dozen, 7.00
Packed 2 dozen to carton
Shipping weight 40 pounds

2428. 8 inch Plate, Ground bottom
Made in the following sizes and colors:

		CRYSTAL	STIEGEL	RITZ BLUE	RUBY
2427.	7 inch	$3.40	$3.40	$3.40	$4.60
2427½	7½ inch	3.50	3.50	3.50	4.70
2428.	8 inch	3.60	3.60	3.60	4.80

Any one of 3 sizes, 6 dozen to carton
Weight: 7 inch 50 pounds, 7½ inch 60 pounds, 8 inch 65 pounds

46. Saucer Foot Syrup Jug
CRYSTAL, Per dozen, $4.50
STIEGEL GREEN, Per dozen, 4.50
RITZ BLUE, Per dozen, 4.50
AMBER, Per dozen, 4.50
Packed 6 dozen to carton
Shipping weight 60 pounds

63¾D. Low Round Candleholder
CRYSTAL, Per dozen pieces, $3.50
STIEGEL GREEN, Per dozen pieces, 3.50
RITZ BLUE, Per dozen pieces, 3.50
RUBY, Per dozen pieces, 4.50

ROUND

FLANGED

75X. 12½ inch 4-toed Console Bowl
CRYSTAL, STIEGEL GREEN, RITZ BLUE, Per dozen, $10.00 RUBY, $13.50
Packed ½ dozen to carton, shipping weight 45 pounds

75X/63D. 3 piece Console Set, ½ dozen to carton, shipping weight 55 pounds
CRYSTAL, STIEGEL GREEN, RITZ BLUE, Per dozen, $17.00 RUBY, $22.50

6 dozen pieces to carton
Shipping weight 60 pounds

SHIPPING WEIGHTS ARE APPROXIMATED

Illustrations ½ Size

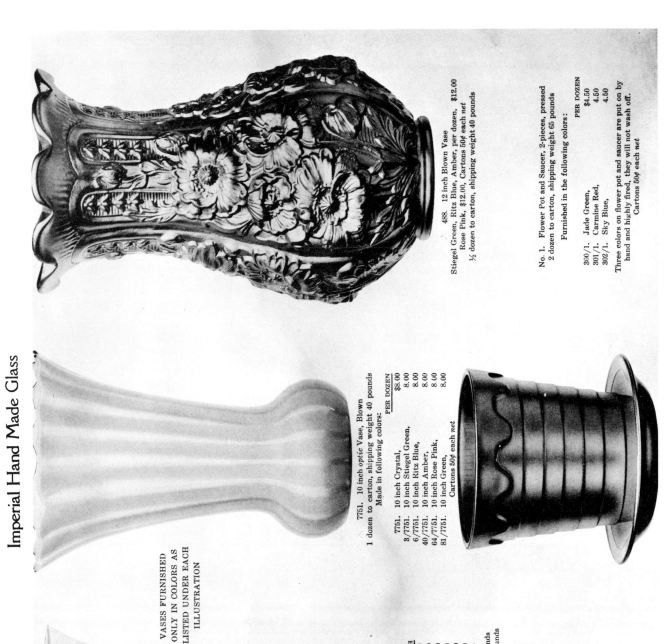

VASES FURNISHED
ONLY IN COLORS AS
LISTED UNDER EACH
ILLUSTRATION

775. 10 inch *plain* Blown Vase
Also made in 12 inch size

In following colors, per dozen

	10 INCH	12 INCH
Crystal,	$6.00	$11.00
Stiegel Green,	6.00	11.00
Ritz Blue,	6.00	11.00
Amber,	6.00	11.00
Rose Pink,	6.00	11.00
Imperial Green,	6.00	11.00
Ruby,	12.00	—

10 inch, 1 dozen to carton, shipping weight 40 pounds
12 inch, ⅔ dozen to carton, shipping weight 40 pounds

IF ANY ARTICLE ON THIS
PAGE IS ORDERED IN LESS
THAN CARTON LOTS ADD
10%

7751. 10 inch *optic* Vase, Blown
1 dozen to carton, shipping weight 40 pounds
Made in following colors:

		PER DOZEN
7751.	10 inch Crystal,	$8.00
3/7751.	10 inch Stiegel Green,	8.00
6/7751.	10 inch Ritz Blue,	8.00
40/7751.	10 inch Amber,	8.00
64/7751.	10 inch Rose Pink,	8.00
81/7751.	10 inch Green,	8.00

Cartons 50¢ each *net*

488. 12 inch Blown Vase
Stiegel Green, Ritz Blue, Amber, per dozen, $12.00
Rose Pink, $12.00, Cartons 50¢ each *net*
½ dozen to carton, shipping weight 40 pounds

No. 1. Flower Pot and Saucer, 2-pieces, pressed
2 dozen to carton, shipping weight 65 pounds
Furnished in the following colors:

		PER DOZEN
300/1.	Jade Green,	$4.50
301/1.	Carmine Red,	4.50
302/1.	Sky Blue,	4.50

Three colors on flower pot and saucer are put on by
hand and highly fired, they will not wash off.
Cartons 50¢ each *net*

Illustrations ½ Size

Product of Imperial

Imperial Milk or Opal Glass (Opaque)

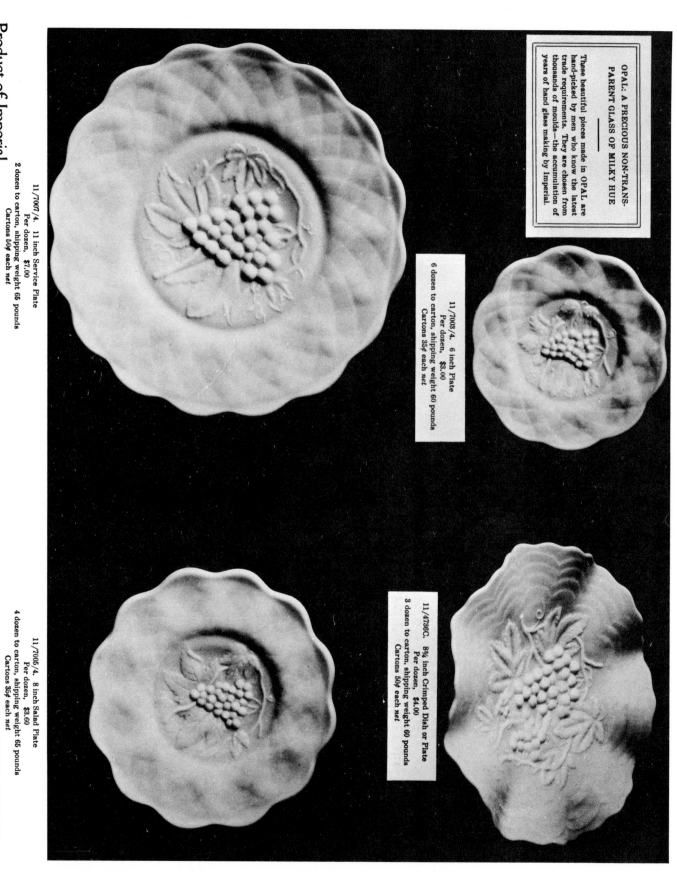

OPAL: A PRECIOUS NON-TRANS-
PARENT GLASS OF MILKY HUE

These beautiful pieces made in OPAL are
hand-picked by men who know the latest
trade requirements. They are chosen from
thousands of moulds—the accumulation of
years of hand glass making by Imperial.

11/7003/4. 6 inch Plate
Per dozen, $3.00
6 dozen to carton, shipping weight 60 pounds
Cartons 35¢ each net

11/7007/4. 11 inch Service Plate
Per dozen, $7.00
2 dozen to carton, shipping weight 65 pounds
Cartons 60¢ each net

11/4736C. 8¾ inch Crimped Dish or Plate
Per dozen, $4.00
3 dozen to carton, shipping weight 60 pounds
Cartons 50¢ each net

11/7005/4. 8 inch Salad Plate
Per dozen, $3.60
4 dozen to carton, shipping weight 65 pounds
Cartons 35¢ each net
CARTONS CHARGED AT NET PRICES

Illustrations ½ Size

210

Imperial Milk or Opal Glass (Opaque)

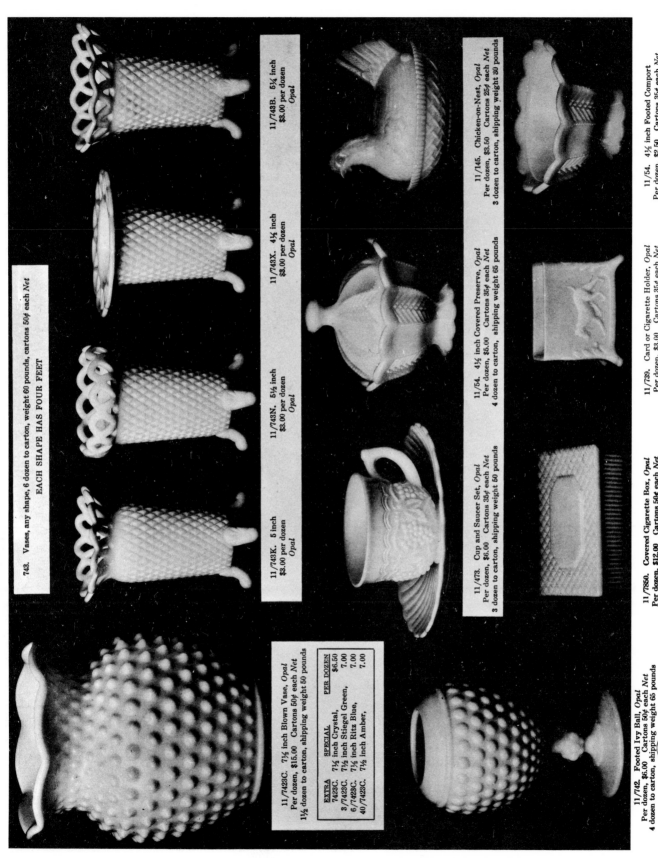

743. Vases, any shape, 6 dozen to carton, weight 60 pounds, cartons 50¢ each Net
EACH SHAPE HAS FOUR FEET

11/743K.   5 inch
$3.00 per dozen
Opal

11/743N.   5¼ inch
$3.00 per dozen
Opal

11/743X.   4½ inch
$3.00 per dozen
Opal

11/743B.   5¼ inch
$3.00 per dozen
Opal

11/145.   Chicken-on-Nest, *Opal*
Per dozen, $3.50   Cartons 25¢ each Net
3 dozen to carton, shipping weight 30 pounds

11/54.   4½ inch Footed Comport
Per dozen, $2.50   Cartons 35¢ each Net
6 dozen to carton, shipping weight 55 pounds

11/54.   4½ inch Covered Preserve, *Opal*
Per dozen, $5.00   Cartons 35¢ each Net
4 dozen to carton, shipping weight 65 pounds

11/739.   Card or Cigarette Holder, *Opal*
Per dozen, $3.00   Cartons 35¢ each Net
6 dozen to carton, shipping weight 35 pounds

11/473.   Cup and Saucer Set, *Opal*
Per dozen, $6.00   Cartons 35¢ each Net
3 dozen to carton, shipping weight 60 pounds

11/7850.   Covered Cigarette Box, *Opal*
Per dozen, $12.00   Cartons 50¢ each Net
6 dozen to carton, shipping weight 65 pounds

11/7423C.   7½ inch Blown Vase, *Opal*
Per dozen, $15.00   Cartons 50¢ each Net
1½ dozen to carton, shipping weight 50 pounds

EXTRA	SPECIAL	PER DOZEN
7423C.	7½ inch Crystal,	$6.50
3/7423C.	7½ inch Stiegel Green,	7.00
6/7423C.	7½ inch Ritz Blue,	7.00
40/7423C.	7½ inch Amber,	7.00

11/742.   Footed Ivy Ball, *Opal*
Per dozen, $6.00   Cartons 50¢ each Net
4 dozen to carton, shipping weight 65 pounds

Illustrations ½ Size

Product of [HAND MADE]

211

Product of Imperial

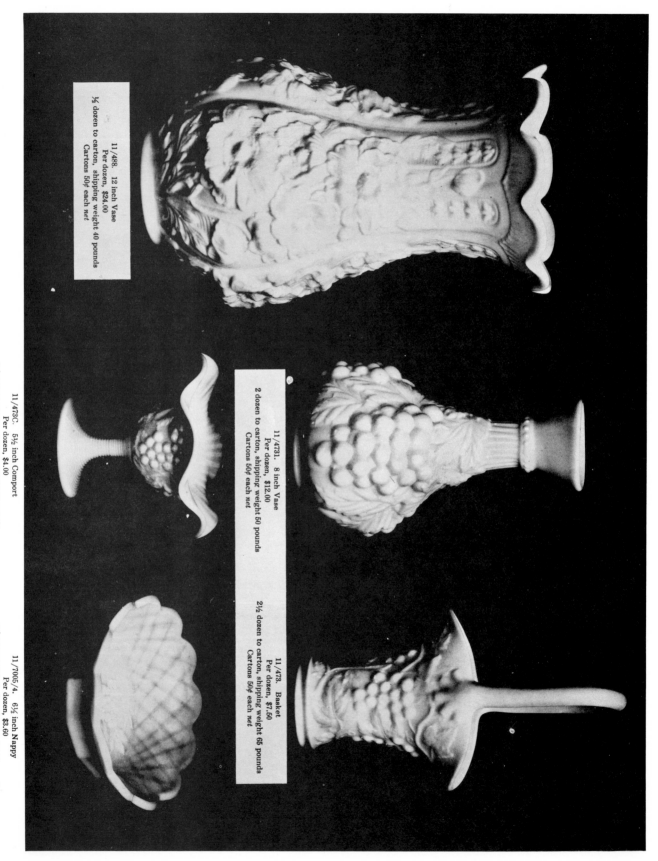

11/488. 12 inch Vase
Per dozen, $24.00
½ dozen to carton, shipping weight 40 pounds
Cartons 50¢ each *net*

11/4731. 8 inch Vase
Per dozen, $12.00
2 dozen to carton, shipping weight 50 pounds
Cartons 50¢ each *net*

11/473. Basket
Per dozen, $7.50
2½ dozen to carton, shipping weight 65 pounds
Cartons 50¢ each *net*

11/473C. 5½ inch Comport
Per dozen, $4.00
3 dozen to carton, shipping weight 50 pounds
Cartons 50¢ each *net*
Illustrations ½ Size

11/7005/4. 6½ inch Nappy
Per dozen, $3.60
4 dozen to carton, shipping weight 65 pounds
Cartons 35¢ each *net*
CARTONS CHARGED AT NET PRICES

212